DEFINING MOMENTS
THE VOTING RIGHTS ACT
OF 1965

DEFINING MOMENTS
THE VOTING RIGHTS ACT
OF 1965

Laurie Collier Hillstrom

Omnigraphics

P.O. Box 31-1640
Detroit, MI 48231

Omnigraphics, Inc.

Kevin Hillstrom, *Series Editor*
Cherie D. Abbey, *Managing Editor*

Peter E. Ruffner, *Publisher*
Matthew P. Barbour, *Senior Vice President*

Elizabeth Collins, *Research and Permissions Coordinator*
Kevin Hayes, *Operations Manager*

Allison A. Beckett and Mary Butler, *Research Staff*
Cherry Stockdale, *Permissions Assistant*
Shirley Amore, Martha Johns, and Kirk Kauffman, *Administrative Staff*

Library of Congress Cataloging-in-Publication Data

Hillstrom, Laurie Collier, 1965-
 The Voting Rights Act of 1965 / by Laurie Collier Hillstrom.
 p. cm. -- (Defining moments)
 Includes bibliographical references and index.
 Summary: "Explains the events that led to the Voting Rights Act of 1965. Details both the racial discrimination and violence that pervaded the South and the civil rights protests that changed American voting rights. Features include a narrative overview, biographies, primary source documents, chronology, glossary, bibliography, and index"--Provided by publisher.
 ISBN 978-0-7808-1048-8 (hardcover : alk. paper) 1. African Americans--Suffrage. 2. United States. Voting Rights Act of 1965 3. Suffrage--United States. 4. United States--Politics and government--1963-1969. 5. Election law--United States. I. Title.
 JK1924.H55 2008
 324.6'20973--dc22
                                                                    2008038392

TABLE OF CONTENTS

PRIMARY SOURCES

PREFACE

Throughout the course of America's existence, its people, culture, and institutions have been periodically challenged—and in many cases transformed—by profound historical events. Some of these momentous events, such as women's suffrage, the civil rights movement, and U.S. involvement in World War II, invigorated the nation and strengthened American confidence and capabilities. Others, such as the McCarthy era, the Vietnam War, and Watergate, have prompted troubled assessments and heated debates about the country's core beliefs and character.

Some of these defining moments in American history were years or even decades in the making. The Harlem Renaissance and the New Deal, for example, unfurled over the span of several years, while the American labor movement and the Cold War evolved over the course of decades. Other defining moments, such as the Cuban missile crisis and the terrorist attacks of September 11, 2001, transpired over a matter of days or weeks.

But although significant differences exist among these events in terms of their duration and their place in the timeline of American history, all share the same basic characteristic: they transformed the United States' political, cultural, and social landscape for future generations of Americans.

Taking heed of this fundamental reality, American citizens, schools, and other institutions are increasingly emphasizing the importance of understanding our nation's history. Omnigraphics' *Defining Moments* series was created for the express purpose of meeting this growing appetite for authoritative, useful historical resources. This series will be of enduring value to anyone interested in learning more about America's past—and in understanding how those historical events continue to reverberate in the 21st century.

Each individual volume of *Defining Moments* provides a valuable one-stop resource for readers interested in learning about the most profound events in our nation's history. Each volume is organized into three distinct sections—Narrative Overview, Biographies, and Primary Sources.

- The **Narrative Overview** provides readers with a detailed, factual account of the origins and progression of the "defining moment" being examined. It also explores the event's lasting impact on America's political and cultural landscape.

- The **Biographies** section provides valuable biographical background on leading figures associated with the event in question. Each biography concludes with a list of sources for further information on the profiled individual.

- The **Primary Sources** section collects a wide variety of pertinent primary source materials from the era under discussion, including official documents, papers and resolutions, letters, oral histories, memoirs, editorials, and other important works.

Individually, each of these sections is a rich resource for users. Together, they comprise an authoritative, balanced, and absorbing examination of some of the most significant events in U.S. history.

Other notable features contained within each volume in the series include a glossary of important individuals, places, and terms; a detailed chronology featuring page references to relevant sections of the narrative; an annotated bibliography of sources for further study; an extensive general bibliography that reflects the wide range of historical sources consulted by the author; and a subject index.

Acknowledgements

This series was developed in consultation with a distinguished Advisory Board comprised of public librarians, school librarians, and educators. They evaluated the series as it developed, and their comments and suggestions were invaluable throughout the production process. Any errors in this and other volumes in the series are ours alone. Following is a list of board members who contributed to the *Defining Moments* series:

Gail Beaver, M.A., M.A.L.S.
Adjunct Lecturer, University of Michigan
Ann Arbor, MI

Melissa C. Bergin, L.M.S., NBCT
Library Media Specialist, Niskayuna High School
Niskayuna, NY

Rose Davenport, M.S.L.S., Ed. Specialist
Library Media Specialist, Pershing High School Library
Detroit, MI

Karen Imarisio, A.M.L.S.
Assistant Head of Adult Services, Bloomfield Twp. Public Library
Bloomfield Hills, MI

Nancy Larsen, M.L.S., M.S. Ed.
Library Media Specialist, Clarkston High School
Clarkston, MI

Marilyn Mast, M.I.L.S.
Kingswood Campus Librarian, Cranbrook Kingswood Upper School
Bloomfield Hills, MI

Rosemary Orlando, M.L.I.S.
Library Director, St. Clair Shores Public Library
St. Clair Shores, MI

The author also wishes to thank Jeff Hill for his assistance with the biographies section.

Comments and Suggestions

We welcome your comments on *Defining Moments: The Voting Rights Act* and suggestions for other events in U.S. history that warrant treatment in the *Defining Moments* series. Correspondence should be addressed to:

Editor, *Defining Moments*
Omnigraphics, Inc.
P.O. Box 31-1640
Detroit, MI 48231-1640
E-mail: editorial@omnigraphics.com

HOW TO USE THIS BOOK

*D*efining Moments: The Voting Rights Act of 1965 provides users with a detailed and authoritative overview of the passage of this landmark legislation, as well as background information on the principal figures involved in this pivotal episode in U.S. history. The preparation and arrangement of this volume—and all other books in the *Defining Moments* series— reflect an emphasis on providing a thorough and objective account of events that shaped our nation, presented in an easy-to-use reference work.

Defining Moments: The Voting Rights Act of 1965 is divided into three primary sections. The first of these sections, the **Narrative Overview**, provides a detailed, factual account of the events that led to the signing of the historic bill. It details the racial discrimination and violence that pervaded the Jim Crow South, tracks the rising influence of Martin Luther King, Jr., and other civil rights leaders, and explains the ways in which boycotts, sit-ins, freedom rides, and other forms of social protest developed. In addition to covering significant milestones in the civil rights movement, the overview provides special emphasis on events related to the fight for black voting rights, such as the 1964 Freedom Summer voter registration drives in Mississippi and the 1965 Selma-Montgomery march in Alabama.

The second section, **Biographies**, provides valuable biographical background on leading individuals associated with the voting rights campaign, including civil rights legends such as Martin Luther King, Jr., John Lewis, Ella Baker, James Farmer, and Fannie Lou Hamer. Each biography concludes with a list of sources for further information on the profiled individual.

The third section, **Primary Sources**, collects essential documents that illuminate how the Voting Rights Act progressed from dream to reality. Featured sources include James Farmer's recollections of the early Freedom Rides across the South, John Lewis's account of the infamous "Bloody Sunday" attack carried out by Alabama law enforcement officers against peaceful civil rights marchers, and President Lyndon B. Johnson's historic address urging Congress to pass the Voting Rights Act.

Other valuable features in *Defining Moments: The Voting Rights Act of 1965* include the following:

- Attribution and referencing of primary sources and other quoted material to help guide users to other valuable historical research resources.

- Glossary of Important People, Places, and Terms.

- Detailed Chronology of events with a *see reference* feature. Under this arrangement, events listed in the chronology include a reference to page numbers within the Narrative Overview wherein users can find additional information on the event in question.

- Photographs of the leading figures and major events associated with the Voting Rights Act of 1965.

- Sources for Further Study, an annotated list of noteworthy works about the voting-rights movement.

- Extensive bibliography of works consulted in the creation of this book, including books, periodicals, Internet sites, and videotape materials.

- A Subject Index.

NARRATIVE OVERVIEW

PROLOGUE

For Americans in the twenty-first century, registering to vote is easy. U.S. citizens age 18 or older—regardless of race, religion, or gender—can register by filling out a simple application form. Copies of this form are widely available at colleges, libraries, post offices, and state or local government agencies across the country. Prospective voters can even download a form from the Internet and mail it in. Once the state election office verifies an applicant's name, address, and date of birth, the newly registered voter receives a postcard with information about their election district and polling place.

The process of registering to vote has become so routine that many people do not realize this was not always the case. As recently as the 1960s, millions of American citizens found it nearly impossible to register to vote—and extremely dangerous even to try.

Prior to 1965, many states in the South used elaborate voter-registration procedures to determine which citizens were "qualified" to vote. Prospective voters were often required to fill out complicated application forms, pass tough literacy tests, pay prohibitive poll taxes, and provide proof of their good moral character. But these requirements were not applied equally to all citizens. Their main purpose was to give white political leaders a way to deny African Americans and members of other minority groups their constitutional right to vote.

In those days, people who wanted to register to vote had to take time off from work and travel to a distant county courthouse to appear before a registrar. Unlike the convenient options available today, county registrars in the South were usually open one or two days per month, for only a few hours. Local law enforcement officers often lingered nearby to insult, threaten, beat, or arrest any African Americans who dared to try to enter the building.

Black citizens who managed to overcome these hurdles and appear before the registrar were then subjected to a series of qualification tests. They might be required to read a complex section of the U.S. Constitution aloud, for instance, and then explain its meaning to the registrar. They might also be expected to write out a section of the document as the registrar read it aloud, making sure to spell all of the difficult legal terminology correctly. Finally, prospective voters might have to answer several pages of written questions about the inner workings of state and federal government. Whether an applicant passed or failed these tests was left to the sole judgment of the local registrar, who was invariably white. Most white applicants passed—even if they were unable to read or write—while nearly all black applicants failed.

For the few black applicants who passed these elaborate voter-registration tests, their ordeal was still not over. The next step in the process usually involved having their names and addresses published in the local newspaper for a period of one to two weeks. Many white citizens kept an eye on these lists and found ways to punish any blacks whose names appeared. African Americans who tried to register to vote in the South were often fired from their jobs or evicted from their homes. Some became the victims of violent crimes, including assault, kidnapping, rape, arson, or even murder.

Students today might wonder why states in the South resorted to such awful measures to prevent black citizens from registering to vote. The main goal of such policies was to ensure that whites maintained control of social, economic, and political life throughout the region. The surest way for whites to continue to hold the reins of power was to deny black voting rights. After all, if African Americans were allowed to participate in the democratic process, the South's longstanding system of racial segregation and discrimination would be put in jeopardy. African Americans who possessed full voting rights were certain to demand freedom and equality in other areas of society as well.

In the early 1960s, securing black voting rights in the South became the primary focus of the civil rights movement. Martin Luther King, Jr., and other movement leaders realized that gaining access to the ballot would be invaluable in helping African Americans end discrimination and improve their lives. Civil rights organizations held a series of voter-registration drives and protest marches across the South, including Freedom Summer in Mississippi in 1964 and the Selma-Montgomery Voting Rights March in Alabama in 1965. These activities were designed to raise public awareness of the unjust system and force the federal government to take action to end it.

On August 6, 1965, this campaign culminated in the passage of the Voting Rights Act. Widely considered to be one of the most effective civil rights laws in U.S. history, this landmark legislation outlawed the various practices used to deny black voting rights and led to an immediate increase in the number of black registered voters and elected officials throughout the South.

The impact of the Voting Rights Act of 1965 continued to be felt in the twenty-first century. Not only did discriminatory voter-registration procedures disappear, but African Americans and members of other minority groups enjoyed unprecedented influence in state and federal government. Senator Barack Obama of Illinois—a Democrat who went on to make history as the first black candidate to win a major party's nomination for president of the United States—assessed the law's legacy on the 40th anniversary of its passage:

> Forty years ago, the Voting Rights Act of 1965 was made law by millions of ordinary Americans who showed the extraordinary courage to overcome.
>
> These heroes of our past didn't wait for their government to act or complain idly when it didn't. They believed in the promise first articulated by our founding fathers; that in America, we have it in our power to begin the world anew.
>
> And so they marched. Women who were willing to walk instead of ride the bus after a long day's work of doing somebody else's laundry and looking after somebody else's children because they believed in freedom. Young people of every race and every creed who were willing to take a bus down to Mississippi and Alabama to register voters even though some would never return. And the brave Americans who faced hate and violence one Sunday on the Edmund Pettus Bridge [in Selma, Alabama] a few months before the Voting Rights Act delivered them redemption.
>
> Since that day, the Voting Rights Act has been a critical tool in ensuring that minority voters and all Americans not only have the right to vote, but to have their vote counted.[1]

Notes

1 Obama, Barack. "Obama Statement on the 40th Anniversary of the Voting Rights Act," August 6, 2005. Available online at http://obama.senate.gov/press/050806.

Chapter One

THE JIM CROW SOUTH

Keep the black man from the ballot and we'll treat him as we
please.

With no means for protection, we will rule with perfect ease.

—Lizelia Augusta Jenkins Moorer, "The Negro Ballot,"
in *Prejudice Unveiled and Other Poems,* 1907

Voting rights are the foundation of American democracy. When U.S. citizens vote to elect people to represent their interests in government, it gives them a voice in the way the country is run. Partly because voting rights are so important, they have been a source of intense social and political conflict during various times in the nation's history. Voting rights have been denied to many groups at one time or another, including immigrants, Jews, women, Native Americans, and people who did not own property. Those who already held power in government knew that the best way to maintain control was to prevent other groups from electing representatives with different views and philosophies.

It took a long time and the hard work of countless activists to ensure that the nation lived up to its founding principles and guaranteed all citizens the right to vote. American women, for example, finally gained the right to vote in 1920, after a battle that lasted 70 years. African Americans, meanwhile, received the right to vote following the Civil War, but they struggled for almost 100 years to fully exercise that right.

Emancipation and Reconstruction

Before the Civil War, states in the southern half of the country practiced slavery. Millions of African Americans were considered the property of white owners. They could be bought and sold and forced to work without pay. The North's victory in the Civil War ended this inhumane practice. The Thirteenth Amendment to the U.S. Constitution, passed in 1865, made slavery illegal across the country.

Even after slavery was abolished, however, many whites in the South were not willing to treat African Americans as equals. Determined to keep their place at the top of the social order, they passed a variety of laws that discriminated against blacks. These laws—known as Black Codes—severely restricted the behavior of freed slaves and returned them to a condition very close to slavery. For example, the laws prevented African Americans from owning weapons, purchasing land in certain areas, and attending white schools.

Before long, the federal government stepped in to address this situation. Led by members of the Republican party from the North, the U.S. Congress passed a series of laws to protect the civil rights of freed slaves. The federal government also sent federal troops to the South to enforce these laws. This period in U.S. history, which lasted from 1866 to 1877, became known as Reconstruction.

Congress added two key amendments to the Constitution during Reconstruction. The Fourteenth Amendment, passed in 1868, granted citizenship to all persons born or naturalized in the United States, regardless of the color of their skin. It also guaranteed all U.S. citizens equal protection under the law and prohibited anyone from taking away a citizen's rights without due process of law. The Fifteenth Amendment, passed in 1870, gave black men the right to vote throughout the United States. It also made it illegal to deny a citizen's voting rights on the basis of race, color, or previous condition of servitude (slavery).

Under the protection of these constitutional amendments and the watchful eye of federal troops, African Americans made significant gains during Reconstruction, especially in the South. Many communities elected black mayors, sheriffs, and school principals. Two African Americans were elected to the U.S. Senate, and 20 black legislators occupied seats in the U.S. House of Representatives. These black leaders launched ambitious programs to provide former slaves with land, education, and jobs to help them recover from their years of enslavement and become self-sufficient.

Who Was Jim Crow?

The name Jim Crow, which was applied to the state and local laws that segregated white and black residents of the South from the 1870s to the 1950s, originated in an 1832 song called "Jump Jim Crow" by Thomas "Daddy" Rice. Rice may have named his song after a slave he knew, or he may have created the name from the common expression "black as a crow."

Rice was best known for appearing in minstrel shows, a type of entertainment in which white performers wore dark makeup and pretended to be African Americans. Minstrel performers sang, danced, and did skits that presented a stereotypical image of black people as silly, simple-minded, and inferior to whites. Over time, Jim Crow became a standard character in minstrel shows.

By the early 1900s, Jim Crow had evolved into a general term for the segregation and discrimination that affected many aspects of American life. The term was commonly used in references to Jim Crow laws, the Jim Crow era, and the Jim Crow South. A century later, however, this historical meaning began to fade. Polls showed that less than 20 percent of American college students recognized the term or were aware of its significance.

The Rise of Jim Crow

Many white Southerners resented the changes that took place during Reconstruction. Some resorted to intimidation and violence to keep African Americans from exercising their newly established rights. Secret organizations like the Ku Klux Klan (KKK)—known as white supremacist groups because they believed that whites were superior to blacks—terrorized, tortured, or killed thousands of blacks during the late 1860s and 1870s. The groups' goals were to prevent blacks from voting, force elected black officials out of office, and restore white control over Southern society.

White supremacists largely achieved these goals after Reconstruction ended in 1877. As part of an agreement to settle the outcome of a disputed presidential election, Republican President Rutherford B. Hayes withdrew federal troops from the South in March of that year. Without federal protection, African Americans had little hope of exercising their rights in the face of mob violence and lynchings. Once whites regained political power in the South, they enacted a wide range of laws that blatantly discriminated against blacks. Known as Jim Crow laws (see sidebar "Who Was Jim Crow?", p. 9), these state and local regulations deprived African Americans of their civil rights and made them subordinate to whites.

The first Jim Crow law was enacted in Tennessee in 1875, and many others soon followed throughout the South. The main intention of these laws was to segregate black and white residents, or keep the races separate, in all areas of public life. During the Jim Crow era, various cities and states passed laws that banned African Americans from hospitals, schools, parks, theaters, and restaurants. All across the South, signs that specified "White Only" or "Colored" were placed on public parks, restrooms, and drinking fountains. In virtually all cases, the facilities set aside for African Americans were markedly inferior to the ones reserved for whites.

The formal Jim Crow laws passed by state and local governments were not the only sources of segregation in the South. Many private businesses—such as stores, restaurants, and factories—had policies that prevented blacks from shopping or working there. In addition, many labor unions, political parties, community groups, and other organizations enforced their own Jim Crow rules. These rules were designed to prevent African Americans from working in certain industries, living in certain neighborhoods, and shopping in certain stores.

Segregation Becomes Legal

Despite their discriminatory nature, the South's Jim Crow laws and policies received validation from the U.S. Supreme Court. The Court found segregation allowable under the Constitution in several controversial decisions during the late 1800s. In 1883, for instance, the Court ruled that the Equal Protection Clause of the Fourteenth Amendment only applied to government-run facilities and agencies. This decision essentially meant that private individuals and businesses were free to discriminate against African Americans.

In 1896 the Court declared that the segregation of public facilities was legal, as long as the separate facilities provided for black and white citizens were equal. The case in question concerned a Louisiana law that required separate railroad cars for white, black, and colored (mixed race) passengers. On

June 7, 1892, a light-skinned carpenter named Homer Plessy challenged the law. After sitting down in a car reserved for whites, he informed railroad officials that he was actually one-eighth African American. Plessy was arrested, and he pursued the matter all the way to the U.S. Supreme Court. The "separate but equal" ruling in *Plessy v. Ferguson* legalized the segregation of public transportation, public buildings, and public schools throughout the South.

Although the separate facilities for blacks and whites were supposed to be equal, this was rarely the case. Instead, the facilities available to African Americans remained inferior to those available to whites. In theaters, for instance, the colored entrances were usually located in a back alley, and the colored seating section in a distant balcony. Sim-

Lynching of African Americans was a common practice in the post-Reconstruction South.

ilarly, colored wards in hospitals and public schools for black children received only a fraction of the financial support that white institutions received for hiring staff, purchasing supplies, and maintaining facilities. Segregation thus amounted to legalized discrimination that placed black citizens at significant economic, social, and educational disadvantages in American society.

Rules of Behavior under Jim Crow

Even in the segregated Jim Crow South, black and white citizens often found themselves in situations where they had to interact with one another. In these instances, African Americans were expected to follow strict rules of behavior that demonstrated respect and submission toward whites. "The whole intent of Jim Crow etiquette boiled down to one simple rule: blacks must demonstrate their inferiority to whites by actions, words, and manners,"[1] explained one scholar.

When speaking with a white person, African Americans had to be passive and agreeable. They were expected to address whites using respectful terms like Boss, Captain, Mr., Mrs., or Miss. Whites, on the other hand, were never supposed to use such terms in reference to blacks. Instead, they usually addressed blacks in condescending or derogatory terms like boy, girl, uncle, auntie, or nigger.

If groups of whites and blacks approached each other on a city sidewalk, the blacks were expected to step aside to let the whites pass. African Americans also had to wait patiently while store clerks routinely served all white customers first. Most stores did not allow black customers to try on clothing, because they knew that white customers would not buy items that had touched black skin. African Americans could not eat inside restaurants that served whites, either. Blacks were sometimes allowed to order takeout food, but they had to bring their own plates and eating utensils.

African Americans who broke these rules of acceptable conduct put their lives—as well as those of their family members—at grave risk from racist violence. Most blacks in the Jim Crow South tried to keep a low profile and avoid calling attention to themselves. They understood that appearing successful, or standing out in any way, could be considered a challenge to white supremacy. Leaders of the black community—including ministers, newspaper editors, and civil rights activists—often became the targets of violence. To minimize such dangers, many African Americans who managed to scrape together savings still chose to live in unpainted houses, operate rundown stores, and avoid buying fancy clothes or new carriages.

Denial of Voting Rights

African Americans in the Jim Crow South felt great anger, frustration, and despair regarding the formal segregation laws and informal rules of conduct that affected every aspect of their lives. But most people felt powerless to change the situation. The constant threat of violence prevented many individuals from speaking out against or defying the Jim Crow laws. Another important reason that the laws went unchallenged, though, was that African Americans had no political influence.

White leaders in the South managed to keep the discriminatory Jim Crow system in place by denying voting rights to African Americans. Immediately after federal troops left the South in 1877, conservative white Democrats wrestled control of state after state from Republican Reconstruction

Robbed of political power, African Americans were helpless to stop the segregation of businesses and public facilities across the South.

governments. Then, in order to remain in power, the Democrats enacted a series of measures designed to disenfranchise black voters.

Many Southern states passed laws that forced citizens to meet a wide range of new requirements in order to be eligible to vote. Some states made citizens pay fees, known as poll taxes, if they wanted to vote. Other states required prospective voters to prove that they could read and write by passing literacy tests (see "Alabama Literacy Test Samples," p. 163).

In many cases, these measures would have excluded poor, rural white men from voting as well as African Americans. To address this problem, many state governments created loopholes that allowed white voters to avoid the new requirements. Oklahoma, for instance, passed a law that said anyone who had been qualified to vote prior to 1866, or who was related to someone who was qualified to vote at that time, did not have to take a literacy test. This type of law became known as a "grandfather clause." Since blacks did not have the right to vote in 1866, only whites could use the grandfather clause to avoid the tests.

The introduction of discriminatory voting requirements led to a dramatic decline in the number of registered African-American voters throughout the South. Less than half of the black men who voted in Georgia and South Carolina in 1880 qualified to vote in 1888 under the new laws. After Louisiana adopted voting restrictions in 1896, the percentage of black residents who were registered to vote dropped from 44.8 percent to 4.0 percent in four years. The federal government was reluctant to challenge the laws, however, because state and local governments generally had the authority to establish their own voting regulations.

Obstacles to Black Voter Registration

By the 1890s, it had become virtually impossible for African Americans to register to vote anywhere in the South. State and local governments made the voter registration process extremely cumbersome, confusing, and time-consuming. For example, a prospective voter might have to take time off work—at the risk of losing his job—to appear in person at a distant courthouse on a specific day. He would likely be met on the steps by white law enforcement officers who proceeded to insult and intimidate him. If he continued inside, he would be subjected to a series of complicated tests. In some cases, a prospective voter was required to bring a registered voter along to vouch for his good moral character. Since very few black men managed to register—and few white voters were willing to vouch for a black man—this barrier was difficult to overcome.

In addition, prospective voters could not prepare in advance for the requirements because they changed all the time. "While in theory there were standard state-wide registration procedures, in real life the individual registrars and clerks did things their own way," one historian noted. "The exact procedures varied from county to county, and within a county it varied from day to day according to the mood of the registrar. And, of course, it almost always varied according to the race of the applicant."[2]

14

In addition to complicated registration rules and procedures, African Americans often faced negative consequences if they attempted to exercise their voting rights in the Jim Crow South. Some government officials and community leaders punished black voters by firing them from their jobs, evicting them from their homes, calling in their loans, or organizing boycotts of their businesses. In more extreme cases, white supremacists used threats, intimidation, and violence to deny African-American voting rights. Groups like the KKK resorted to tactics like cross burnings, bombings, beatings, rapes, and lynchings to keep blacks in a perpetual state of fear and powerlessness.

The white supremacist Ku Klux Klan—seen here marching in 1926—terrorized African Americans across the South for a full century after the end of the Civil War.

Survival Strategies

Since the Supreme Court had legalized segregation, and the federal government was unwilling to protect black voting rights, African Americans in the Jim Crow South were left to cope with the discrimination as best they could. Many tried to build a strong, supportive black community that operated separately from the world of whites. For instance, they formed lodges and social clubs to give people safe places to gather and make friends or cultivate business relationships. They also built schools and taught their children to read and write, despite white hostility to such efforts. The hard work of black teachers in these segregated schools led to a steady increase in the literacy rate among African Americans, from 7 percent in 1865 to 45 percent in 1880 to 77 percent in 1930. These educational advances provided the foundation for the growth of a small but influential black middle class in the South.

Many other African Americans responded to the lynchings and humiliations of the Jim Crow South by leaving the region entirely. "As long as Jim Crow ruled the South, that system of segregation, subordination, and terror created powerful incentives for leaving and staying away,"[3] explained one

Weary of the segregation that ruled virtually every aspect of social life in the South—even including the use of water fountains—many African Americans fled to the North in the 1910s and 1920s.

historian. The promise of free land lured thousands of black farmers westward to Kansas and Oklahoma during the 1880s and 1890s. As Jim Crow voting rights abuses and violence escalated in the 1890s, many other African Americans migrated to the large cities of the East Coast and Midwest. Still, U.S. Census Bureau figures show that 90 percent of the nation's black population remained in the South at the turn of the twentieth century. The mass migration of blacks to the North began in earnest during World War I. Half a million blacks left the South between 1916 and 1919 to seek work in the industrial cities of New York, Pittsburgh, Detroit, and Chicago. Another million African Americans migrated north and west out of the South during the 1920s.

Although these migrants escaped the formal segregation of the Jim Crow South, they did not always receive a warm welcome in their new surroundings. Many white northerners resented the influx of black workers and the increased competition for good jobs and housing. They also found newly arrived blacks to be a convenient target for their anger, frustration, and concern about political corruption, labor disputes, and other social and economic changes taking place during that time. These tensions erupted into violent race riots in more than twenty large cities—including Chicago and Washington, D.C.—during the "Red Summer" of 1919. Most of the people injured or killed in these riots were African Americans.

Early Resistance

In the meantime, educated blacks in the North debated about how best to attack segregation. Some African-American leaders, including educator Booker T. Washington, felt that the best course of action was to accept Jim Crow for the time being. Washington argued that blacks in the South should continue establishing their own farms, businesses, and schools. He believed that it would be easier to challenge segregation once African Americans had gained greater economic security.

Other African-American leaders, like writer W.E.B. DuBois, chafed at the idea of accepting segregation. Instead, DuBois believed that blacks should insist on equal rights and work to end discrimination. He tried to organize educated blacks in the North to lead a campaign of political and economic resistance to Jim Crow. When DuBois publicly criticized Washington's approach in his 1903 book *The Souls of Black Folk*, it created a rift between the two black leaders.

DuBois and his supporters went on to establish an influential new organization, the National Association for the Advancement of Colored People (NAACP), in 1909. The NAACP's mission was to promote civil rights for African Americans and mount legal and political challenges to Jim Crow. It lobbied the federal government to pass strong anti-lynching laws and protect black voting rights. During the 1920s, the NAACP launched the first in a long series of lawsuits aimed at ending segregation. Organizations such as the National Urban League and the National Negro Congress also launched protests against segregation and disenfranchisement of blacks around this time.

In addition to legal and political resistance, some African Americans used music, art, and literature to express their feelings about racial discrimination in the United States. This cultural resistance reached a peak during the

W.E.B. DuBois stood at the forefront of a new generation of African-American leaders who condemned segregation as a great moral evil.

Harlem Renaissance of the 1920s. Black musicians popularized rich new musical forms like ragtime, jazz, and blues. These sophisticated sounds not only showcased the musicians' talents and originality, but also provided an outlet for their frustrations. Black writers of the period produced literature that pointed out the unfairness and brutality of Jim Crow, encouraged readers to fight segregation, and expressed pride in their racial heritage.

A number of African-American entertainers, artists, and literary figures attracted widespread attention and acclaim from white audiences during this period, which helped change public perceptions about the ability of blacks to contribute to society. In addition, their successes gave African Americans an infusion of pride and confidence that laid the groundwork for the civil rights gains of coming decades.

Voting Rights Expand

Even though white segregationists continued to deny voting rights to African-American men in the Jim Crow South in the 1920s, overall voting rights expanded during that decade. Following a 70-year struggle, American women finally gained the right to vote in 1920 with the passage of the Nineteenth Amendment to the Constitution.

The women's suffrage movement originated in the 1850s. Many of the early leaders of the movement, including Susan B. Anthony and Elizabeth Cady Stanton, got started as political activists by working to abolish slavery. Some women hoped that they would gain the right to vote following the Civil War, as part of the Fourteenth or Fifteenth Amendments. Ultimately, though, lawmakers decided to secure civil rights for the freed slaves first. They argued that making women's suffrage part of these amendments would only make them more controversial and difficult to pass.

Opponents of women's voting rights claimed that a woman's proper place was in the home, caring for a family. They said that participating in politics would distract women from their domestic duties, cause harm to families, and disrupt the social order. Despite such arguments, women gained voting rights in several states and territories from the 1870s to the 1890s. Suffrage activists introduced a number of constitutional amendments that would have provided for national women's voting rights in the early 1900s, but none of these measures made it through Congress.

The women's suffrage movement grew more radical in the 1910s. Activists held large-scale protest marches and rallies, set up picket lines in front of the White House, and went on hunger strikes in prison. These controversial tactics made it increasingly difficult for lawmakers to ignore the movement's demands. Congress finally passed the Nineteenth Amendment in 1919, and it was ratified by the required number of states in 1920. The amendment prohibited the government from restricting voting rights on the basis of sex, and it thus expanded the nation's eligible voting population by 50 percent.

Four years later, Native Americans were granted full citizenship in the United States through the passage of the Indian Citizenship Act of 1924. Although the Fourteenth Amendment had guaranteed the rights of citizenship to all people born in the United States, it only applied to people who were "subject to the jurisdiction" of the federal government. This clause excluded most Native Americans, who were considered members of sovereign nations. Over the years, many Native Americans became U.S. citizens through treaties or other means, such as marrying a citizen or serving in the military. Although the act granted citizenship to all Native Americans, many still struggled to exercise their voting rights in the face of discriminatory state laws.

Notes

1. Davis, Ronald L. F. "Racial Etiquette: The Racial Customs and Rules of Racial Behavior in Jim Crow America," *The History of Jim Crow,* n.d. Available online at http://www.jimcrowhistory.org/resources /lessonplans/hs_es_etiquette.htm.
2. *Veterans of the Civil Rights Movement,* "Voting Rights: Are You Qualified to Vote?" n.d. Available online at http://www.crmvet.org/info/lithome.htm.
3. Gregory, James N. *The Southern Diaspora: How the Great Migrations of Black and White Southerners Transformed America.* Chapel Hill: University of North Carolina Press, 2007.

Chapter Two

BOYCOTTS, SIT-INS, AND FREEDOM RIDES

When a black pays their way to ride the public bus, they shouldn't go up and pay and then go back in the back door and sit in the back of the bus. They pay the same amount that white people pay. They are American citizens. Let them go sit where a seat's available, where they want to sit. That's just basic.

—Federal Judge Frank M. Johnson, explaining his order desegregating public transportation in Montgomery, Alabama

African Americans continued to face segregation and discrimination in the Jim Crow South throughout the first half of the twentieth century. Anger and frustration over this situation increased following World War II—when blacks made important contributions to the war effort as soldiers and defense-industry workers—and helped launch the civil rights movement. Activists started out by attacking the segregation of public schools, then moved on to protest against the segregation of public transportation and private businesses. Although the movement achieved many important legal victories during the 1950s, African Americans still faced a difficult struggle to overcome white resistance that often turned violent.

Black Activism Increases after World War II

The extension of voting rights to American women in 1920 had little effect on African Americans in the Jim Crow South. Black women, like black men, found it virtually impossible to register to vote in the face of poll taxes, literacy tests, harassment, and violence. By 1940, only 3 percent of eligible

Gandhi and Nonviolent Resistance

Nonviolent resistance—peaceful refusal to obey unjust laws and passive acceptance of the consequences of such action—was one of the most effective tools in the American civil rights movement. Martin Luther King, Jr., James Lawson, and other promoters of nonviolent resistance were influenced by the example of Mohandas Gandhi, a religious leader who used the philosophy to combat injustice in India and South Africa earlier in the twentieth century.

Gandhi was born on October 2, 1869, in western India. At that time, his country was a colony of England. British colonial rulers exploited India's people and resources and used unfair laws and high taxes to maintain control.

After studying law in England as a young man, Gandhi took a job in South Africa. Indian immigrants were a minority in that country, and Gandhi was exposed to racial prejudice. In 1906 he called a meeting of 3,000 fellow Indians and convinced them to disobey unfair laws that required them to register with the government. The protesters applied the concept of nonviolent resistance developed by Gandhi and also outlined by the American writer Henry David Thoreau in his *Essay on Civil Disobedience.*

Gandhi returned to India in 1914 determined to resist British colonial rule and gain his nation's independence. He arranged a number of labor

black men were registered to vote in the South. Without the means to participate in government, African Americans throughout the region continued to live as second-class citizens under segregation.

During World War II, this sort of discrimination extended to U.S. military forces. When the United States entered the conflict in 1941, thousands of African Americans volunteered to serve in the military. But they were placed in segregated units, under the command of white officers. Since white military leaders considered black soldiers unfit for combat, the units were generally assigned support tasks, like cooking or moving supplies.

strikes and other protests over the next 30 years. One of his best-known efforts came in 1930, when he organized a nationwide campaign against British Salt Laws. These laws forbade Indians from evaporating seawater to obtain salt. Instead of using this method, they were forced to pay high taxes to buy salt from British authorities. Over 60,000 people were sent to prison for disobeying the laws during the campaign, demonstrating the unity and commitment of the Indian people.

In 1947 Gandhi launched a hunger strike in prison to draw attention to social problems in India. His protest convinced the national Congress to pass a historic resolution making it illegal to discriminate against members of the lowest class in Indian society, known as the Untouchables.

Later that year, British authorities created two separate independent states, India and Pakistan, out of the Hindu and Muslim parts of its former colony. Although it was a hard-fought victory in the movement for independence, Gandhi was disappointed in the arrangement. He had hoped to forge a single, unified nation out of India's various religious and ethnic groups.

Gandhi was assassinated on January 30, 1948, in New Delhi, India. During his lifetime, though, he showed the world that nonviolent resistance had the power to spark revolutionary social change. His philosophy inspired King and formed the backbone of the American civil rights movement.

Many African-American soldiers recognized that they were fighting a two-pronged battle. "The symbol of black participation at that time was the 'Double V,'" according to Bill De Shields, founder of the Black Military History Institute of America. "'Double V' meant two victories: victory against the enemy abroad, and victory against the enemy at home. The enemy at home of course being racism, discrimination, prejudice, and Jim Crow."[1]

Many black leaders pressured the federal government to desegregate the armed forces. The U.S. military eventually agreed to train a few all-black units for combat missions to see if they could perform as well as white units. The most famous among these units was the small group of black pilots known as the Tuskegee Airmen. After receiving training in Alabama, the Tuskegee Airmen flew important missions in North Africa and Europe beginning in 1943. They became the only American unit to sink a German destroyer during the war, and they never lost a bomber to enemy fire in 200 missions. In 1944, facing a desperate shortage of men, General Dwight D. Eisenhower temporarily desegregated the army and allowed black soldiers to fight on the front lines in Europe.

Meanwhile, the fight against discrimination continued on the home front. As millions of American men went off to war, many of the nation's factories and offices scrambled to find enough workers. African-American leaders like A. Philip Randolph recognized that the shortage of workers gave blacks an opportunity to demand greater equality in pay and promotion opportunities regarding wartime jobs. In 1941, Randolph threatened to lead 100,000 protesters in a nonviolent March on Washington if President Franklin D. Roosevelt did not meet this demand. Roosevelt responded by issuing an executive order that guaranteed equal employment opportunities for black workers in government jobs and defense industries. Throughout the war years, more than 2 million African Americans went to work in defense-related jobs and 2 million more joined the civil service.

These wartime jobs gave black workers greater economic power and encouraged the growth of the black middle class. In addition, as African Americans and whites worked together in factories and in the military, it became more difficult for people of both races to accept segregation. Recognizing the contributions made by black soldiers and defense workers, a growing number of whites expressed concern about racial discrimination. At the same time, blacks who took advantage of wartime opportunities were no longer willing to be treated like second-class citizens. African Americans who served in the military, like civil rights leader Medgar Evers, also gained leadership and organizational skills that they could put to use in the fight against segregation at home. In this way, "World War II really gave the Civil Rights movement its spark,"[2] said historian Stephen Ambrose.

In 1948, President Harry S. Truman signed executive order 9981, which officially desegregated the U.S. military. This policy change took some time to implement, however, and the armed forces were not fully integrated until the Vietnam War. In addition, Truman's order did nothing to address the continued segregation of schools, transportation, restaurants, and other facilities throughout the South.

The NAACP Attacks School Segregation

The 1896 Supreme Court ruling in *Plessy v. Ferguson* made segregation of public facilities legal, as long as the facilities provided for blacks and whites were "separate but equal." The fundamental inequality of segregation was most apparent in the public schools in the Jim Crow South. A 1930 study, for instance, showed that South Carolina spent 10 times more money educating a white child than it did a black child. Such disparities occurred in other states, as well. All across the South, African-American students could be found attending classes in unheated shacks, while white students went to school in brick buildings.

Howard University law professor Charles Houston traveled through the region documenting the differences in education for black and white children. He then trained a group of talented black lawyers, including future Supreme Court Justice Thurgood Marshall, to challenge segregation laws in federal court. Houston and his team achieved their first victory in 1935, when they forced the University of Maryland law school to admit its first African-American student, Donald Murray.

Most of these early legal cases tried to give black students access to equal educational opportunities, especially in graduate programs, which were not widely available at all-black colleges. As the civil rights movement blossomed following World War II, however, the strategy shifted. Marshall and other members of the NAACP Legal Defense Committee used the federal courts to challenge the basic concept of "separate but equal." They charged that segregation could never provide equal treatment for African Americans.

In 1950 the NAACP lawyers launched an attack on the constitutionality of the *Plessy* ruling as it applied to public schools. They compiled extensive evidence to show how segregated schools discriminated against black students and placed them at an educational disadvantage compared to white students. They filed a number of lawsuits on behalf of black children whose educational opportunities were limited by segregation. One of these cases, *Brown v. Board of Education of Topeka, Kansas*, concerned a little girl named Linda Brown. A public school for white children was located near her home. Because of the state's segregation laws, however, she had to cross a busy railroad switching yard in order to catch a bus to attend a distant school for black children.

Another case, *Briggs v. Clarendon County, South Carolina*, pointed out the extreme differences in the quality of education provided to white and black

Studies of black children carried out by psychologist Kenneth Clark were a potent weapon in the NAACP's efforts to end segregation in America's public schools.

students in segregated schools. School administrators in Clarendon County spent $179 per year to educate each white child, compared to $43 per year for each black child. In addition, the school district provided one teacher for every 28 white students, compared to one teacher for every 47 black students.

The NAACP lawyers hoped to secure a broad Supreme Court ruling that would overturn *Plessy* and find segregation of public schools unconstitutional. They presented arguments in *Brown, Briggs,* and several other related cases before the Supreme Court on December 9, 1952. During the trial, some of the most convincing evidence of the damaging effects of segregated schools came from psychologist Kenneth Clark. He conducted a series of interviews with black children that showed how segregation lowered their self-esteem. "Segregation was, is, the way in which a society tells a group of human beings that they are inferior to other groups of human beings in the society," Clark explained. "It really is internalized in children, learning they cannot go to the same schools as other children, that they are required to attend clearly inferior schools than others are permitted to attend. It influences the child's view of himself."[3]

As the Supreme Court struggled to reach a decision, Chief Justice Fred M. Vinson died of a heart attack. The remaining justices decided to rehear the case in December 1953 under the new chief justice, Earl Warren. On May 17, 1954, the Court announced its decision. "We conclude, unanimously, that in the field of public education the doctrine of 'separate but equal' has no place," the opinion stated. "Separate educational facilities are inherently unequal." The landmark *Brown* ruling overturned *Plessy* and declared state-mandated segregation in public schools to be unconstitutional.

School Desegregation Efforts Meet with Massive Resistance

Although civil rights activists hailed the *Brown* ruling as a major legal blow against segregation, they knew that it would be difficult to change the longstanding system of Jim Crow laws. As soon as the Supreme Court decision was announced, a number of Southern politicians declared their intention to ignore or defy it. Georgia Governor Herman Talmadge, for instance, claimed that "no force whatever could compel" desegregation in his state. Virginia Senator Harry F. Byrd urged fellow white Southerners to mount a campaign of "massive resistance" to school integration. Mississippi Senator James Eastland told the people of his state that "You are not obliged to obey the decisions of any court which are plainly fraudulent."[4]

The initial *Brown* ruling did not include instructions on how the states should go about desegregating schools. After hearing further arguments on the issue, the Supreme Court released a second decision on May 31, 1955. Instead of offering a specific remedy for the wrongs of school segregation, this vaguely worded ruling—which came to be known as *Brown II*—only said that states must admit black children "to public schools on a racially nondiscriminatory basis with all deliberate speed."

Some Southern communities came up with desegregation plans and implemented them without incident. Many others, however, either delayed compliance or openly defied the ruling. One of the key school integration battles took place in Little Rock, Arkansas, where nine African-American students attempted to enroll in the formerly all-white Central High School in the fall of 1957.

Arkansas Governor Orval Faubus threatened that "blood will run in the streets" if federal authorities tried to enforce the desegregation order. He then surrounded Central High School with Arkansas National Guard troops to prevent the black students from entering. President Eisenhower was reluctant to intervene, but he eventually sent federal troops to Little Rock to control the violent white mobs outside the school and enforce the *Brown* ruling. The crisis in Little Rock resulted in a tense, year-long standoff between the state and federal governments. The bravery of the black students known as the Little Rock Nine, who remained at Central High despite harassment and intimidation, served as an inspiration for the growing civil rights movement.

Maintaining Segregation through Violence and Fear

Encouraged by the defiant attitudes of their political leaders, many white Southerners resisted desegregation efforts with threats or violence. Some middle-class whites formed community organizations called White Cit-

African-American high school students enter a formerly all-white school in Clinton, Tennessee, in 1956.

izens Councils. The purpose of these groups, as one council leader explained, was to use their economic resources "to make it difficult, if not impossible, for any Negro who advocates desegregation to find and hold a job, get credit, or renew a mortgage."[5] In more extreme cases, white supremacist gangs tried to maintain the Jim Crow system by beating, raping, burning, or lynching African Americans who dared to support desegregation.

Mississippi experienced a particularly violent backlash against the *Brown* ruling. In early 1955, for instance, NAACP activists Lamar Smith and the Reverend George W. Lee were killed for trying to help African Americans register to vote in the state. Countless other violent incidents occurred in Mississippi as white racists created an atmosphere of fear to keep segregation in place (see "Learning the Bitter Truth about Jim Crow," p. 167).

The most infamous incident took place in the summer of 1955. A 14-year-old African-American boy from Chicago, Emmett Till, traveled south with a cousin to visit an older relative, Mose Wright, in Money, Mississippi. In Till's hometown, African Americans enjoyed decent job opportunities and held some political influence. Till's mother, Mamie Bradley, had warned her son that the situation was very different for blacks in the South. Till was nevertheless unprepared for the strict rules of appropriate behavior he encountered in Mississippi.

One night during his visit, Till went to a country store and bragged to the black boys outside about having a white girlfriend back home in Chicago. The boys dared him to go into the store and talk to the attractive white woman inside. Till entered the store, bought some candy, and said "Bye, Baby" to the white woman as he left.

A few days later, the woman's husband, Roy Bryant, learned about the incident. He and his brother-in-law went to Mose Wright's cabin looking for vengeance. Wright tried to explain that Till was just a boy and did not understand the way things worked in the South. But the two white men dragged Till outside, threw him into their car, and drove away. Authorities found the teenager's mangled body three days later in the Tallahatchie River. Till had been beaten severely and shot in the head.

Unlike many other incidents of racist violence in the South, the murder of Emmett Till received a great deal of media attention. A grief-stricken Mamie Bradley insisted that her son's body be shipped home to Chicago and displayed in an open casket, so that the whole world could see the results of racist brutality. Thousands of people attended the funeral, and pictures of Till's body were published nationwide in *Jet* magazine.

A few weeks later, Roy Bryant and his accomplice went on trial for murder. Despite constant threats and harassment, Mose Wright testified against the men in court. His brave and defiant act encouraged several other African-American witnesses to come forward. Despite all the evidence against them, Bryant and his brother-in-law were found not guilty by an all-white jury on September 23.

The brutal murder of Emmett Till and the injustice of the jury's verdict had a profound effect on black America. Countless African Americans expressed their outrage in passionate speeches and editorials, and contributions to the NAACP reached record levels. "The murder of Emmett Till had a powerful impact on a new generation of blacks," noted one historian. "It was this generation, those who were adolescents when Till was killed, that would soon demand justice and freedom in a way unknown in America before."[6]

The Montgomery Bus Boycott

Just a few months after the Till verdict was announced, African Americans in Montgomery, Alabama, launched one of the first large-scale protests against segregation. Activists organized a boycott of the city's bus system in an effort to extend desegregation to the area of public transportation.

The Montgomery Bus Boycott started on December 1, 1955, when a seamstress named Rosa Parks refused to give up her seat on a public bus to a white passenger. At that time, the front few rows of every city bus were reserved for white passengers, and the back few rows were reserved for colored passengers. African Americans were required to board through the back doors and fill the seats from back to front, while whites were required to board through the front doors and fill the seats from front to back. When a white passenger got onto a full bus, the black passengers in the row closest to the front had to get up and move to the back.

When Parks refused to obey the segregated seating policy, she was arrested and taken to jail. Several African Americans had been arrested in the past for similar actions, and Parks did not expect that her defiance would spark a city-wide bus boycott. But given her good standing in the community, black leaders in Montgomery decided that Parks's arrest provided them with an ideal opportunity to launch a protest.

Jo Ann Robinson, president of the Women's Political Council, prepared a flyer that described the situation and called on Montgomery's black population to boycott the bus system the following Monday, December 5. "Another Negro woman has been arrested and thrown in jail because she refused to get up out of her seat on the bus for a white person to sit down," the flyer stated. "Three-fourths of the riders are Negroes, yet we are arrested, or have to stand over empty seats. If we do not do something to stop these arrests, they will continue. The next time it may be you, or your daughter, or mother. This woman's case will come up on Monday. We are, therefore, asking every Negro to stay off the buses Monday in protest."[7] The Women's Political Council distributed 35,000 copies of the flyer around the city.

When Monday came, the buses that ran through the streets of Montgomery were nearly empty. Thousands of African Americans who usually rode the bus to work or school either stayed home, walked, took taxis, or got rides from church carpools or white employers. When Rosa Parks appeared in court that day, she was found guilty of violating the city's segregation ordinance and fined $14.

When Rosa Parks—shown here being fingerprinted by a Montgomery police officer—was arrested for refusing to give up her bus seat to a white man, the incident touched off a massive bus boycott by African-American residents.

Organizers originally expected the bus boycott to last only one day. But the tremendous success of the initial effort made them consider extending it. Thousands of supporters turned out for a mass meeting that night at Holt Street Baptist Church. After hearing a stirring civil rights speech by a relatively unknown young minister, the Reverend Martin Luther King, Jr. (see King biography, p. 146), attendees voted to continue the boycott until the city agreed to desegregate the bus system.

King became president of the newly formed Montgomery Improvement Association (MIA), which tried to negotiate with city leaders. But Montgomery Mayor W.A. Gayle refused to compromise with the protesters. "We are going to hold our stand," he declared. "We are not going to be a part of any program that will get Negroes to ride the buses again at the price of the destruction of our heritage and way of life."[8] Although King and other leaders of the boycott faced intimidation and violence from angry whites, these tactics only increased the unity and sense of purpose in Montgomery's black community.

The Montgomery Bus Boycott lasted 381 days and involved an estimated 42,000 black residents of the city. It ended as a result of a federal lawsuit brought by the MIA, *Browder v. Gayle*. MIA lawyers argued that the *Brown* ruling that desegregated public schools should apply to all forms of state-mandated segregation, including public transportation. On May 11, 1956, federal circuit court judges Frank M. Johnson and Richard T. Rives accepted the MIA's argument and ordered the city to desegregate its bus system. The U.S. Supreme Court upheld the lower court's ruling on November 13, and the boycott ended when Montgomery city officials obeyed the court order on December 20 (see "White Support for the Montgomery Bus Boycott," p. 172).

The Greensboro Lunch Counter Sit-ins

The success of the Montgomery Bus Boycott encouraged African Americans in other cities across the South to challenge segregation laws. Even after the Supreme Court declared the segregation of public schools and public transportation to be illegal, segregation was still widely practiced in private businesses, such as stores and restaurants. Many white Southerners felt that business owners—as private citizens—had a right to associate with whomever they chose. They claimed that the federal government should not be able to force them to serve African Americans. The growing civil rights movement, on the other hand, argued that African Americans had the right to shop or eat anywhere they wanted. They felt that the same rules against segregation that applied to state and federal governments should also apply to private businesses.

Many civil rights activists found the segregation of lunch counters in the South to be particularly unfair. Large chain department stores like Woolworth's, which operated in towns throughout the North and South, often

The Founding of SCLC

The success of the Montgomery Bus Boycott got civil rights activists thinking about ways to expand anti-segregation protests to other cities in the South. In 1956 Bayard Rustin presented several ideas in a series of working papers. One of his key suggestions involved forming a central organization to coordinate such efforts.

Martin Luther King, Jr., followed up on this suggestion the following year. He organized the Negro Leaders Conference on Nonviolent Integration, a meeting of 60 black ministers held at Ebenezer Baptist Church in Atlanta. This meeting led to the formation of the Southern Christian Leadership Conference (SCLC) as an umbrella organization to coordinate direct-action protests by local affiliates across the South. Under King's leadership, SCLC defined racism and segregation as moral issues and explained its mission as "redeeming the soul of America" through nonviolent protest.

Using the power of black churches, SCLC activists trained local communities across the South in the use of Christian nonviolence. The organization coordinated major civil rights protests in several cities during the early 1960s, including Albany, Georgia, and Birmingham, Alabama. It also played an important role in organizing the 1963 March on Washington and the 1965 Selma-Montgomery Voting Rights March.

With the charismatic King as its spokesman, SCLC brought increased visibility to the civil rights struggle. Following the passage of the Voting Rights Act of 1965, however, tensions grew between SCLC and more militant groups over the continued value of nonviolence. Although the assassination of King in 1968 led to a decline in membership, SCLC continued to exist into the twenty-first century. It expanded its activities nationwide and remained committed to using nonviolent action to achieve social, economic, and political justice.

adapted their policies to local conditions. Since whites in the North generally accepted the presence of blacks in the stores and restaurants they frequented, Woolworth's in that region were fully desegregated. In the South, on the other

Angry whites attack a sit-in demonstrator at a segregated Nashville lunch counter in February 1960.

hand, most Woolworth's stores had policies that prohibited blacks from eating alongside whites at the lunch counter.

On February 1, 1960, four African-American students from North Carolina Agricultural & Technical State University—Franklin McCain, Joseph McNeil, Ezell Blair, Jr., and David Richmond—decided to challenge this policy. Tired of just complaining to each other about the situation, they went to the lunch counter at the Woolworth's in Greensboro, North Carolina, and sat down. The young men knew that the store owner would refuse to serve them. But they planned to continue sitting there in peaceful protest until they were dragged out or arrested. "With their very bodies they obstructed the wheels of injustice,"[9] wrote civil rights leader James Farmer.

The Greensboro Lunch Counter Sit-in expanded quickly in the ensuing weeks. As the crowd of protesters grew, the sit-in received coverage on national television news programs. Before long, students at black colleges throughout the South launched their own sit-ins at segregated lunch counters in their towns. Over the next few months, the sit-in movement spread to nine states in the South, but the impact was felt all across the country. As residents of the North became more aware of the unfair policies that Woolworth's and other national retail chains used in the South, many people—both black and white—boycotted the stores to show their support for the students.

The sit-in participants faced harassment from angry whites. Some protesters were beaten, spat upon, or had food dumped on them. But they steadfastly refused to respond to the taunting and stuck to a philosophy of nonviolent resistance (see sidebar "Gandhi and Nonviolent Resistance," p. 22). Their outright defiance of segregation eventually took such a financial toll on Woolworth's and other targeted national retailers that the chains gave in and integrated lunch counters throughout the South. The sit-ins also led to the creation of a new, student-based arm of the civil rights movement that would have a strong influence on the fight for African-American voting rights.

Founding of the Student Nonviolent Coordinating Committee

In the midst of the student-led sit-ins at lunch counters throughout the South, activist Ella Baker (see Baker biography, p. 127) of the Southern Christian Leadership Conference (see sidebar "The Founding of SCLC," p. 33) recognized that the protesters would benefit from increased leadership and direction. She invited representatives from various student and civil rights groups—including the NAACP, SCLC, Congress on Racial Equality (CORE), and Students for a Democratic Society (SDS)—to a conference on the campus of Shaw University in Raleigh, North Carolina. Baker expected about 100 people to attend the meeting and instead ended up with more than 300 participants.

Some leaders of long-established civil rights organizations like the NAACP felt that the student sit-ins were counterproductive. They argued that African Americans could best achieve their long-term goal of racial equality through legal and political means. But Baker was impressed by the enthusiasm and dedication of the student protesters. She knew that some members of the younger generation felt dissatisfied with the slow pace of desegregation and the strategies applied by established civil rights groups. She sensed that they were eager to chart a new course. Baker later said that the conference made it "crystal clear that the current sit-in and other demonstrations are

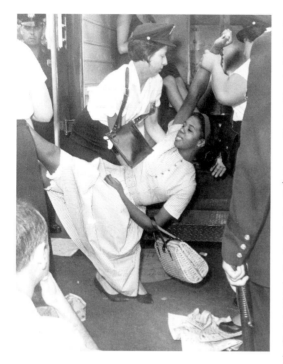

Young African Americans—such as this woman being arrested during a civil rights demonstration in Brooklyn, New York—were the leading foot soldiers in the civil rights movement.

concerned with something bigger than a hamburger.... The Negro and white students, North and South, are seeking to rid America of the scourge of racial segregation and discrimination—not only at lunch counters but in every aspect of life."[10]

Rather than asking the students to join the youth councils of the NAACP or SCLC, Baker encouraged them to establish a new organization and pursue their own goals. The students took her advice and founded the Student Nonviolent Coordinating Committee (SNCC, pronounced Snick) (see "Ella Baker Describes the Founding of SNCC," p. 174). The first mission of the new organization involved coordinating and publicizing the lunch counter sit-ins, but it soon moved on to play an active role in other protests. SNCC recruited student leaders from college campuses and sent them into rural areas to organize local protest movements. The organization introduced future black leaders like John Lewis (see Lewis biography, p. 151), Julian Bond, and Marion Barry to civil rights activism.

The Election of 1960

As the sit-ins continued into the summer of 1960, the United States prepared to elect a new president. The Republican vice president, Richard M. Nixon, faced off against a charismatic young Democratic senator from Massachusetts, John F. Kennedy. Both candidates generally tried to avoid addressing civil rights issues on the campaign trail. To win the presidency, they knew they needed support from black voters and moderate whites in the North. But they also wanted to avoid alienating the white segregationists who held political power in the South. Nixon especially had to court these voters, because many of them still resented President Eisenhower's decision to send federal troops to enforce school integration in Little Rock. Kennedy expressed support for gradual desegregation, calling the Supreme Court's vague *Brown II* ruling "satisfactory."

With neither candidate willing to take a strong stand, many civil rights activists had trouble deciding which one should get their vote. Historically, most African-American voters had tended to favor the Republican party. Republican President Abraham Lincoln was responsible for ending slavery, after all, and Republicans had granted blacks citizenship and voting rights during Reconstruction. Furthermore, the white segregationists who came to power in the South following Reconstruction—and created the Jim Crow system—were Democrats. The party affiliation of some African Americans started to waver during the Great Depression of the 1930s, however, when Democrat Franklin Roosevelt passed a number of economic programs that helped poor blacks. By the 1960 election, many African Americans were willing to support whichever candidate promised to do more to advance civil rights.

The tide turned in October 1960, just a month before American voters went to the polls to elect a new president. Civil rights leader Martin Luther King, Jr., was arrested for participating in a restaurant sit-in in Atlanta and sentenced to four months in prison. Nixon decided not to intervene. But Kennedy called King's wife, Coretta Scott King, personally to express his support, then used political connections to help King get out of jail. Afterward, King broke with tradition and publicly endorsed the Democrat. Kennedy's campaign literature described him as "the candidate with a heart," in contrast to "no-comment Nixon."[11]

Kennedy ended up winning 68 percent of the black vote nationwide, which helped him gain the presidency by a very narrow margin. Convinced that Kennedy owed them a political debt, some African Americans were disappointed when the new president did not immediately take steps to introduce new civil rights legislation. A few months after Kennedy took office, civil rights leaders decided to test his willingness to use the power of the federal government to enforce desegregation.

The Freedom Rides

In December 1960, the Supreme Court issued yet another decision that outlawed segregation in public facilities. Its ruling in *Boynton v. Virginia* declared that federal laws governing interstate commerce prohibited states from forcing black and white travelers to use separate bus and train terminals, restrooms, and waiting areas. As had been the case with earlier desegregation orders, however, many states simply ignored the ruling. By the spring of 1961, most transportation facilities remained segregated in the Jim Crow South.

Civil rights leaders came up with a plan to defy the local segregation laws through nonviolent resistance. They recruited groups of black and white protesters to take Freedom Rides—or integrated bus trips—through the segregated South. Whenever they reached a major city, the protesters planned to enter the bus terminals together and exercise their legal right to use the public facilities, without regard to the signs designating those facilities for white or colored travelers.

The first Freedom Ride left Washington, D.C., on May 4, 1961. The group of six white and seven black riders, including CORE director James Farmer (see Farmer biography, p. 132, and "James Farmer Remembers the Freedom Rides," p. 176) and SNCC activist John Lewis, planned to follow a route through several Southern cities on the way to New Orleans. They knew that they were likely to encounter violent resistance on their journey. "We were told that the racists, the segregationists, would go to any extent to hold the line on segregation in interstate travel," remembered Farmer. "So when we began the ride I think all of us were prepared for as much violence as could be thrown at us. We were prepared for the possibility of death."[12]

The Freedom Riders passed through Virginia and North Carolina without incident. In Rock Hill, South Carolina, however, they were attacked by a white mob as they tried to enter a whites-only waiting room at the Greyhound bus terminal. Local police showed up to disperse the mob and let the protesters enter the waiting room. After continuing on through Georgia, the bus carrying the Freedom Riders was stopped at the Alabama border. An angry white mob surrounded the bus, slashed its tires, and set it on fire. Some members of the mob held the bus doors shut in an attempt to trap the Freedom Riders inside the burning vehicle. A potential tragedy was averted when an undercover police officer drew his gun and forced the mob to let the protesters exit the bus.

Even after the first vehicle was destroyed, the Freedom Riders continued their journey through Alabama on another bus. In the town of Anniston, a group of white segregationists boarded the bus and beat the protesters with iron pipes and baseball bats. Several of the Freedom Riders had to be treated at a hospital for injuries afterward. Although they wanted to continue their

A Freedom Rider bus goes up in flames in May 1961 outside Anniston, Alabama, after a fire bomb attack.

journey, they could not find a bus driver willing to take them any further. The protesters had to fly to New Orleans, ending the first Freedom Ride.

Despite the violent reception that the initial effort received, SNCC leaders were determined to continue pursuing the Freedom Ride strategy. "If the Freedom Ride had been stopped as a result of violence, I strongly felt that the future of the movement was going to be, just cut short," organizer Diane Nash recalled in a 1985 interview. "Because the impression would have been given that whenever a movement starts, all that has to be done is that you attack it, massive violence, and the blacks would stop. And I thought that was a very dangerous thing to happen."[13]

Nash quickly organized a second group of riders, who started in Nashville, Tennessee, on May 17. Upon reaching Birmingham, Alabama, the protesters were arrested by Police Chief Eugene "Bull" Connor. The Freedom Riders responded by going on a hunger strike and singing protest songs in the city jail. Connor then arranged for their release and transported them back to the Tennessee line, where his officers dropped them off alongside the highway.

At this point, President Kennedy called Alabama Governor John Patterson and told him that the state had a responsibility to protect the safety of interstate travelers. Patterson reluctantly sent the state police to escort the Freedom Riders' bus across the state to Montgomery. When they reached the Montgomery bus terminal, however, the police escort suddenly disappeared. A violent mob of 300 white segregationists attacked the Freedom Riders, as well as reporters who tried to take pictures of the assault.

Embarrassed by extensive news coverage of the violence, the Kennedy administration asked civil rights leaders to stop the Freedom Rides and observe a "cooling off period." They rejected this request, however, and continued sponsoring rides. Around 60 different buses carrying a total of more than 400 protesters made their way through the South during the summer of 1961. Following the incident in Montgomery, national guardsmen accompanied the protesters on the buses. Although the presence of armed troops led to a decrease in violence, the number of protesters who were arrested for disobeying local segregation laws rose steadily. Many of the later journeys ended in Jackson, Mississippi, where hundreds of Freedom Riders filled the local jails and state penitentiary.

The persistence and determination of the Freedom Riders, though, finally convinced the Kennedy administration to take action to end discrimination. In September the federal Interstate Commerce Commission issued a formal order requiring the desegregation of all public transportation facilities. When the order took effect on November 1, 1961, interstate travelers gained the legal right to sit wherever they wanted on buses and trains and use the same terminals, waiting rooms, restrooms, and lunch counters—regardless of race.

The Freedom Rides thus increased the credibility of the entire civil rights movement. People across the United States had watched with horror as both black and white Americans endured savage beatings in an effort to end segregation in interstate transportation. To many Americans, these scenes had underscored the bravery of the civil rights activists and the legitimacy of their cause. In addition, the successful protests demonstrated the effectiveness of nonviolent resistance and gave many others the courage to defy Jim Crow laws. The Freedom Rides were particularly inspiring for rural blacks in the South, who became the backbone of future campaigns for voting rights.

Notes

[1] Quoted in "African-American Soldiers in World War II Helped Pave the Way for Integration of U.S. Military," *Voice of America News*, May 10, 2005. Available online at http://www.voanews.com /english/archive/2005-05/2005-05-10-voa47.cfm.

2   Quoted in Krause, Lisa. "Black Soldiers in World War II: Fighting Enemies at Home and Abroad." *National Geographic News,* February 15, 2001. Available online at http://news.nationalgeographic.com/news/2001/02/0215_tuskegee.html.

3   Quoted in Williams, Juan. *Eyes on the Prize: America's Civil Rights Years, 1954-1965.* New York: Viking Penguin, 1987, p. 20.

4   Quoted in Telgen, Diane. *Defining Moments: Brown v. Board of Education.* Detroit: Omnigraphics, 2005, p. 75.

5   Quoted in Williams, p. 39.

6   Williams, p. 57.

7   Quoted in Hare, Ken. "They Changed the World: The Story of the Montgomery Bus Boycott," *Montgomery Advertiser,* June 7, 2005. Available online at http://www.montgomeryboycott.com/article_overview.htm.

8   Quoted in Hare.

9   Quoted in Schlosser, Jim. "The Story of the Greensboro Sit-Ins," *News and Record,* 1998. Available online at http://www.sitins.com/story.shtml.

10 Baker, Ella. "Bigger Than a Hamburger." *The Southern Patriot,* May 1960.

11 Wofford, Harris. *Of Kennedys and Kings: Making Sense of the Sixties.* Pittsburgh, PA: University of Pittsburgh Press, 1992, p. 16.

12 Farmer, James. *Heart Lay Bare the Heart: An Autobiography of the Civil Rights Movement.* 1985. Fort Worth: Texas Christian University Press, 1998.

13 Nash, Diane. Quoted in an interview conducted November 12, 1985. Available online at http://www.teachersdomain.org/resources/iml04/soc/ush/civil/nash/assets/iml04_doc_fullnash/iml04_doc_fullnash.pdf.

Chapter Three

THE MARCH
ON WASHINGTON

—⫘⫘⫘⫘—

We are confronted primarily with a moral issue.... The heart of the question is whether all Americans are going to be afforded equal rights and equal opportunities, whether we are going to treat our fellow Americans as we want to be treated.

—President John F. Kennedy, nationally televised address,
June 11, 1963

Beginning with the Supreme Court's landmark *Brown v. Board of Education* ruling in 1954—and continuing through the Montgomery bus boycott, Greensboro lunch counter sit-ins, and Freedom Rides of the late 1950s and early 1960s—African Americans made a number of important legal gains in the fight to end segregation. Civil rights activists faced further battles, however, to ensure the compliance of white leaders in the South.

Several of these battles took place in 1963 and helped increase public awareness of and support for the civil rights movement. For instance, many Americans were horrified by television news footage of police brutality toward peaceful protesters in Birmingham, Alabama. Others were outraged by racist comments made by Alabama Governor George Wallace as he attempted to block two black students from attending classes at the University of Alabama. These and other events helped convince President John F. Kennedy to introduce sweeping new civil rights legislation in Congress. In an unprecedented display of unity and determination, a quarter-million people demonstrated their support for the bill by participating in the triumphant March on Washington.

The Albany Movement

Supreme Court rulings and federal orders did little to convince diehard segregationists in the South to abandon their discriminatory practices. Instead, they often looked for ways to ignore, delay, resist, or obstruct desegregation efforts. With the law on their side, however, civil rights activists continued to organize nonviolent protests in an attempt to force white leaders to comply. One such campaign was launched in the fall of 1961 in Albany, Georgia, a farming community with a population that was 40 percent black.

Following the September 1961 Interstate Commerce Commission order requiring the desegregation of interstate transportation facilities, a group of students from Albany State College decided to test whether local officials would comply with the ruling. When the black students went to Albany's bus terminal, they found that the facilities were still segregated. Albany's police chief, Laurie Pritchett, had the students arrested.

Various civil rights groups, including SNCC and SCLC, quickly mobilized the community in protest. They arranged Freedom Rides to the bus terminal and launched sit-ins and boycotts of local businesses. Martin Luther King, Jr., came to town to give a speech and was arrested for participating in the protests. But Pritchett proved to be a wily adversary for King and other civil rights leaders. Instead of charging the activists with violating local segregation laws—which he knew to be illegal—the police chief charged them with crimes that were more difficult to contest in court, such as trespassing, loitering, failing to obey a police officer, and marching without a permit.

King left Albany after city leaders insisted that they would only negotiate with local residents, not "outside agitators." But the two sides could not reach an agreement, and the Albany Movement continued fighting segregation in the city for several more years. King viewed his involvement in the protests as a failure, but Albany provided the SCLC with experience in community organizing that soon proved valuable in Birmingham, Alabama.

Children March in Birmingham

Birmingham had a poor history of race relations. The city closed dozens of parks, playgrounds, and swimming pools rather than obey orders to allow black residents to use them. When the Freedom Rides passed through Birmingham, Police Commissioner Eugene "Bull" Connor made no effort to protect the protesters from being attacked by violent white mobs. In addition, there had been 18 unsolved bombings in the city's black neighborhoods over the previous five years.

In recognition of the city's dismal civil rights record, King chose Birmingham as the site of the SCLC's next major direct-action protest. The campaign got started in April 1963, when the prominent minister was arrested on Good Friday and spent the Easter holiday in prison. Following King's arrest, a group of local white clergymen published a full-page advertisement in the *Birmingham News* condemning him as a troublemaker. King responded by writing his famous "Letter from a Birmingham Jail," in which he explained the philosophy of nonviolent resistance to his fellow pastors:

> You may well ask, "Why direct action? Why sit-ins, marches, and so forth? Isn't negotiation a better path?" You are quite right in calling for negotiations. Indeed, this is the very purpose of direct action. Nonviolent direct action seeks to create such a crisis and foster such a tension that a community which has constantly refused to negotiate is forced to confront the issue. It seeks so to dramatize the issue that it can no longer be ignored.[1]

In accordance with this philosophy, SCLC activists recruited schoolchildren to participate in desegregation protests in Birmingham. On May 2, more than 900 children were arrested as they marched toward downtown from the Sixteenth Street Baptist Church. City police turned the local fairgrounds into a makeshift jail to hold all of the protesters. The following day, 1,000 more children skipped school and prepared to make another march. But Connor ordered his officers to use police dogs and fire hoses to break up the demonstration. People across the country saw television footage of black children being blasted off their feet and rolled down the street by the force of the water cannons. Photos showing the brutal treatment of the young protesters by Birmingham Police appeared in magazines and newspapers around the world.

The violence in Birmingham shocked and outraged many Americans, including President Kennedy. He sent Justice Department official Burke Marshall to the city to help negotiate a settlement between the protesters and white business leaders. On May 10, representatives of the city's business owners agreed to integrate lunch counters and hire more black workers in exchange for an end to the demonstrations and boycotts.

Encouraged by Connor, however, white segregationists refused to accept the settlement. Instead of a truce, a new wave of violence hit Birmingham. The Ku Klux Klan held a rally, and bombs exploded at the motel where King was staying as well as at his brother's home. Some angry and frustrated African Americans abandoned nonviolent resistance and began rioting, resulting in violent clashes with the police. President Kennedy addressed the situation by sending federal troops to Fort McClellan, about 30 miles outside Birmingham, and threatening to use them to restore order in the city. The conflict ended a short time later, however, when Albert Boutwell became the new mayor of Birmingham and agreed to honor the settlement.

George Wallace Obstructs Desegregation

The effort to secure civil rights for African Americans in Alabama soon reached another crisis point, however. The new governor of the state, George Wallace (see Wallace biography, p. 156), was an ardent supporter of the Jim Crow system who had been elected on a campaign slogan of "Segregation now! Segregation tomorrow! Segregation forever!" When a federal court ordered the University of Alabama to admit black students, Wallace claimed that the ruling was a violation of states' rights. On June 11, 1963, Wallace stood in the doorway of a university building to prevent two African-American students, James Hood and Vivian Malone, from entering. Wallace reluctantly stepped aside when confronted by federal marshals, though, and the University of Alabama was finally integrated almost a decade after the Supreme Court declared school segregation illegal.

Later that night, President Kennedy appeared on national television to address the nation about civil rights. He framed it as a moral issue and announced his intention to introduce a new bill in Congress to promote desegregation in the South.

> We face ... a moral crisis as a country and as a people. It cannot be met by repressive police action. It cannot be left to increased demonstrations in the streets. It cannot be quieted by token moves or talk. It is a time to act in Congress, in your state and local legislative bodies and, above all, in all of our daily lives. I am therefore asking the Congress to enact legislation giving all Americans the right to be served in facilities which are open to the public—hotels, restaurants, theaters,

Gov. George Wallace (left, standing between officers) stands in the doorway of the University of Alabama administration building to display his anger about federal efforts to integrate the school.

retail stores and similar establishments. This seems to me to be an elementary right. Its denial is an arbitrary indignity that no American in 1963 should have to endure.

True to his word, Kennedy introduced a sweeping new civil rights bill in Congress on June 19. The proposed bill outlawed segregation in all types of public accommodations, allowed the attorney general to file lawsuits to enforce school integration, and shut off federal funding for any programs that discriminated against African Americans. It also addressed the South's systematic denial of black voting rights with a provision establishing that any adult with a sixth-grade education was eligible to vote.

The Murder of Medgar Evers

On the very evening that President Kennedy made his historic speech about civil rights, a tragic incident occurred that shed new light on the hate

Myrlie Evers comforts her grieving son Darrell at her husband's funeral.

and fear that continued to reign in parts of the South. Medgar Evers, a prominent civil rights activist, was shot and killed in the driveway of his home in Jackson, Mississippi.

A Mississippi native, Evers had experienced racial discrimination throughout his life. After serving overseas with the U.S. military in World War II, he returned home and registered to vote. When he went to the polls, however, a mob of white segregationists wielding guns and knives prevented the veteran from exercising his rights. Evers was a standout student at Alcorn College, and he dreamed of becoming a lawyer. Even after the *Brown* ruling outlawed segregation in public schools, however, he was denied admission to law school at the University of Mississippi because of his race.

These experiences convinced Evers to join the NAACP in 1954, and he soon became the organization's first Mississippi field director. Although the population of Mississippi was 45 percent black, only 5 percent of eligible African Americans were registered to vote. The Jim Crow system was well-entrenched in the state, and African Americans who did not follow the rules faced harassment and violence.

Evers's job with the NAACP included investigating unsolved murders of African Americans. For instance, he worked on the case of Emmett Till, a black teenager from Chicago who was killed for speaking to a white woman. During the summer of 1961, Evers also worked with SNCC volunteers to teach voter registration clinics and nonviolent protest methods. The following year, he helped African-American student James Meredith launch a successful lawsuit to gain admission to the University of Mississippi. When Mississippi Governor Ross Barnett defied a federal court order to integrate the school,

President Kennedy had to send in federal troops to enforce it. Evers supported Meredith throughout his graduate studies and shared in the victory when he became the first African American to earn a degree from the school in 1963.

In May 1963, Jackson Mayor Allen C. Thompson made a televised address warning the city's black residents not to cooperate with "outside agitators" who came to stir up racial trouble. Evers convinced the local TV station to provide him with air time to respond. He delivered a passionate speech, calling on African Americans to use nonviolent resistance methods to create social change. Jackson residents listened to his message and volunteered for sit-ins, boycotts, and other protests. Evers was widely viewed as the inspirational force behind the movement.

On June 12, though, Evers was ambushed by an assassin who hid in the bushes across the street from his home. Neighbors rushed to help, but Evers died before he reached the hospital. The next night his widow, Myrlie Evers, spoke at a rally in Jackson and asked supporters to continue the fight for civil rights. "Nothing can bring Medgar back, but the cause can live on," she declared. "It was his wish that this movement be one of the most successful that this nation has ever known. We cannot let his death be in vain."[2] Following a funeral that was attended by black and white leaders from across the country, Evers was buried at Arlington National Cemetery near Washington, D.C. Afterward, his wife and young children were invited to meet with President Kennedy at the White House.

A short time later, Jackson police arrested white supremacist Byron de la Beckwith and charged him with the murder of Medgar Evers. Although prosecutors presented a great deal of evidence against Beckwith, he was treated like a hero by many high-profile white segregationists, including Governor Barnett. All-white juries failed to reach a verdict in two separate 1964 trials, so Beckwith was allowed to go free. Thirty years later, he faced trial for a third time and was finally convicted (see sidebar "Belated Justice for Medgar Evers," p. 50).

The March on Washington

Heeding Myrlie Evers's words, civil rights leaders began organizing a large-scale demonstration in support of President Kennedy's civil rights bill. One of the guiding forces behind this effort was A. Philip Randolph, who had been active in the labor and civil rights movements since founding the Brotherhood of Sleeping Car Porters in 1925. He convinced other prominent black

Belated Justice for Medgar Evers

The *New York Times* called the 1963 murder of Mississippi NAACP organizer Medgar Evers "one of the most notorious events in the violence that marked the civil rights era." Byron de la Beckwith, a well-known white supremacist, was soon arrested and charged with the crime.

Beckwith went on trial two times in 1964, and the prosecution presented convincing evidence against him. The murder weapon belonged to him, for instance, and his fingerprints were on it. In addition, witnesses testified that they saw both Beckwith and his car near the scene of the crime. A cab driver even recalled Beckwith asking for directions to Evers's house.

But the racial atmosphere in Mississippi at that time made it unlikely that Beckwith would be convicted. Many whites tended to dismiss violence against blacks when it served the purpose of preserving segregation. Mississippi Governor Ross Barnett demonstrated this attitude when he shook Beckwith's hand in the middle of a crowded courtroom. In both trials, the all-white, all-male juries failed to reach a verdict. The charges against Beckwith were dismissed, and he was allowed to go free.

leaders—such as Martin Luther King, Jr., of SCLC, James Farmer of CORE, Roy Wilkins of the NAACP, John Lewis of SNCC, and Whitney Young of the National Urban League—to set aside their differences and work together to encourage Congress to pass the legislation.

Although the various civil rights groups had many goals in common, they prioritized their goals differently and pursued different strategies toward achieving them. Some groups continued to focus on direct action aimed at ending segregation, which remained widespread even though nine years had passed since the *Brown* ruling. Others preferred to use legal and political means to attack problems like poverty and unemployment. They pointed out that unemployment rates among blacks, at 11 percent, were more than twice as high as the unemployment rates among whites. They also noted that the average annual income for black families was $3,500, compared to $6,500 for whites. They wanted the federal government to take action to address these discrepancies.

In 1979 Beckwith was arrested again for having a bomb in his car. He allegedly intended to use it to destroy the home of a Jewish activist in New Orleans. Beckwith was found guilty of transporting explosives without a permit and sent to a Louisiana prison. While there, he threatened to kill a black nurse in the prison infirmary the way he had gotten rid of the "uppity" Medgar Evers. A prison guard who overheard this statement later testified against him.

In the early 1990s a newspaper investigation revealed that the Mississippi Sovereignty Commission—a state agency that favored segregation—had given Beckwith advice on jury selection for his 1964 trials. Based on this and other new information, Beckwith was put on trial a third time for the murder of Medgar Evers. On February 5, 1994, a jury consisting of eight blacks and four whites convicted him of the crime, and he was sentenced to spend the rest of his life in prison. Beckwith died behind bars in 2001, at the age of 80. Many people pointed to his eventual conviction as evidence of how much race relations in Mississippi had improved in the three decades since his first trial.

Source:
Stout, David. "Byron De La Beckwith Dies," *New York Times,* January 23, 2001.

After negotiating about goals and strategies, the major civil rights groups agreed to jointly sponsor the March on Washington for Jobs and Freedom, to be held on August 28, 1963. The stated goals of the event included the full integration of public schools within a year and the enactment of federal legislation prohibiting job discrimination by race. It was also intended to demonstrate the movement's unity of purpose and convince Congress to pass Kennedy's civil rights bill.

The president initially asked organizers to call off the march. He worried that it would further anger white segregationists and make it more difficult to convince Southern Democrats to support his civil rights legislation. But organizers worked hard to reassure Kennedy that the demonstration would benefit the civil rights cause. To make sure that problems did not arise, Bayard Rustin of SCLC oversaw every detail of the march, from transportation and public safety to restrooms and garbage collection.

African-American marchers participating in the historic March on Washington on August 28, 1963.

Civil rights leaders spread word of the march nationwide. They initially hoped to attract 100,000 marchers, but instead an estimated 250,000 people—60,000 of them white—participated in the one-day event. They arrived in Washington, D.C., on buses and trains from across the country, proudly carrying signs demanding voting rights, desegregation, and equal employment opportunities for African Americans. They marched down Constitution and Independence Avenues and then gathered in front of the Lincoln Memorial, which honored the president who had signed the Emancipation Proclamation a century earlier.

After hearing inspirational songs by performers like Bob Dylan and Mahalia Jackson, the crowd listened to a series of speeches by prominent civil rights leaders. Many of the speakers presented upbeat, hopeful assessments of the movement's progress. The most memorable speech of the day was Martin Luther King's famous "I Have a Dream" speech, which envisioned a future of racial harmony.

Martin Luther King, Jr., delivers his famous "I Have a Dream" speech from the steps of the Lincoln Memorial.

Most of the speakers offered praise for the Kennedy administration's efforts to promote equality. But John Lewis, the president of SNCC, had a different view of the situation. In his hard-hitting speech, Lewis criticized the Kennedy administration for failing to protect blacks in the South from discrimination and violence. He also expressed reservations about the president's civil rights bill and promised to continue fighting for real change:

> This bill will not protect young children and old women from police dogs and fire hoses when engaging in peaceful demonstrations.... This bill will not protect the hundreds of people who have been arrested on trumped-up charges.... I want to know, which side is the federal government on? The revolution is a serious one. Mr. Kennedy is trying to take the revolution out of the streets and put it in the courts. Listen, Mr.

> Kennedy, the black masses are on the march for jobs and free-
> dom, and we must say to the politicians that there won't be a
> 'cooling-off period.'[3]

By any measure, the 1963 March on Washington was a major success. Although it was the largest mass demonstration in history up to that time, it was peaceful and orderly from start to finish. Millions of Americans who watched the event live on television were impressed by the dedication of the marchers and inspired by the powerful speeches. "America witnessed an unprecedented spectacle that day," wrote one historian. "The march brought joy and a sense of possibility to people throughout the nation who perhaps had not understood the civil rights movement before or who had felt threatened by it."[4]

Triumph Followed by Tragedy

But even as civil rights leaders basked in the glow of the successful March on Washington, yet another tragedy struck at the heart of the movement. Less than three weeks after the march concluded, a bomb exploded at Sixteenth Street Baptist Church in Birmingham, Alabama. The church had long served as a center of civil rights activities in the city. The blast occurred on the morning of September 15, as young members of the congregation attended Sunday school. It took the lives of four girls between the ages of 11 and 14—Addie Mae Collins, Denise McNair, Carole Robertson, and Cynthia Wesley—and injured 20 other people.

Like the dozens of other bombings that rocked Birmingham in the early 1960s, the church bombing was immediately attributed to local white supremacists. Their goal in these terrorist acts was to create an atmosphere of fear that would stop black residents from fighting to end segregation. The senseless deaths of the four young girls had the opposite effect, however. The tragedy generated an outpouring of grief and outrage in Birmingham and across the country. More than 8,000 mourners attended the funerals, including Martin Luther King, Jr., and other prominent civil rights leaders. The event increased national support for the movement and prompted new calls for Congress to pass Kennedy's civil rights legislation.

The FBI investigated the Birmingham church bombing and uncovered evidence pointing to several members of the local Ku Klux Klan. But FBI director J. Edgar Hoover declined to press charges because he claimed that a conviction was unlikely. One of the men responsible was successfully prosecuted in 1978, after an investigation revealed that Hoover had withheld important evidence in the case. Two other men were convicted of murder in 2000 for their involvement in the bombing.

The nation was gripped by shock and grief once again on November 22, 1963, when President John F. Kennedy was shot and killed while traveling in an official motorcade through Dallas, Texas. His vice president, Lyndon B. Johnson, immediately took the oath of office and assumed the presidency. By the time of his death, Kennedy was widely viewed as a valuable supporter of the civil rights movement. Many people wondered whether Johnson, who came from Texas, would continue on this course.

The assassination of John F. Kennedy, seen here delivering his historic June 1963 address on civil rights, cast a long shadow over the civil rights movement.

Notes

1 Quoted in Carson, Clayborne, et al, eds. *The Eyes on the Prize Civil Rights Reader: Documents, Speeches, and Firsthand Accounts from the Black Freedom Struggle, 1954-1990*. New York: Penguin, 1991, p. 155.

2 Quoted in Williams, Juan. *Eyes on the Prize: America's Civil Rights Years, 1954-1965*. New York: Viking Penguin, 1987, p. 225.

3 Quoted in "SNCC 1960-66: Six Years of the Student Nonviolent Coordinating Committee." Available online at http://www.ibiblio.org/sncc/march.html.

4 Williams, p. 202.

Chapter Four

FREEDOM SUMMER

⟫⟪

The open and flagrant violation of constitutional guarantees in Mississippi has precipitated serious conflict which, on several occasions, has reached the point of crisis.... Citizens of the United States have been shot, set upon by vicious dogs, beaten, and otherwise terrorized because they sought to vote.

—"Interim Report of the United States Commission on Civil Rights," April 16, 1963

After a year-long battle, the Civil Rights Act of 1964 finally became law. The landmark legislation took important steps toward ending discrimination in employment and public accommodations. It also included some provisions aimed at securing African-American voting rights, which were still being systematically denied through much of the South. Still, many people felt that the law's voting rights provisions did not go far enough.

In 1964, civil rights leaders decided to focus on voting rights as the key to ending segregation and promoting racial equality. They launched a major voter registration drive in Mississippi that became known as Freedom Summer. This initiative culminated in the formation of the Mississippi Freedom Democratic Party (MFDP) as an all-inclusive alternative to the segregationist state Democratic Party. In the summer of 1964, the MFDP delegation made an eloquent, emotional appeal to be recognized as the state's official representatives to the Democratic National Convention in Atlantic City, New Jersey. While this effort was unsuccessful, it attracted a great deal of attention and sympathy to the cause.

Pushing Congress to Take Action

The civil rights movement of the mid-1960s was greatly aided by President Lyndon B. Johnson (see Johnson biography, p. 141), who turned out to be a vocal supporter of civil rights. Shortly after taking office, he presided over the ratification of the Twenty-Fourth Amendment to the U.S. Constitution. This amendment, which had first been proposed under Kennedy in 1962, outlawed the use of poll taxes as a condition of voting in federal elections. It took effect on February 4, 1964, after Johnson persuaded the state legislatures of Maine and South Dakota to ratify it.

Johnson also actively pushed the U.S. Congress to pass the civil rights legislation that Kennedy had introduced. "No memorial or eulogy could more eloquently honor President Kennedy's memory than the earliest possible passage of the civil rights bill for which he fought," Johnson declared in an address to a joint session of Congress.

Prior to Kennedy's assassination, the civil rights bill had been held up in the House Rules Committee, where a number of changes were introduced to it. The chairman of the committee, Representative Howard W. Smith of Virginia, added gender to the protected categories that could not be used as the basis for discrimination (the others were race, color, religion, and national origin). Some critics believed that he changed the bill to make it more controversial and reduce the likelihood of its passage. But Smith claimed that he introduced the change in an honest attempt to address the concerns of women's rights activists.

After Kennedy's death, Smith and other members of the House of Representatives faced increasing public pressure to pass the civil rights bill. They finally did so in February 1964, and the legislation moved on to the Senate. Determined to prevent it from coming up for a vote, a group of senators from the South launched a filibuster. The procedural rules used in Congress allow members to extend the debate over a bill indefinitely by continuing to speak without interruption. As long as the members involved in a filibuster hold the floor—and the other members do not have enough votes to cut off debate—no other business can be conducted.

The Senate filibuster against the civil rights bill lasted for 57 days. During this time, a number of prominent civil rights leaders appeared in Washington to watch the debate, which demonstrated the lengths to which Southern political leaders were willing to go to deny equal rights to African Ameri-

President Lyndon B. Johnson (center) meets with civil rights leaders (from left to right) Martin Luther King, Jr., Whitney Young, and James Farmer.

cans. One of those present was Malcolm X, who had gained influence in black America as a minister in the Nation of Islam. His disgust over the filibuster led him to make one of his most famous speeches, "The Ballot or the Bullet."

In this speech, which he delivered on April 12 in Detroit, Malcolm X discussed the importance of voting rights in the fight for racial equality. He insisted that African Americans, by voting together as a bloc, had the power to determine the outcome of elections and remove segregationists from office. But Malcolm X acknowledged that voting rights were systematically denied to blacks in the South. He warned that African Americans must be allowed full participation in the democratic process ("the ballot"), or the next step in the civil rights movement would be a violent revolution ("the bullet"):

> Today, our people are disillusioned. They've become disenchant-
> ed. They've become dissatisfied, and in their frustrations they

59

want action.... We don't see any American dream; we've experienced only the American nightmare. We haven't benefited from America's democracy; we've only suffered from America's hypocrisy. And the generation that's coming up now can see it and are not afraid to say it.... It's the ballot or the bullet. It's liberty or death. It's freedom for everybody or freedom for nobody.[1]

Under pressure from President Johnson, Senate leaders finally mustered enough votes to end the filibuster and pass the civil rights legislation that Kennedy had introduced a year earlier. Johnson signed the Civil Rights Act of 1964 into law on July 2. Although the act had been weakened by compromises during its long stay in Congress, the final version contained many important new protections against discrimination on the basis of race, color, religion, sex, or national origin.

The law prohibited discrimination in all public accommodations—including hotels, restaurants, and theaters—and forbade state and local governments from denying access to such facilities. It gave the U.S. attorney general the authority to investigate discrimination claims, file lawsuits to enforce school integration, and deny federal funding to government agencies that used discriminatory practices. The Civil Rights Act also prohibited discrimination in employment—including decisions about hiring, firing, promotion, wages, and training—and established the Equal Opportunity Employment Commission (EEOC) to handle discrimination cases.

Finally, the 1964 law made some effort to address discrimination in voting rights. For instance, it said that state and local governments must apply voter registration requirements equally to all citizens, regardless of race, religion, gender, or other factors. In what soon came to be regarded as a major flaw, however, the law did not specifically outlaw literacy tests or other qualification methods commonly used to disenfranchise black voters. It also failed to address the intimidation, violence, and economic retaliation that segregationists in the South used to prevent blacks from exercising their voting rights.

The Civil Rights Act of 1964, therefore, was only of limited effectiveness in giving African Americans full voting rights. It made it easier for black citizens to challenge discriminatory voting practices in federal court, but this approach was not effective in ending the worst abuses of black voting rights. Often, when a court ruling overturned a specific voting requirement, the state or local government simply substituted a new, slightly different requirement

Martin Luther King, Jr., seen here talking with an African-American family in Mississippi, recognized that voting rights were the key to increased black political and economic power.

that skirted the ruling. In addition, the process of challenging voting laws on a case-by-case basis turned out to be expensive and time consuming.

These problems convinced civil rights leaders that the new legislation did not go far enough to secure black voting rights. Some began demanding that the federal government take action to prevent state and local governments from coming up with their own elaborate rules and qualifications for voting. They argued that the right to vote was a fundamental right granted to American citizens under the U.S. Constitution and should not be subject to restrictions.

Registering Black Voters in Mississippi

This idea was central to the next phase of the civil rights movement, which focused on securing unrestricted voting rights for African Americans. Leaders such as King acknowledged that federal legislation and Supreme Court rulings had outlawed segregation and racial discrimination in many key areas of public life. But they pointed out that as long as white segregationists held political power in the South, these laws generally met with resistance or defiance. Many civil rights activists came to view voting rights as the key to concluding the seemingly endless struggle to convince white political leaders to follow the law. Voting would give African Americans the power to remove segregationist officials from office and elect political leaders who supported desegregation.

Mississippi was the target of many voting rights campaigns. After all, Mississippi society remained strictly segregated more than a decade after the *Brown* ruling. The state required residents to be able to "read and interpret" the U.S. Constitution in order to qualify to vote. In the absence of a clear definition of that terminology, white registrars were free to make their own determination about whether a prospective voter met the requirement, so even well-educated African-American applicants failed. In addition, African Americans who even attempted to register still faced harassment, intimidation, violence, and the potential loss of jobs or homes. As a result of all these factors, only 5 percent of eligible black residents of Mississippi were registered to vote.

Civil rights leaders also selected Mississippi because of its population mix. The state had the highest percentage of black residents in the country, at 45 percent. African Americans formed the majority of the population in many counties. If they ever received the voting rights they deserved, they had the potential to wield a strong influence over state and local politics.

Activists from the Student Nonviolent Coordinating Committee (SNCC) launched their first voter registration project in Mississippi in 1961. As a pamphlet outlining the project's goals explained, "SNCC voter registration efforts give disenfranchised Negroes the right to vote in areas where they have been denied this right since Reconstruction. And, fully as important, the program deepens an awareness of the meaning of first-class citizenship, develops a community of action, and creates mutual trust and support among people who too often have been suspicious and divided by fear."[2] Although the project succeeded in building grassroots leadership in Mississippi, few blacks registered to vote because of the threat of economic reprisals, police harassment, and racist violence.

SNCC activists returned to Mississippi in 1963 to launch a new initiative called the Freedom Ballot. Some white political leaders claimed that the

A white Freedom Summer volunteer discusses voter registration with a Mississippi resident, July 1964.

state's black residents had no interest in politics and no desire to vote in elections. To prove otherwise, SNCC organized a mock election in which a team of volunteer candidates—Aaron Henry, a black NAACP leader; and Edwin King, a white civil rights activist—ran for governor and lieutenant governor on a platform that called for ending segregation. More than 90,000 people participated in the mock election, demonstrating that blacks in Mississippi were ready and willing to vote if they were given the opportunity. "What we have discovered is that the people who run Mississippi today can only do so by force," said Freedom Ballot organizer Allard Lowenstein. "They cannot allow free elections in Mississippi, because if they did, they wouldn't run Mississippi."[3]

63

The 1964 Mississippi Summer Project

The success of the Freedom Ballot encouraged civil rights leaders to mount a larger voter registration effort in 1964. The Mississippi Summer Project, better known as Freedom Summer, was organized by the Council of Federated Organizations (COFO). Led by Mississippi activist Bob Moses, COFO was an association of four established civil rights groups—SNCC, CORE, NAACP, and SCLC—and several local organizations. In addition to helping African Americans register to vote, the project involved setting up Freedom Schools for black children and organizing an integrated alternative to the all-white state Democratic Party.

The key to Freedom Summer was the arrival of more than 1,000 college students from across the country—most of them white and from middle-class or privileged backgrounds. The brochure SNCC used to recruit students for the program noted that "As the winds of change grow stronger, the threatened political elite of Mississippi becomes more intransigent and fanatical.... Negro efforts to win the right to vote cannot succeed without a nationwide mobilization of support. A program is planned for this summer which will involve the massive participation of Americans dedicated to the elimination of racial oppression."[4]

The young activists were determined to bring national attention to the discrimination and violence used to prevent blacks from voting in Mississippi. In order to show their commitment to the cause, they worked for subsistence wages and lived in the same conditions as poor blacks in rural Mississippi. They lived in the communities they organized and worked to help local residents overcome their fears and gain the confidence to demand their rights. Although the activists knew that their activities could place them in danger, they were willing to take the risk. In fact, some felt that violence directed at young, educated, white volunteers might bring national attention to the cause and force the federal government to take action (see sidebar "A Letter Home from Freedom Summer," p. 65).

Three Voting Rights Activists Are Murdered

Mississippi political leaders viewed the arrival of Freedom Summer student volunteers as a hostile invasion of their state. They took a number of steps to try to limit the effectiveness of the voter registration project. For instance, the state legislature made it illegal to distribute flyers calling for boy-

A Letter Home from Freedom Summer

During the Mississippi Summer Project of 1964—better known as Freedom Summer—more than 1,000 college students from across the country descended on the South to help African Americans register to vote. Most of the student volunteers were white and came from middle-class or privileged backgrounds. Although they underwent extensive training and were deeply committed to the cause of civil rights, many of the young activists were unprepared for the racial tension and hostility they encountered during the voter registration campaign. In the following excerpt from a letter published in the collection *Letters from Mississippi,* a Freedom Summer volunteer expresses great longing to return to his normal, relaxed existence as a college student in California.

Holly Springs, August 9
Dear Ruth and Carl,

It is Sunday, and I have driven over 2,000 miles in the last three days. I am tired. I want to go very much to a movie, or to watch TV even. I want to be in Berkeley and do stupid things and don't look behind me in the rearview mirror. I want to look at a white man and not hate his guts, and know he doesn't hate me either. I want to talk about the White Sox and be admired by somebody who isn't going through worse than I am. I want to get out of the 90 degree weather and go swimming....

Love to you,
Bob

Source:

Martinez, Elizabeth Sutherland. *Letters from Mississippi: Personal Reports from Civil Rights Volunteers of the 1964 Freedom Summer.* Brookline, MA: Zephyr Press, 2002, p. 227.

cotts and to operate schools without a license. Many local governments also hired additional police officers and purchased guns, vehicles, and other law enforcement equipment to stamp out any African-American demonstrations.

The situation was tense when the first 300 student activists arrived in Mississippi on June 20, 1964. One day later, three civil rights workers disappeared. One of the missing persons was a 21-year-old black Mississippi native who worked for CORE, James Chaney. The other two were white men: 20-year-old student volunteer Andrew Goodman and 24-year-old civil rights activist Michael Schwerner. As part of the project to register black voters, the three men had driven together to Philadelphia, Mississippi, to investigate the burning of a black church.

Although it did not become clear what had happened for several weeks, most people assumed that the men had been murdered. The FBI launched a massive search for the missing activists, and the remains of their burned car were found a few days later. The case attracted heavy media coverage, and millions of Americans followed news of the search on television or in newspapers.

Some black civil rights leaders resented the fact that the disappearance of two white men created such a stir, when black people disappeared in Mississippi on a regular basis. In the process of searching for Chaney, Goodman, and Schwerner, in fact, the FBI discovered the corpses of several African Americans whose missing-person cases had not generated national media attention. As Schwerner's widow, Rita Schwerner, explained, "If [my husband] and Andrew Goodman had been Negroes, the world would have taken little notice of their deaths. After all, the slaying of a Negro in Mississippi is not news. It is only because my husband and Andrew Goodman were white that the national alarm had been sounded."[5] The special attention given to the disappearance of the white activists contributed to an atmosphere of mistrust between white volunteers and black Mississippians and limited the effectiveness of the voter-registration project (see "Registering Voters during Freedom Summer," p. 179).

After 44 days of searching, the bodies of the three men were found buried in an earthen dam. They had been beaten and shot to death. The facts that eventually came out indicated that local police had arrested them for speeding, held them in custody until after dark, and then released them into the hands of the Ku Klux Klan.

The FBI arrested 18 men in connection with the murders in October but had trouble getting convictions. Some of the men were acquitted by all-white juries, and a few others received light sentences for conspiracy from a federal judge. For decades, it appeared that no one would ever be punished for the Freedom Summer murders. But thanks to the work of an investigative reporter in Jackson, Mississippi, the man who planned the murders, local KKK leader

On June 24, 1964, searchers found the burned car of three civil rights workers who disappeared in Mississippi; their bodies were found later that summer.

Edgar Ray Killen, was finally convicted of manslaughter on the 41st anniversary of the crime in 2005.

The Mississippi Freedom Democratic Party

Although most student volunteers continued working on the Freedom Summer voter registration drive following the murders of James Chaney, Andrew Goodman, and Michael Schwerner, the tension and fear triggered by the activists' disappearance limited the effectiveness of the project. Activists from SNCC and COFO only managed to register 1,200 new black voters over the course of the summer, which increased the percentage of registered voters to 6.7 percent of the state's African-American population.

In other ways, however, Freedom Summer helped instill a sense of hope and pride in black Mississippi residents. Activists with the program established 50 Freedom Schools to provide African-American children with an alternative to segregated public schools. In addition to improving literacy and other academic skills, the schools also worked to increase students' self-image and confidence. They encouraged black children to participate in community organizing and demand equality, in hopes that their bold attitudes would inspire their parents to join the civil rights movement as well.

Freedom Summer activists also brought national attention to the plight of black Mississippi residents by organizing the Mississippi Freedom Democratic Party (MFDP). The regular state Democratic Party was controlled by white segregationists who denied black voting rights, rejected the national party platform on civil rights, and adopted their own platform promoting segregation. By presenting Mississippi residents with an alternative that was open to everyone, regardless of race, the MFDP attracted 80,000 members.

Following party rules, the MFDP held local caucuses and a statewide meeting to elect delegates to the Democratic National Convention, which was held in August in Atlantic City, New Jersey. As the convention approached, the MFDP delegation formally petitioned to be seated in place of the regular state party. They argued that the regular party delegation had been elected through a segregated process, in violation of party guidelines and federal law, and thus had no right to participate in the convention. The MFDP's position gained the support of a number of other state Democratic parties.

A High-Profile Hearing

The Credentials Committee—a group of party officials charged with issuing passes to the convention—agreed to hear the MFDP's challenge. The hearings were broadcast live on national television. Dozens of black Mississippi residents, along with a number of white supporters, spoke about the discrimination and violence that prevented them from exercising their right to vote. "The Saturday before the convention began, they presented their case to the Credentials Committee, and through television, to the nation and to the world," SNCC leader Charles M. Sherrod remembered. "No human being

Aaron Henry, chair of the Mississippi Freedom Democratic Party, testifies before the Credentials Committee at the Democratic National Convention in 1964.

confronted with the truth of our testimony could remain indifferent to it. Many tears fell. Our position was valid and our cause was just."[6]

Some of the most powerful testimony came from longtime voting-rights activist Fannie Lou Hamer (see Hamer biography, p. 137, and "Powerful Testimony from Fannie Lou Hamer," p. 181). The youngest of 20 children in a poor black family, she grew up working as a sharecropper on a plantation owned by Mississippi Congressman Jamie Whitten, chairman of the House Agricultural Committee. Hamer only had a third-grade education, but she spoke eloquently about how segregation turned African Americans into second-class citizens in the South. She also described the harassment and brutality she and other activists had endured as they worked to change this system. Finally, Hamer challenged the party—and the nation—to live up to their stated ideals of freedom and equality. "Is this America?," she demanded. "The land of the free and the home of the brave? Where we have to sleep with our telephones off the hook, because our lives be threatened daily?"[7]

President Johnson, who was poised to become the Democratic Party's nominee when the convention began, viewed the MFDP's challenge with alarm. Although he generally supported the civil rights movement, he worried that a high-profile controversy at the convention might derail his presidential campaign. Johnson knew that seating the MFDP delegates could offend many white Southerners and cause them to shift their votes to his opponent, conservative Republican Barry Goldwater. At the same time, he knew that denying the MFDP challenge could anger African-American voters in the North.

Johnson did his best to draw attention away from the controversy. For instance, he hurriedly scheduled a press conference so that the television networks would break off their live coverage of the MFDP delegates' testimony before the Credentials Committee. Johnson also worked with influential liberal Democrats and civil rights leaders to try to negotiate a compromise to end the MFDP protest.

The Democratic Party eventually offered the MFDP delegation two non-voting seats at the convention, meaning that they could observe as "delegates at large" but not officially represent their state or participate in the nomination process. Some civil rights leaders encouraged the delegates to take the deal, saying that they had made their point and now needed to form an alliance with the liberal wing of the Democratic Party. But MFDP leaders felt that they could not return to Mississippi with the token victory the party offered. "It would have been a lie to accept that particular compromise," Sherrod noted. "It would have said to blacks across the nation and the world that we share the power, and that is a lie!"[8]

The MFDP delegates refused to accept the compromise and continued trying to claim the seats they felt rightfully belonged to them. On the first day of the convention, three members of the regular Mississippi Democratic Party walked out in protest over the national party platform supporting civil rights. Three MFDP delegates borrowed passes from sympathetic members of other state delegations and sat in the empty seats. When party officials responded by removing the chairs, the MFDP delegates stood and sang freedom songs to disrupt the convention.

Fallout from the Convention Fight

The MFDP's spirited fight to be seated at the 1964 Democratic National Convention, and other Freedom Summer events, inspired many people to

By the end of 1964, securing voting rights and higher levels of black voter registration were the top priorities of civil rights organizations.

support the civil rights movement. The project, for example, generated new enthusiasm for grassroots activism among Mississippi's black residents. "There was no civil rights movement in the Negro community in Mississippi before the 1964 Summer Project," Hamer recalled. "There were people that wanted change, but they hadn't dared to come out and try to do something, to try to change the way things were. But after the 1964 project when all of the young people came down for the summer—an exciting and remarkable summer—Negro people in the Delta began moving."[9]

At the same time, though, Johnson's decision to block the MFDP delegates from full participation in the convention left many civil rights activists feeling angry and disappointed. Some felt that the experience showed that the federal government, and white America in general, was not truly committed to racial equality. "The rejection of the compromise was a major turning point in the history of the southern black movement," wrote one historian. "Bitterness over the outcome of that convention challenge exacerbated many of the racial tensions that had festered during the summer's unprecedented interactions between black activists and white volunteers in Mississippi. Many black organizers in SNCC became increasingly dubious about the merits of interracialism as a strategy of black advancement, and more determined to seek fundamental social change rather than merely civil rights legislation."[10]

After 1964, a significant rift began to form in the civil rights movement. Some mainstream leaders, like Martin Luther King, Jr., continued to insist that nonviolent resistance and political change would eventually result in an end to segregation and discrimination. But a new generation of black leaders began promoting a more militant approach. Having concluded that it was impossible to achieve true racial equality through peaceful means, Malcolm X and other angry African-American leaders began planning for a revolutionary change in tactics.

Notes

[1] X, Malcolm. "The Ballot or the Bullet," April 12, 1964. Available online at http://www.american rhetoric.com/speeches/malcolmxballotorbullet.htm.

[2] Quoted in "SNCC: Structure and Leadership" (pamphlet), August 1963. Available online at http://www.ibiblio.org/sncc/index.html.

[3] Quoted in Williams, Juan. *Eyes on the Prize: America's Civil Rights Years, 1954-1965.* New York: Viking Penguin, 1987, p. 228.

[4] Quoted in "SNCC 1960-66: Six Years of the Student Nonviolent Coordinating Committee." Available online at http://www.ibiblio.org/sncc/mfdp.html.

[5] Schwerner, Rita. Quoted in a statement to the press, August 4, 1964. Available online at http://www .spartacus.schoolnet.co.uk/USASchwerner.htm.

[6] Sherrod, Charles M. "Mississippi at Atlantic City." *In The Eyes on the Prize Civil Rights Reader.* Edited by Clayborne Carson, et al. New York: Penguin, 1991, p. 187.

[7] Hamer, Fannie Lou. "Testimony before the Credentials Committee, Democratic National Convention," 1964. Available online at http://www.americanrhetoric.com/speeches/fannielouhamercreden tialscommittee.htm.

[8] Sherrod, "Mississippi in Atlantic City," p. 189.

[9] Quoted in Williams, p. 249.

[10] Carson, Clayborne. "Mississippi: Is This America?" *In The Eyes on the Prize Civil Rights Reader.* New York: Penguin, 1991, pp. 167-69.

Chapter Five

SHOWDOWN IN SELMA

—⟨⟨⟨⟩⟩⟩—

History is going to reflect that the savagery of Bloody Sunday in Selma put a face on racist hatred that could not be ignored. The whole nation watched on television. It is questionable that most viewers understood that this had been going on for nearly a century. What mattered was that, finally, people were watching.

—Tavis Smiley, in *The Unfinished Agenda of the Selma-Montgomery Voting Rights March*

The events of 1964 convinced Martin Luther King, Jr., and other civil rights leaders that federal intervention was necessary to overcome the barriers erected in the South to prevent African Americans from voting. With this in mind, strong voting rights legislation became the main focus of the civil rights movement in the spring of 1965. The Southern Christian Leadership Conference chose Selma, Alabama, as the target for a series of protests designed to force the federal government to take action. On March 7—a date which became known as Bloody Sunday—these protests culminated in a brutal police assault on peaceful marchers attempting to cross the Edmund Pettus Bridge. The racist violence helped convince President Lyndon B. Johnson to introduce a voting rights bill to Congress and created a surge of public support for its passage.

Calling for Direct Federal Action

The credentials fight at the Democratic National Convention did not seem to hurt the reelection campaign of President Lyndon B. Johnson. He

After winning the November 1964 election, President Lyndon B. Johnson watched anxiously to see if the South would obey the various provisions of the Civil Rights Act.

earned a landslide victory in the November 1964 presidential election, winning 44 states. Civil rights leaders felt that Johnson's overwhelming victory gave the president a mandate to pass additional civil rights legislation. Specifically, they wanted the federal government to outlaw the various tactics—like poll taxes and literacy tests—that some state and local governments in the South still used to prevent African Americans from voting. They also wanted the federal government to send federal registrars to oversee the registration of black voters and federal marshals to protect black voters from harassment by local law enforcement officials.

Johnson suspected that a strong voting rights act might eventually be needed if African Americans were ever going to receive their full constitutional rights in the South. He instructed Attorney General Nicholas Katzenbach to research voting rights abuses and determine what should be included in a new bill. But Johnson and many others in Washington were reluctant to try to pass additional civil rights legislation right away. They hoped that once people in the South had time to adjust to the new reality of the Civil Rights Act of 1964, discriminatory voting practices would gradually disappear on their own. "We felt we had made some real honest-to-God progress [in 1964]," said the Senate minority leader, Republican Everett M. Dirksen of Illinois. "We felt everything would fall into its slot. We thought we were out of the civil rights woods, but we weren't."[1]

Many towns in the South removed "white" and "colored" designations from hotels, restaurants, theaters, bus stations, and other public accommodations following the passage of the Civil Rights Act of 1964. But white resistance to integration remained strong in some places. Many segregationists were willing to use whatever means necessary—from defying federal law to police harassment and physical violence—to prevent blacks from voting. A string of reports of continued voting rights abuses made their way to Washington, but Congress and the White House remained hesitant to intervene. Civil rights leaders decided to organize a series of voting-rights protests in an effort to force the federal government to take action.

The Situation in Selma

The target they chose for the protests was Selma, Alabama, a busy commercial town in Dallas County, in the middle of the state. Both Selma and the surrounding county had a poor voting rights record. Although African Americans accounted for half of Dallas County's 30,000 residents, only 1 percent of eligible blacks (a total of 156 people) were registered to vote, compared to 65 percent of eligible whites.

Local officials strongly discouraged black residents from attempting to register to vote. When SNCC activists held a Freedom Day voter registration drive in Selma in 1963, for instance, Dallas County Sheriff James G. Clark (see sidebar "Sheriff Jim Clark and the Showdown in Selma," p. 78) and his police force mounted a campaign of harassment. Volunteers from SNCC convinced 250 local African Americans to march to the county courthouse and wait in line to register to vote. Clark and his deputies showed up at the demonstration wearing helmets and carrying guns and billy clubs. The sheriff took photographs of everyone in the line and threatened to show the pictures to their employers and the Ku Klux Klan. His men also beat and arrested SNCC volunteers when they tried to bring food and water to the people in line.

Sheriff Jim Clark and the Showdown in Selma

After civil rights leaders decided to stage voting rights protests in Selma, Alabama, Sheriff James G. Clark, Jr., became one of their most bitter foes. Confronting Clark carried no small amount of danger. He had already taken a prominent role in suppressing civil rights activism, not only in Selma but also in other southern cities. On numerous occasions in the previous two years, his heavily armed sheriff's posse had used nightsticks, tear gas, and electric cattle prods to break up civil rights rallies and intimidate peaceful protestors.

When the Selma courthouse protests got underway in the spring of 1965, Clark added a new accessory to his uniform—a button that simply read "Never"—which served as his reply to the activists' calls for reform. Despite pleas for restraint from Selma city officials, Clark's hotheaded personality soon showed itself. The images of the sheriff personally manhandling and striking protestors—and in one case being floored by a devastating counter-punch from an angry female activist—kept Selma in the headlines and maintained the campaign's momentum.

On Bloody Sunday, the sheriff and his posse joined Alabama state troopers at the Edmund Pettus Bridge. Clark's input into the decision to attack the marchers is uncertain, but once the order was given, his mounted troops thundered through the line of protestors on horseback and struck them with bullwhips and lengths of rubber tubing wrapped in barbed wire. In news footage of the incident, the sheriff can be heard yelling to his men to "get those god-damned niggers."

While Clark personified the brutality of official resistance, he also came to symbolize the changes that took place following the enactment of the Voting Rights Act of 1965. The following year, with barriers to registration removed, African-American participation in the local elections increased dramatically. Ballots from the county's black wards were decisive in voting Clark out of office.

Even if black residents of Selma made it inside the courthouse, they still found it nearly impossible to register successfully. The voter registration office was only open two days per month for limited and often unpredictable hours. In order to qualify, prospective voters had to complete a four-page form with more than 50 blanks, read passages from the U.S. Constitution and answer questions about them, write part of the Constitution from dictation, answer obscure questions about the American system of government, sign an oath of loyalty to the United States and the state of Alabama, and have a registered voter available to vouch for their good character. Nearly all African-American applicants failed some aspect of the daunting qualification process—even individuals who were better educated than the registrar giving the tests—while the vast majority of white applicants passed. Between May 1962 and August 1964, only 8.5 percent of black applicants successfully registered to vote in Dallas County, compared to 77 percent of white applicants.

The discriminatory nature of the voter registration system created anger and frustration within the black community in Selma. One of the few local African Americans who managed to register, voting rights activist Amelia Platts Boynton, remembered going to the courthouse to vouch for the character of an elderly black man. When the man's application to register was denied, he shared his outrage with the registrar: "I am 65 years old, I own 100 acres of land that is paid for, I am a taxpayer and I have six children. All of them is teachin', workin'," he declared. "If what I done ain't enough to be a registered voter with all the tax I got to pay, then Lord have mercy on America."[2]

King Comes to Selma

In December 1964, Martin Luther King's contributions to the American civil rights movement were recognized with the Nobel Peace Prize. In his acceptance speech for the prestigious award, the SCLC leader described himself as a "trustee for the 22 million Negroes of the United States of America who are engaged in a creative battle to end the night of racial injustice."[3]

King was thus at the height of his fame and influence when he announced his intention to join the campaign for voting rights in Alabama. He traveled to Selma on January 2 and gave a fiery speech at Brown's Chapel AME Church. "We will seek to arouse the federal government by marching by the thousands to the places of registration," he declared. "When we get the right to vote, we

Judge Frank M. Johnson, Jr.

Some of the most important rulings in support of desegregation and civil rights came from the Alabama courtroom of federal judge Frank M. Johnson, Jr. Despite pressure from white political leaders—and threats from white segregationists—Johnson stood firm in promoting racial justice. "You can't intimidate me," he declared in an interview. "If you can be intimidated, you don't have any business being a judge."

Johnson was born on October 30, 1918, in Winston County in northern Alabama. After earning a law degree from the University of Alabama in 1943, he joined the U.S. military and fought overseas during World War II. When the war ended, he returned home and practiced law in Jasper, Alabama.

Although the Democratic Party controlled Alabama politics during that era, Johnson became active in the Republican Party. He worked on Dwight Eisenhower's presidential campaign as the head of his state's Veterans for Eisenhower organization. Once Eisenhower was elected, he appointed Johnson the U.S. attorney for the northern district of Alabama.

In 1955—the year after the Supreme Court's *Brown v. Board of Education* ruling outlawed segregation in public schools—Johnson was appointed to serve on the U.S. District Court of the Middle District of Alabama. As a federal judge, he was responsible for applying the Supreme Court decision to local cases. One of Johnson's first important desegregation rulings came in the 1956 case *Browder v. Gale,* which grew out of the Montgomery bus boycott. Declaring that the *Brown* ruling applied to public transportation as well as public schools, he found the segregation of

will send to the statehouse not men [like Alabama Governor George Wallace] who will stand in the doorways of universities to keep Negroes out, but men who will uphold the cause of Justice. Give us the ballot."[4]

King's decision to throw his weight behind the Selma campaign got the attention of government officials at various levels. A week after he made his city buses illegal. In 1961, following the Freedom Rides, he ordered the desegregation of interstate bus terminals in *Lewis v. Greyhound.*

Johnson also issued a number of important decisions regarding African-American voting rights. In *U.S. v. Alabama*, for instance, he ruled that the state must apply the same qualification standards for voter registration, regardless of the race of the applicant. Johnson also declared poll taxes unconstitutional, required the state to draw legislative districts fairly, and ordered that blacks be allowed to serve on juries. When Alabama Governor George Wallace refused to grant permission for civil rights activists to march from Selma to Montgomery in support of voting rights, Johnson ordered the governor to open the road for the marchers.

Johnson's decisions in support of African-American civil rights made him extremely unpopular among white segregationists. The Ku Klux Klan called him "the most hated man in Alabama," and he received so many death threats he and his family were placed under federal protection for 15 years. Ultimately, though, his decisions helped end centuries of discrimination and transform American society.

Johnson joined the U.S. Court of Appeals in 1978, and he continued to serve on the federal bench until his death on July 23, 1999. By the time of his death, he was one of the most widely admired judges in the country. He received the Presidential Medal of Freedom in 1995, and the federal courthouse in Montgomery is named after him.

Source:

Academy of Achievement, "Frank M. Johnson, Jr.," 2006. Available online at http://www.achievement.org/autodoc/page/joh2pro-1.

speech, the Justice Department announced that it was drafting legislation to outlaw literacy tests as a condition for voting in federal elections. It also filed a lawsuit challenging the statewide voter registration practices used in Alabama. Officials charged that these practices discriminated against African-American residents. Selma's white leaders, meanwhile, knew that King's involvement in the protests would bring a great deal of publicity to the city.

In an effort to limit the negative coverage Selma received, Mayor Joseph Smitherman hired a new director of public safety to supervise the actions of Sheriff Clark and his deputies.

Activists from SCLC and SNCC, along with local residents, launched the first in a series of protest marches in Selma on January 18, 1965. They marched across town to the county courthouse, where they lined up to try to register to vote. Under strict orders from the town's leadership, Clark avoided a violent confrontation on the first day. He merely herded the protesters into an alley behind the courthouse to keep them away from the news reporters covering the march. When the protesters returned the following day, however, they refused to obey the police order to line up in the alley. Clark angrily grabbed Amelia Boynton by the coat, shoved her to the ground with his billy club, and placed her under arrest. Dramatic pictures of the incident appeared on the front page of newspapers across the country.

An important turning point in the Selma protests came on January 22, when a group of 100 black teachers joined the march to the courthouse. Although the teachers served as leaders in the community, they did not usually participate in civil rights protests because they knew they would probably be fired by the white school board. When the teachers accepted this risk and joined the protest, it created a new sense of hope and purpose throughout Selma's black community. Their actions inspired African-American members of other middle-class occupations to begin marching for voting rights, and large groups of local schoolchildren soon joined in as well.

Civil Right No. 1

As more and more people joined the marches, Clark and his officers began arresting large groups of protesters. The Dallas County jails soon became overcrowded and the prisoners endured terrible conditions. On February 1—hoping to bring more media attention to the situation in Selma—Martin Luther King made sure that he was among the 250 protesters arrested.

Following the example of his famous "Letter from a Birmingham Jail," King wrote a letter to be published during his incarceration in Selma (see "Martin Luther King's Letter from a Selma, Alabama, Jail," p. 184). This letter, entitled "Civil Right No. 1: The Right to Vote," was published in the *New York Times* a few days later. "Have you ever been required to answer 100 questions on government, some abstruse even to a political science specialist, merely to vote? Have you ever stood in line with over a hundred others and after wait-ing an entire day seen less than ten given the qualifying test?" he demanded. "This is Selma, Alabama, where there are more Negroes in jail with me than there are on the voting rolls."[5]

While King was still in jail, the militant black activist Malcolm X came to Selma. In an echo of his "Ballot or the Bullet" speech, he encouraged state and local political leaders to meet the protesters' demands and give African Americans full voting rights. If they did not respond to King's nonviolent protest methods, he warned, then they should be prepared to face more extreme measures. Less than three weeks later, Malcolm X was assassinated. But his strong stance resonated with many young civil rights activists, who were beginning to feel frustrated with the slow pace of change.

Political leaders in Washington, meanwhile, monitored events in Selma with great interest. On February 4, President Johnson held a press conference to express his support for African-American voting rights. "All Americans should be indignant when one American is denied the right to vote," he declared. "The loss of that right to a single citizen undermines the freedom of every citizen. That is why all of us should be concerned with the efforts of our fellow Americans to register to vote in Alabama." Once King got out of jail, he met with Johnson on February 8 to make a formal request for new voting rights legislation.

Planning a March for Voting Rights

Meanwhile, the protests continued in Selma and also spread to other towns in Alabama. On February 16, SCLC staff member C.T. Vivian confront-ed Clark and his deputies on the steps of the Dallas County courthouse. Vivian compared the law enforcement officers' racist oppression of black citi-zens to the brutal reign of Adolf Hitler and the Nazi Party in Germany during the Holocaust. Clark responded by punching Vivian in the mouth, sending the activist sprawling and breaking the sheriff's hand in the process.

Two days later, Vivian was invited to speak in the nearby town of Mari-on, Alabama. When a group of protesters began to march afterward, they were attacked by local law enforcement officers and an angry mob of white segregationists. During this violent incident, a 26-year-old black man named Jimmie Lee Jackson fought to protect his mother and 82-year-old grandfather. Jackson was shot in the stomach by a police officer, and he died in the hospi-

Civil rights activist C.T. Vivian (left) confronts Sheriff Jim Clark (center of photo) on the courthouse steps in Selma.

tal a week later. Many other people were badly injured, including NBC News reporter Richard Valeriani, who was hit in the head with an ax handle. He appeared on television the following night, from his hospital bed, to describe the frightening scene.

The brutal treatment of the peaceful protesters made headlines across the country. Instead of being intimidated by the violence, however, many activists grew even more determined to win the fight for voting rights. After Jackson's funeral, where King gave a moving memorial speech, some SCLC members came up with an idea for a dramatic protest march. The original idea involved carrying Jackson's body from Selma to Montgomery and laying it on the steps of the state capitol. Since this was not practical, though, they decided instead to deliver a list of demands to Alabama Governor George Wallace.

The SCLC scheduled the march to begin the following Sunday, March 7. It would begin in Selma, cross the Edmund Pettus Bridge over the Alabama River, and follow Route 80 all the way to Montgomery. The organizers figured that it would take protesters about four days to travel the 50-mile route. King threw his support behind the plan, but SNCC leaders worried about the potential for violence. In the end, SNCC decided not to participate officially, although the organization permitted its members to march as individuals.

Upon hearing about the march, Wallace declared that the state would not allow it to proceed. He claimed that he made this decision out of concern for the safety of the protesters and the need to keep traffic flowing smoothly on public highways. Many white Alabama residents applauded the governor's stand. But others expressed frustration and disgust with the state's determination to prevent African Americans from voting. On March 6, a group of white citizens marched to the Selma courthouse to show their support for the protesters and their goals. "We consider it a shocking injustice that there are still counties in Alabama where there are no Negroes registered to vote and where Negroes have reason to fear hostility and harassment by public officials when they do try to register,"[6] the Reverend Joseph Ellwanger said in a speech at that event.

Bloody Sunday

The Selma-Montgomery voting rights march started on schedule on Sunday, March 7, 1965. Many people expected King to lead the march, but after meeting with President Johnson in Washington the previous day, he decided to preach at his church in Atlanta rather than return to Selma. In his absence, the task of leading the 600-person procession fell to the Reverend Hosea Williams. He was joined in the front row of marchers by SNCC chairman John Lewis.

The protesters did not meet any resistance as they made their way through the streets of Selma. But as they crossed the Edmund Pettus Bridge on the outskirts of town, they found their path blocked by an estimated 200 Alabama state troopers and sheriff's department officers. The police looked menacing as they stood in formation wearing helmets and gas masks and holding billy clubs.

Major John Cloud of the Alabama State Police ordered the protesters to turn around and gave them two minutes to leave the area. When they refused

This image from Bloody Sunday in Selma shows John Lewis (in foreground on knees) being attacked by a club-wielding Alabama state trooper.

and began to pray, the troopers rushed toward the protesters and beat them with their clubs, knocking more than a dozen people to the ground. Then, as marchers bent down to help the injured or tried to run away, the police fired tear gas. Finally, a group of mounted police charged into the crowd, knocking protesters down and trampling those on the ground. "The police were riding along on horseback beating people," SCLC leader Andrew Young remembered. "The tear gas was so thick you couldn't get to where the people needed help."[7]

John Lewis was clubbed on the head during the assault and suffered a fractured skull (see "John Lewis Remembers 'Bloody Sunday,'" p. 186, and "Terror on the Edmund Pettus Bridge," p. 194). Dozens of other demonstrators had to be treated in the hospital for their injuries. "People were left bloodied in the highway. Lewis was on his knees, suffering from two concussions and bleeding like a stuck hog. Women and even children were unconscious, others semiconscious, lying, sitting, trying to run, but literally being run over by horses—and hearing their ribs and limbs cracking. It was the worst day of my life," recalled civil rights lawyer J.L. Chestnut, Jr. "What I witnessed led me to believe America could not be saved and white people were not worth saving."[8]

National television networks interrupted their regular programming to broadcast footage of the brutal police attack. Newscasters referred to the event as "Bloody Sunday." People across the country watched in disbelief and outrage. Although most people were aware that civil rights protests sometimes met with violence in the South, the dramatic footage provided indisputable evidence of the true extent of the problem. Thousands of Americans from all walks of life were inspired to take action. They immediately dropped whatever they were doing and made arrangements to travel to Alabama and join the protests. "When that beating happened at the foot of the bridge, it looked like war," recalled Selma mayor Joseph Smitherman. "That went all over the country. And the people, the wrath of the nation came down on us."[9]

Turnaround Tuesday

The outpouring of public support convinced organizers of the Selma-Montgomery march that the protest should continue as soon as possible. King called on religious leaders across the country to join him in a second march on Tuesday, March 9—two days after Bloody Sunday. Even in the face of escalating national pressure, however, Governor Wallace still refused to allow the march to proceed. He declared his intention to use state and local law enforcement officers to prevent the protesters from blocking traffic on public highways.

SCLC leaders formally requested that U.S. District Court Judge Frank M. Johnson (see sidebar "Judge Frank M. Johnson, Jr.," p. 80) order Wallace not to interfere with the march. Although Johnson agreed to hold a hearing on the request later that week, he also ordered the protesters not to march until after the court date. This order put march organizers in a difficult position. They knew that Johnson had issued a number of important rulings in support of civil rights in the past, so they had hope for a favorable ruling. But they also knew that thousands of people had come to Selma specifically to participate in the protest, and they worried that many of these people would leave town if they delayed the march for several days.

After discussing the matter with SCLC and SNCC leaders, King decided to disobey the court order and proceed with the March 9 protest. He led 1500 marchers—many of them members of the clergy—back to the Edmund Pet-

When Martin Luther King, Jr., and other demonstrators organized another march out of Selma on March 9, 1965, they were turned back by law enforcement officers.

tus Bridge. Once again, a large group of law enforcement officers met the procession at the bridge and ordered the protesters to turn back. This time, however, King obeyed the order and led the marchers back into Selma. He explained that the aborted march had served a purpose by demonstrating that the police were still prepared to use violence against peaceful protesters. But many of the marchers were upset about King's decision and viewed it as a betrayal of their trust. They mockingly called the second attempt to march to Montgomery "Turnaround Tuesday."

Later that night, after the march ended, three white ministers went out for dinner at a black restaurant in Selma. As they left, they were attacked and brutally beaten by local white segregationists. One of the men, Unitarian minister James Reeb, died from his injuries. The murder of Reeb put the Selma protests back in the headlines across the country. Many Americans expressed their outrage about the racist violence by demanding action from their members of Congress.

Johnson Delivers "The American Promise"

Shortly after Bloody Sunday, President Johnson held a press conference to discuss the voting rights protests in Selma. He denounced the brutal police assault on the marchers as "an American tragedy" and said that it "must strengthen the determination of each of us to bring full equality and equal justice to all of our people."

On March 15, Johnson appeared before a joint session of Congress to announce that he was introducing new legislation specifically designed to secure African-American voting rights. This historic speech, entitled "The American Promise," was broadcast live on television to 70 million people. Many viewers were moved when the president repeated a theme from the civil rights movement, telling the American people that "we shall overcome" racism and injustice (see "President Lyndon Johnson Delivers 'The American Promise,'" p. 197).

SCLC activist C.T. Vivian recalled watching Johnson's speech on television in the company of King and other civil rights leaders. "When LBJ said, 'And we shall overcome,' we all cheered," he noted. "And I looked over ... and Martin was very quietly sitting in the chair, and a tear ran down his check. It was a victory like none other. It was an affirmation of the movement."[10] King later described Johnson's address as one "that will live in history as one of the most passionate pleas for human rights ever made by a president of our nation."[11]

The March Finally Reaches Montgomery

In the meantime, federal judge Frank M. Johnson held his court hearing as scheduled to determine whether the march could legally proceed in the face of opposition from Alabama Governor George Wallace and Dallas County Sheriff Jim Clark. The judge ruled that the protesters' right to vote and right to assemble outweighed the state and local governments' concerns about highway safety. "The extent of the wrong is taken into consideration when you are trying to determine whether an extensive protest is justified,"

Johnson explained of his decision. "If they had just deprived one person of the right to use a public fountain, then that wouldn't have justified a march of 100,000 people from Selma to Montgomery on a public highway. But if you have general discrimination, throughout the state, on the right to vote and the right to do other basic things that citizens—white citizens—are entitled to, then you have a right to an extensive protest."[12]

The march was scheduled to depart from Selma on March 21, 1965. To ensure that it proceeded without interference, President Johnson placed the Alabama National Guard under federal control. He also sent 2,000 U.S. Army troops, 100 FBI agents, and 100 federal marshals to protect the protesters on the road to Montgomery.

When the scheduled day arrived, King successfully led a procession of 4,000 marchers—both black and white—over the Edmund Pettus Bridge. Although a few segregationists along the route held up signs and shouted at the protesters, the federal marshals maintained order. The marchers continued walking toward the state capital for four days. Many of them carried signs or American flags and passed the hours by singing freedom songs. They slept in tents by the side of the road at night, and volunteers supplied them with food and water. "The final march was enjoyable and it was tension-filled all at the same time," recalled Ralph David Abernathy. "We knew that victory was in sight. We had to march on one side of the road, and the cars had to move on the other side. A great deal of profanity was yelled from the passing cars, and the old farmers came out, mostly white people, and they looked at us with utter disdain. But we knew that victory was in sight."[13]

By the time the procession reached Montgomery on March 25, it had expanded in size to include 25,000 people. A number of prominent civil rights leaders joined King at the front, including Rosa Parks, John Lewis, and A. Philip Randolph. The national television networks covered the triumphant final leg of the march live, and pictures appeared on the front pages of newspapers across the country and around the world.

The Selma-Montgomery voting rights march concluded with a rally on the steps of the Alabama State Capitol. A group of eight marchers presented a petition to Governor Wallace demanding that the state remove all restrictions on black voter registration. Then King made a speech in which he honored all the people who responded to the Bloody Sunday assault by rushing to join the Selma protests. "Selma, Alabama, became a shining moment in the con-

In the days leading up the triumphant Selma-to-Montgomery march, other demonstrations such as this one in Brooklyn, New York, were organized to show solidarity with the Selma activists.

science of man," he declared. "If the worst in American life lurked in its dark streets, the best of American instincts arose passionately from across the nation to overcome it."[14] King concluded by encouraging the crowd to keep fighting to achieve true racial equality in America.

Support Grows for Strong Legislation

When the rally concluded, organizers and federal marshals encouraged the protesters to leave Montgomery as soon as possible in order to minimize the potential for violence. People who had come from out of town headed to the airport, and a number of volunteers shuttled local marchers back to Selma. One of these volunteers, Viola Liuzzo, was a white homemaker who had come from Michigan to help out. As she drove back toward Montgomery after dropping off a group of marchers in Selma, her car was chased and forced off the road by Ku Klux Klan members. Liuzzo was shot and killed. The black teenager who accompanied her on the drive, Leroy Moton, survived the attack by pretending to be dead. As it turned out, one of the people in the other car was an FBI informant, so the KKK members were arrested a few days later.

This latest incidence of racial violence further increased public support for Johnson's proposed voting rights legislation. "Recent events in Alabama, involving murder, savage brutality, and violence by local police, state troopers, and posses, have so aroused the nation as to make action by this Congress necessary and speedy," declared House Judiciary Committee member Emanuel Celler. "The climate of public opinion has so changed because of the Alabama outrages, as to make assured the passage of this solid bill—a bill that would have been inconceivable a year ago."[15]

Notes

[1] Quoted in "Voting Rights Act of 1965," The Dirksen Congressional Center. Available online at http://www.congresslink.org/print_basics_histmats_votingrights_contents.htm.

[2] Quoted in Williams, Juan. *Eyes on the Prize: America's Civil Rights Years, 1954-1965.* New York: Viking Penguin, 1987, p. 254.

[3] King, Martin Luther, Jr. "Nobel Prize Lecture," December 11, 1964. Available online at http://nobelprize.org/nobel_prizes/peace/laureates/1964/king-lecture.html.

[4] Quoted in Williams, p. 258.

[5] Source: King, Martin Luther Jr. "A Letter from a Selma, Alabama, Jail" [advertisement], *New York Times,* February 5, 1965.

[6] Quoted in Williams, p. 268.

[7] Quoted in Williams, p. 273.

[8] Quoted in *The Unfinished Agenda of the Selma-Montgomery Voting Rights March,* p. 42.

[9] Quoted in Williams, p. 273.

[10] Quoted in Williams, p. 278.

[11] "Our God Is Marching On," speech delivered in Montgomery, Alabama, March 25, 1965. Available online at MLK Papers Project, http://www.stanford.edu/group/King/publications/speeches.

[12] Quoted in Academy of Achievement, "Frank Johnson Interview," 1991. Available online at http://www.achievement.org/autodoc/page/joh2pro-1.

[13] Quoted in Hampton, Henry, and Steve Fayer, with Sarah Flynn. *Voices of Freedom: An Oral History of the Civil Rights Movement from the 1950s through the 1980s.* New York: Bantam, 1991, p. 236.

[14] Quoted in Carson, Clayborne, et al, eds. *The Eyes on the Prize Civil Rights Reader: Documents, Speeches, and Firsthand Accounts from the Black Freedom Struggle, 1954-1990.* New York: Penguin, 1991, p. 225.

[15] Quoted in Williams, p. 283.

Chapter Six

THE VOTING RIGHTS ACT BECOMES LAW

Millions of non-white Americans will now be able to participate for the first time on an equal basis in the government
under which they live.

—U.S. Supreme Court decision upholding the
Voting Rights Act (*South Carolina v. Katzenbach*, 1966)

When President Lyndon B. Johnson signed the Voting Rights Act into law on August 6, 1965, it marked a tremendous victory for the civil rights movement. The law provided for direct federal intervention to secure African-American voting rights in areas where they had been systematically denied in the past. Its passage resulted in a huge increase in the number of black registered voters throughout the South. After this important goal was achieved, however, the civil rights movement splintered into competing factions and faded in influence.

Passing the Landmark Legislation

The events in Selma convinced many Americans that existing federal laws were not strong enough to secure black voting rights in the face of white resistance. The violence that took place on Bloody Sunday made it clear that direct federal intervention was needed to enable African Americans to register and cast ballots in the South. Thousands of people contacted their representatives in Congress and demanded that they support President Johnson's voting rights bill.

The bill passed the U.S. Senate on May 11, 1965. Members of the U.S. House of Representatives then debated over the proposed legislation for five weeks. One of the main issues under debate involved whether or not the new law should include an outright ban on states' use of poll taxes. Many lawmakers felt that making voters pay a fee to cast a ballot discriminated against the poor. For this reason, the use of poll taxes was already prohibited in national elections. But some legislators worried that striking down a state election practice by federal statute might be unconstitutional.

As a compromise on the issue, Johnson asked Attorney General Nicholas Katzenbach to challenge the poll tax in federal court. The Justice Department filed a lawsuit against the four states where poll taxes were still used (Alabama, Mississippi, Texas, and Virginia), arguing that the practice violated the equal protection clause of the Fourteenth Amendment. In its decision in the 1966 case *Harper v. Virginia State Board of Elections*, the Supreme Court agreed with the argument and struck down poll taxes as a requirement in state or local elections nationwide.

With the poll tax question left to the courts to decide, the House finally passed the legislation on July 10, 1965. After the two chambers of Congress held a conference to reconcile the differences between their two versions of the bill, they voted again on the final version. The House approved the conference report on August 3 by a vote of 328-74, and the Senate approved it the following day by a vote of 79-18.

On August 6, 1965, President Johnson signed the Voting Rights Act into law in the President's Room off the Capitol Rotunda. He chose this room partly for its historic symbolism: it was the same place where President Abraham Lincoln had signed the Emancipation Proclamation 104 years earlier, marking the end of slavery in the United States. During the signing ceremony, Johnson gave a moving speech about the power of the vote to break down the barriers of discrimination and injustice. He called the Voting Rights Act "one of the most monumental laws in the entire history of American freedom" (see "Johnson Signs the Voting Rights Act of 1965," p. 207).

A number of leaders of the civil rights movement watched the president sign the landmark legislation, including Martin Luther King, Jr., and Rosa Parks. Everyone in attendance recognized the historic significance of the occasion. "That day was a culmination, a climax, the end of a very long road," SNCC leader and Selma marcher John Lewis recalled in his autobiography, *Walking with the Wind*. "In a sense, it represented a high point in modern America, probably the finest hour in terms of civil rights."[1]

President Lyndon B. Johnson signs the Voting Rights Act as Martin Luther King, Jr., and other civil rights leaders look on.

Provisions of the VRA

The Voting Rights Act of 1965 (VRA) contained a number of provisions designed to ensure that African Americans gained an equal opportunity to register and vote in states where that right had been denied in the past. The VRA differed from previous civil rights laws, which had mostly allowed black citizens to challenge discriminatory state voter-registration requirements in federal court. Since attacking such election practices on a case-by-case basis had not worked, the new law provided for direct federal action to secure black voting rights.

The VRA included both general provisions and special or emergency provisions. The general provisions applied to every state in the nation and were permanent. The most important of these general provisions prohibited the use of voter-registration tests, procedures, or standards "in a manner which results in a denial or abridgement of the right of any citizen of the

President Bill Clinton Commemorates "Bloody Sunday"

In 2000 President Bill Clinton led thousands of marchers in a ceremonial procession across the Edmund Pettus Bridge in Selma, Alabama, to commemorate the 35th anniversary of Bloody Sunday. In a speech prepared for the occasion, which is excerpted below, Clinton thanked the protesters for risking their lives to bring greater freedom and opportunity to all Americans.

> Thirty-five years ago, a single day in Selma became a seminal moment in the history of our country. On this bridge, America's long march to freedom met a roadblock of violent resistance. But the marchers, thank God, would not take a detour on the road to freedom....

> On this Bloody Sunday, about 600 foot soldiers, some of whom, thankfully, remain with us today, absorbed with uncommon dignity the unbridled force of racism, putting their lives on the line for that most basic American right: the simple right to vote, a right which already had been long guaranteed and long denied.

> Here in Dallas County, there were no black elected officials because only one percent of voting-age blacks, about 250 people, were registered. They were kept from the polls, not by

United States to vote on account of race or color." This provision applied to literacy tests, educational achievement requirements, government and citizenship questionnaires, good moral character vouchers, and other devices used to assess people's qualifications for voting.

The special or emergency provisions of the VRA only applied to areas (mostly in the South) where widespread abuses of minority voting rights had occurred. The law defined these "covered jurisdictions" as areas where literacy tests or similar devices had been used to determine citizens' eligibility to vote, or where voter turnout for the 1964 presidential election was less than 50 percent of eligible adults. The jurisdictions originally covered under the special provisions of the VRA were Alabama, their own indifference or alienation but by systematic exclusion, by the poll tax, by intimidation, by literacy testing that even the testers, themselves, could not pass. And they were kept away from the polls by violence.

It must be hard for the young people in this audience to believe, but just 35 years ago, Americans, both black and white, lost their lives in the voting rights crusade.... They did not die in vain.... Six months later, President Johnson signed the Voting Rights Act, proclaiming that the vote is the most powerful instrument ever devised for breaking down injustice.... It has been said that the Voting Rights Act was signed in ink in Washington, but it first was signed in blood in Selma.

Those who walked by faith across this bridge led us all to a better tomorrow.... After Selma, free white and black southerners crossed the bridge to the new South, leaving hatred and isolation on the far side.... We could not have done it if brave Americans had not first walked across the Edmund Pettus Bridge.

Source:
Clinton, William J. "Remarks on the 35th Anniversary of the 1965 Voting Rights March in Selma, Alabama." *Weekly Compilation of Presidential Documents*, March 13, 2000, p. 470.

Georgia, Louisiana, Mississippi, South Carolina, Virginia, 40 counties in North Carolina, and Alaska.

The law allowed the Justice Department to send federal registrars to the covered jurisdictions to register voters in place of local officials. It also provided for federal observers to go to polling sites during elections and oversee state voting practices. Most importantly, the special provisions of the VRA required covered jurisdictions to obtain federal approval before making any changes to their election laws or voting procedures. Known as "preclearance," this provision applied to "any voting qualification or prerequisite to voting, or standard, practice, or procedure with respect to voting." The covered states and counties had to prove that any proposed change—from the design of a ballot to the location of a polling place—did not have a discriminatory purpose or effect.

The special provisions of the VRA were temporary. They were set to expire in five years unless Congress voted to renew them. The law also provided opportunities for covered jurisdictions to "bail out" or be excused from the preclearance provision. In the original VRA of 1965, states or counties could bail out by proving in federal court that the voting tests they had used in the past did not discriminate against minorities. Later versions of the law allowed a covered jurisdiction to bail out of the preclearance requirement by demonstrating that it had used nondiscriminatory voting practices for at least ten years and had taken affirmative steps to improve minority voting opportunities. Eleven counties in Virginia eventually took advantage of this method to end federal oversight of their election practices.

Although the VRA provided for direct federal action to prevent states from discriminating against minority voters, the law did not establish the right to vote as an entitlement granted by the federal government. The states continued to control many aspects of the election process, and some nondiscriminatory requirements for voter registration remained valid. For instance, state governments were still allowed to establish time frames for voter registration, require voters to show identification, and prohibit people from voting if they had been convicted of a felony.

Efforts to Limit the VRA

Almost immediately after the VRA passed Congress, white political leaders in the South challenged the constitutionality of the new law in court. They pointed out that the Constitution granted the power to regulate elections to the states. They claimed that the VRA violated states' rights by providing for federal government intervention in voter registration and oversight of election practices. The Supreme Court disagreed with this reasoning, however, and upheld the constitutionality of the VRA several times over the next few years.

In the 1966 case *South Carolina v. Katzenbach,* for instance, the Court ruled that the VRA's preclearance provision was justified by the southern states' long history of denying black voting rights. "After enduring nearly a century of systematic resistance to the Fifteenth Amendment, Congress might well decide to shift the advantage of time and inertia from the perpetrators of the evil to its victims," the justices wrote.

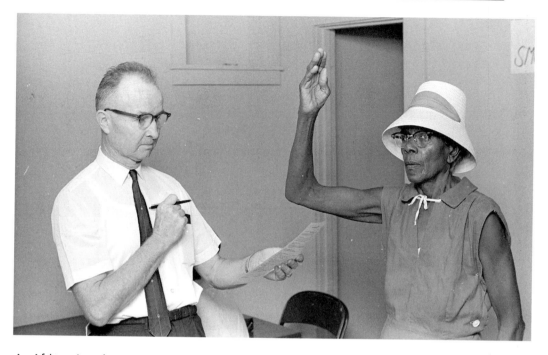

An African-American woman registers to vote in Mississippi after passage of the Voting Rights Act.

The Court upheld the VRA again in the 1969 case *Allen v. State Board of Elections*. In this decision, the justices said that the law served its intended purpose—"to rid the country of racial discrimination in voting"—by providing "new remedies against those practices which had most frequently denied citizens the right to vote on the basis of their race."

Immediate Impact on Voter Registration

The passage of the VRA had an immediate impact on voter registration, especially in the South. Thousands of African Americans rushed to take advantage of the hard-fought opportunity to be part of the democratic process. "There was a substantial jump in black voter registration in a relatively short period of time," noted one historian. "Given the opportunity, through the reduction of barriers, blacks would eagerly seek to participate in the governance that determines their status in American society."[2]

During the first six months after Johnson signed the VRA, federal registrars processed the applications of more than 100,000 black voters in the

South. Local officials, recognizing the new reality, registered another 200,000 African-American voters during that period. In Dallas County, Alabama—where the Selma-Montgomery voting rights marchers were attacked by police on Bloody Sunday—more than 9,000 black residents registered to vote within a year, up from 156 who had managed to register at the time of the march. The man most responsible for the police brutality toward the marchers, Sheriff Jim Clark, was voted out of office in the next election. Although Alabama Governor George Wallace kept his job for several more terms, many other segregationists were voted out of office throughout the South on the strength of the black vote.

Perhaps the most dramatic impact of the VRA occurred in Mississippi, where SNCC activists had held voter registration drives during Freedom Summer in 1964. The percentage of African Americans registered to vote in the state increased from 6.7 percent in 1965 to 59.8 percent in 1968. On average, the jurisdictions covered under the VRA saw a 25 percent increase in black registered voters by the 1968 presidential election. An impressive 52 percent of voting-age African Americans cast ballots in the South during that election, which approached the 62 percent of southern whites who voted.

The increase in black registered voters helped create a surge in the number of black elected officials across the country. Following the 1968 elections, there were 11 African-American members of the U.S. Congress, including the first black woman—Shirley Chisholm of New York. Two years later, Representative Charles Diggs, Jr., of Michigan established the Congressional Black Caucus to promote issues of importance to African Americans. In 1972 SCLC activist Andrew Young was elected to the U.S. House of Representatives from Georgia, becoming the first black member of Congress to be elected from the South since Reconstruction.

President Johnson also appointed black men to several powerful positions in the federal government. In 1966 he named Robert Weaver to his cabinet as the head of the Department of Housing and Urban Development. The following year, Johnson nominated Thurgood Marshall—who had won the landmark 1954 *Brown v. Board of Education* case as a lawyer for the NAACP—as the first African-American justice of the U.S. Supreme Court.

The End of the Civil Rights Movement

The passage of the VRA was a tremendous victory for the civil rights movement. It marked the end of a decade-long fight to end segregation and dis-

As the Vietnam War dragged on, pulling greater numbers of white and black American soldiers into the conflict, the nation's attention shifted away from civil rights.

crimination in American society. Starting with the *Brown* ruling that desegregated the nation's public schools, the movement had achieved a series of major legal and political gains in the late 1950s and early 1960s. Voting rights represented the ultimate prize in the minds of many activists. Fair and equal access to the ballot allowed African Americans to participate in the democratic process and have a say in the future direction of the country. Once the VRA secured black voting rights, many people felt that further gains would occur naturally.

The VRA, though, did not have an immediate impact on other problems that disproportionately affected African Americans, such as unemployment, poverty, crime, inadequate health care, and poor education. Many civil rights activists felt disappointed that the movement did not make more progress toward solving these problems. "The journey on the road from Selma to Montgomery did not just promise to lead to the right to vote or the privilege of African Americans serving in public office," said Henry Sanders, a black member of the Alabama State Senate. "It promised to lead to a better life. That promise remains largely unfulfilled."[3]

Although protest marches and sit-ins were used to call attention to such problems, these nonviolent tools of the southern civil rights movement did not hold as much appeal for the black residents of northern cities. Trapped in lives of hopelessness and despair in urban ghettoes, some African Americans lashed out in violent race riots. Rioting broke out in a number of black neighborhoods in 1965, including Watts in Los Angeles and Harlem in New York.

The violence in the black ghettoes shook up some civil rights groups. Organizations like SNCC and CORE experienced inner turmoil as members struggled to figure out how to continue fighting for true racial equality. Some black activists wanted to work within the system and use their new political power to make needed changes. But others argued that blacks could not trust whites to give them real equality. Instead, they claimed that African Americans must build their own sources of power to achieve a transformation in American society.

These competing philosophies led to a split in the civil rights movement following the signing of the VRA. Looking back, many activists viewed the Selma-Montgomery Voting Rights March as the closing chapter in the history of the civil rights movement. "It was certainly the last act for the movement as I knew it," John Lewis recalled in *Walking with the Wind*. "Something was born in Selma during the course of that year, but something died there, too. The road of nonviolence had essentially run out. Selma was the last act.... It had been Selma that held us together as long as we did. After that, we just came apart."[4]

Black Power

Lewis stepped down as head of SNCC in 1966 and was replaced by Stokely Carmichael, a militant activist who rejected nonviolence. He claimed that violent uprising was sometimes necessary to promote revolutionary change. "The only way we gonna stop them white men from whuppin' us is to take over," Carmichael declared at a 1966 rally. "What we gonna start sayin' now is Black Power!"

Black Power became the slogan for a new movement that emphasized racial pride. Supporters of the movement rejected the old goals of integration

A man collapses in grief after reading about the assassination of Martin Luther King, Jr., in April 1968.

into white society and cooperation with the white power structure. Instead, they said that African-American interests would be better served by pursuing new goals of racial separation and black autonomy. The radical message of the Black Power movement disturbed many moderate black civil rights leaders. SCLC founder Bayard Rustin, for example, argued that it was harmful to black interests because it encouraged anti-black sentiment.

Martin Luther King, Jr., also found the increased militancy upsetting. He continued to lead the mainstream civil rights movement and to advocate the use of nonviolent protest methods. After the VRA passed, however, he turned his attention away from segregation and voting rights and began fighting against poverty, unemployment, and other problems affecting urban areas. He tried to build a coalition of urban blacks and poor whites to pressure government and business leaders to solve these problems.

King also moved away from his traditional civil rights focus to speak out against American involvement in the Vietnam War. Like other black leaders, he was initially reluctant to criticize Johnson's decision to send U.S. troops to Vietnam because the president had supported the VRA. But King changed his mind when it became clear that the war drew the U.S. government's money and attention away from programs designed to fight poverty and other problems at home. He also pointed out that African-American soldiers accounted for a disproportionate share of casualties in the newly integrated U.S. military.

In April 1968 King traveled to Memphis, Tennessee, to show his support for the city's black sanitation workers, who had gone on strike to protest unequal wages and working conditions. His flight there was delayed by a bomb threat. Once he arrived in Memphis, he tried to reassure and encourage his supporters in a speech entitled "I've Been to the Mountaintop," delivered on April 3:

> Like anybody, I would like to live a long life. Longevity has its place. But I'm not concerned about that now. I just want to do God's will. And He's allowed me to go up to the mountain. And I've looked over. And I've seen the promised land. I may not get there with you. But I want you to know tonight, that we, as a people, will get to the promised land![5]

The following day, King was shot and killed as he stood on the second-floor balcony of the Memphis motel where he had been staying. People around the world were devastated by the news of the inspirational leader's death. Upon learning that the assassin was believed to be a white man, many African Americans reacted with rage and violence. Riots broke out in dozens of cities across the country, despite King's lifelong adherence to the philosophy of nonviolence.

Notes

[1] Lewis, John, with Michael D'Orso. *Walking with the Wind: A Memoir of the Movement.* New York: Simon and Schuster, 1998.

[2] Walters, Ronald. "The Partisan Landscape: How Blacks Became the Indispensable Democrats." In *Editors of Black Issues in Higher Education, The Unfinished Agenda of the Selma-Montgomery Voting Rights March.* Hoboken, NJ: John Wiley and Sons, 2005, p. 46.

[3] Quoted in Walters, p. 77.

[4] Lewis, *Walking with the Wind.*

[5] King, Martin Luther, Jr. "I've Been to the Mountaintop." Speech delivered in Memphis, Tennessee, April 13, 1968. Available online at http://www.americanrhetoric.com/speeches/mlkivebeentothe mountaintop.htm.

Chapter Seven

LEGACY OF THE VOTING RIGHTS ACT

[Georgia is] not the same state that it was ... in 1965 or in 1975 or even 1980 or 1990. We've changed. We have come a great distance. It's not just Georgia but the American South. I think people are preparing to lay down the burden of race.

—U.S. Representative John Lewis
testifying in a voting rights trial, 2004

The Voting Rights Act of 1965 ranks among the most important and influential laws in U.S. history. Nearly a century after the Fifteenth Amendment enshrined black voting rights in the Constitution, the VRA finally turned the promise of these rights into a reality. The law put an end to the discriminatory practices that had been used to prevent African Americans from voting in the South, and it spurred a dramatic increase in the number of black registered voters and elected officials. "The VRA, considered the most successful civil rights legislation ever passed, has touched virtually every corner of our society and empowered millions of citizens with the vote,"[1] according to the NAACP Legal Defense Fund.

While the basic provisions of the VRA remained in place into the twenty-first century, the law changed somewhat over time. It was renewed or extended four times after its initial passage, in 1970, 1975, 1982, and 2006. The U.S. Supreme Court also interpreted the law in several decisions and adjusted the ways in which it was applied. Through all the changes, however, it was clear that the VRA achieved its original goal of removing discriminatory barriers to voter registration. Later challenges and interpretations focused on subtler techniques used to limit minority influence in elections, such as redrawing voting-district boundaries. Since the VRA had such a significant impact on minority representation in government, some critics questioned whether the law was still necessary. But the overwhelming bipartisan support for its 25-year renewal in 2006 showed that the VRA retained its landmark status.

VRA of 1975 Protects Language Minorities

When the VRA of 1965 originally passed, the special or emergency provisions of the legislation were set to expire after a period of five years (Congress often adds an expiration date to legislation so that its effectiveness can be evaluated later and changes made if needed). After assessing the VRA in 1970, Congress voted to extend it for five more years. Lawmakers also revised the law in a few significant ways at that time. The VRA of 1970 established 18 as the voting age in federal elections, for instance, and permanently banned the use of literacy tests in all states, rather than only in covered jurisdictions.

In 1974 the U.S. Supreme Court issued an important ruling regarding minority voting rights. The case of *Torres v. Sachs* concerned a New York law that required ballots and other election materials to be produced only in the English language. The justices found that this law discriminated against American citizens who primarily spoke a language other than English—a segment of the population collectively known as "language minorities." "In order that the phrase 'the right to vote' be more than an empty platitude," the majority opinion stated, "a voter must be able effectively to register his or her political choice, and this involves more than physically being able to pull a lever or mark a ballot."

With the special provisions of the VRA set to expire again in 1975, the U.S. Commission on Civil Rights conducted a study of minority voting rights. It found that language minorities—including Native Americans, Native Alaskans, Hispanic Americans, and Asian Americans—experienced significant problems when trying to vote. Congress decided to address this situation with the VRA of 1975. Legislators amended the law to require all jurisdictions in which 5 percent or more of eligible voters belonged to a language minority group to provide voting materials and assistance in other languages.

The 1975 renewal thus expanded the areas covered by the VRA beyond the South to include 513 new jurisdictions in 30 states. Some critics objected to the new provisions aimed at helping language minorities. They argued that the changes should not be necessary because new immigrants to the United States were required to be proficient in English in order to become citizens.

They also complained about the high cost of holding bilingual elections and charged that it was difficult to obtain accurate translations of voting materials. Supporters of the new provisions, on the other hand, insisted that they were consistent with the main goal of the VRA: to remove barriers that denied minorities equal voting rights.

VRA of 1982
Addresses Race-Based Districting

By most accounts, the VRA of 1965 and its first two extensions were effective in getting rid of discriminatory voter-registration procedures. Within the first decade after its passage, most African Americans and members of other minority groups were able to register without incident—even in regions where blacks who attempted to register had risked death only a few years before.

In 1972 Andrew Young became one of the first two blacks elected to represent Southern states in the U.S. Congress since 1901.

In some states, however, election officials came up with new, subtler ways to limit the influence of minority voters. For instance, some switched from district-by-district voting to at-large elections. In states where certain districts had large minority populations—but whites made up the majority of the overall population—at-large elections often had the effect of preventing minority candidates from being elected to office.

Redrawing the boundaries of voting districts, or gerrymandering, was the most controversial method used to limit the ability of minority voters to elect candidates of their choice. The Supreme Court weighed in on this practice in several important decisions. In the 1973 case *White v. Regester,* the justices declared that it was unconstitutional to change voting district boundaries if such changes diluted minority voting strength. With its 1980 decision in *City of Mobile v. Bolden,* however, the Court said it was not enough for election practices or district boundaries to have the effect of discriminating against minority voters. Instead, the justices required minority voters to prove that these procedures were intentionally designed with the purpose of discriminating.

When Congress extended the VRA for a third time in 1982, it specifically addressed the issue of race-based districting. Effectively overturning the *Mobile v. Bolden* ruling, the VRA of 1982 prohibited state and local governments from making any election law change that diluted the voting influence of minority groups—whether that was the intent or merely the effect of the change in question. The renewal also allowed blind, disabled, or illiterate citizens to receive assistance in voting from a person of their choice.

In the 1986 case *Thornburg v. Gingles,* the Supreme Court interpreted the VRA of 1982 to mean that states should consider race as a factor in drawing voting district boundaries. In situations where a minority population had been unable to elect candidates of choice in the past, the justices ruled, states had an obligation to create districts in which minorities made up the majority of voters. Such race-based districts became known as "majority-minority" districts. Some people criticized the Court's decision, claiming that it went far beyond the original intent of the VRA and led to racial polarization of the electorate. "The Voting Rights Act was designed to ensure equal access to the ballot," wrote one critic. "But soon the law was seized upon as a means to attain not just ballot access but the spoils of politics. The Voting Rights Act was interpreted to mandate not equal opportunity but equal outcomes."[2]

The Question of Descriptive vs. Substantive Representation

Following the 1990 Census, many states launched major redistricting efforts in order to comply with the *Thornburg v. Gingles* ruling. These efforts contributed to significant growth in the number of minorities elected to office nationwide. For example, the number of African-American members of the U.S. Congress increased from 27 to 39 in the 1992 election. Yet some observers claimed that these and later election results actually gave minority voters less influence in national politics.

Ever since Presidents Kennedy and Johnson gave valuable support to the civil rights movement, African-American citizens have shown a strong tendency to vote for Democratic candidates. In fact, black voters typically account for 20 to 25 percent of the Democratic total in national elections. Many minority voters feel that the stated policy goals of the Republican Party—such as reducing the size of the federal government and limiting spending on social programs—do not reflect their priorities and concerns as well as those of the Democratic Party.

Given the political leanings of the black community, it would seem to be in the best interest of African-American voters to elect as many Democratic candidates as possible. But the race-based redistricting plans of the early 1990s had the opposite effect. Critics claimed that these plans actually contributed to a significant increase in the number of Republicans elected to office, and even helped the Republican Party gain control of Congress in the 1994 elections. "Under the prevailing interpretation of [the VRA], redistricters are obliged to maximize the number of districts with majorities or near majorities of blacks and Hispanics," one analyst explained. "That means that redistricters bunch very large numbers of heavily Democratic precincts into a few districts and keep them out of adjacent districts where the political balance is much closer. The Voting Rights Act, thus interpreted, tends to result in the election of more blacks and Hispanics and fewer Democrats."[3] In other words, Democratic candidates easily win a few elections in majority-minority districts, but lose closer races in many other districts because one of the party's core constituencies is barely present.

Race-based redistricting thus raises the question of whether race is the most important factor in ensuring adequate political representation. In other words, can only minority officeholders truly represent the interests of minority voters? Political scientists talk about the difference between descriptive representation (in which a candidate has the same personal or social characteristics—such as race, religion, or gender—as the voter) and substantive representation (in which a candidate holds the same policy positions as the voter). Although race-based redistricting under the VRA gave minority voters greater descriptive representation, some critics argue that it simultaneously reduced their substantive representation.

In any case, many white voters felt that race-based redistricting was unfair and challenged the plans in court. One such case, *Shaw v. Reno*, concerned the 12th Congressional District in North Carolina. After the boundaries were redrawn to create a majority-minority district, voters elected a black representative to Congress for the first time since Reconstruction. But the U.S. Supreme Court ruled in 1993 that the district was so bizarrely shaped—resembling an ink splatter—that it violated the rights of white voters. The justices decided that race could not be the primary factor used to determine political district boundaries.

The Court weighed in on the districting issue once again in the 2003 case of *Georgia v. Ashcroft*. This ruling allowed states to redraw voting districts in ways that reduced the likelihood of electing minority candidates, as long as the new boundaries did not diminish the overall influence of minority voters. In effect, the ruling said states could "unpack" the majority-minority districts that they had created in the early 1990s. Although some critics viewed this decision as contradicting or weakening the VRA, it won the support of some prominent African Americans. Congressman John Lewis, for instance, argued that unpacking would serve the interests of black voters by increasing the number of Democrats elected to office.

Minority Disenfranchisement in the 2000 Election

The tendency for minority voters to favor Democratic candidates has led to a number of Democratic initiatives aimed at increasing minority voter participation in elections. It has also led to accusations that some Republican initiatives have been specifically designed to reduce participation by minorities and other Democratic-leaning voters. After all, minority turnout can determine the outcome of close elections (see sidebar "Exercising the Right to Vote," p. 116). Some critics claim that disenfranchisement of minority voters contributed to the results of the disputed 2000 presidential election.

This contest between Republican candidate George W. Bush and Democratic candidate Al Gore was one of the closest in U.S. history. The outcome of the entire election eventually came down to the results of voting in a single state, Florida. Following a series of controversial recounts and legal battles that lasted for five weeks, the U.S. Supreme Court finally stepped in to halt the process and declare Bush the winner.

Afterward, the U.S. Civil Rights Commission and the NAACP held a series of hearings about minority participation in the 2000 election. Their findings indicated that minority voters nationwide experienced a number of problems in trying to cast their ballots. Some people went to local polling places only to find that they had been moved to new locations without notice. Others waited in long lines only to have the polls close before they got a chance to vote. Finally, thousands of minority voters were turned away because their names had incorrectly been removed from lists of registered voters.

This last problem occurred frequently in Florida. Prior to the presidential election, Republican Secretary of State Katherine Harris ordered a purge

Felon Disenfranchisement Laws

Approximately 4.2 million U.S. citizens nationwide, or about 1 out of every 50 American adults, are not eligible to vote because they were convicted of a felony. The Fourteenth Amendment to the Constitution allows the states to deny voting rights to people who have been found guilty of "serious crimes." In its 1974 decision *Richardson v. Ramirez,* the U.S. Supreme Court interpreted this amendment to mean that state legislatures may deny convicted felons the right to vote—either temporarily during their prison terms, or permanently after they are released.

Supporters of felon disenfranchisement laws claim that prohibiting former criminals from voting serves important social goals, such as punishing lawbreakers and deterring crime. Some argue that people who have committed felonies are morally unworthy to hold the privilege of voting. Proponents also worry that if ex-convicts held full voting rights, they could band together and vote as a bloc to remove tough sheriffs, judges, and other elected officials from office.

Opponents of felon disenfranchisement, on the other hand, claim that such laws do nothing to deter crime and punish ex-convicts long after they have paid their debts to society. They also argue that the wide variation in state laws governing felon disenfranchisement violates the equal protection clause of the Fourteenth Amendment.

Finally, some critics contend that felon disenfranchisement laws discriminate against African Americans. State laws prohibiting felons from voting affect 1.4 million black men, or about 13 percent of the black male population of the United States. Some of these laws were first enacted following Reconstruction with the express aim of disqualifying black voters and maintaining white rule. Critics assert that instead of turning felons into a class of political outcasts, states should encourage ex-convicts to vote and become contributing members of law-abiding society.

of 57,700 names from the list of people registered to vote in Florida. She claimed that this action was necessary to eliminate convicted felons, who were not allowed to vote under state law (see sidebar "Felon Disenfranchise-

In January 2005 Condoleezza Rice became the first African-American woman to serve as U.S. Secretary of State.

ment Laws," p. 113), and people who had died since the last election. As it turned out, though, more than 90 percent of the voters targeted in the purge had their names removed in error. Critics noted that 54 percent of these voters were black or Hispanic citizens who were statistically more likely to favor Democratic candidates.

Studies conducted after the 2000 election also found high rates of invalidated ballots in Florida counties that were home to large numbers of African-American voters. Ballots could be considered invalid or spoiled if they had stray marks on them, for example, or if the voter wrote in the name of a candidate whose name already appeared. Such ballots were discarded and did not count toward the vote totals.

The percentage of invalidated ballots in Florida varied widely by county. In mostly black Gadsden County, for instance, 1 out of every 8 ballots (12.5 percent) were invalidated. In mostly white Leon County next door, however, only 1 out of every 500 ballots (0.2 percent) were invalidated. Statewide figures indicated that 14.4 percent of the votes cast by African Americans were not counted, compared to 1.6 percent of those cast by whites.

A Harvard University study of the 2000 election found that similar percentages of minority ballots were invalidated nationwide. "National figures indicate that Florida is, surprisingly, typical," said Philip Klinkner, co-author of the study. "Given the proportion of nonwhite to white voters in America, then, it appears that about half of all ballots spoiled in the USA, as many as 1 million votes, were cast by nonwhite voters."[4] Since minorities account for only 31 percent of the U.S. population, some critics charged that these figures represented an alarming trend toward minority disenfranchisement.

New Challenges to Equal Voting Rights

The controversy surrounding the 2000 election led many states to update their voting procedures and equipment. As part of this election-reform movement, Congress passed the Help America Vote Act in 2002. One of the main provisions of this law required states to computerize their lists of registered voters and remove the names of "suspect" voters, including deceased citizens and convicted felons. The Bush administration argued that this measure would help prevent illegal voting, also known as voter fraud. But critics worried that it would result in the elimination of legitimate minority voters instead.

A bipartisan report by the U.S. Election Assistance Commission, reported in *USA Today*, found that "there is little polling-place fraud, or at least much less than is claimed, including voter impersonation, 'dead' voters, noncitizen voting, and felon voters."[5] In fact, only 24 people were convicted of illegal voting at the federal level between 2002 and 2005. Nevertheless, a number of states enacted laws aimed at preventing voter fraud. Many of these laws required citizens to show some form of government-issued identification—such as a driver's license or passport—in order to vote.

Critics claimed that the main effect of such laws was to make it more difficult for poor, elderly, and minority citizens to vote. These groups ranked among the segments of the U.S. population that were least likely to possess the required forms of identification. According to a report by the Brennan Center for Justice, 25 percent of African-American adults do not have a government-issued ID card.

Exercising the Right to Vote

Surveys show that more than 90 percent of Americans believe that voting is an important duty of citizenship. Yet only about 50 percent of eligible voters actually participate in most national elections. Historically, Americans who are young, have less education, and earn low levels of income are half as likely to vote as those who are older, better-educated, and wealthier. Experts offer a wide range of explanations for low turnout among voters in the United States, including feelings of indifference about the candidates, powerlessness to affect the outcome, or disenchantment with the political system.

Many veterans of the civil rights movement are appalled by the low voter turnout rates. They argue that voting is both a privilege that citizens should appreciate, and an obligation that they should take seriously. After all, civil rights activists worked hard—and even put their lives at risk—to ensure that all American citizens could vote. "It is my belief that a limited franchise and limited voter participation hurts our nation: in order to function as a true democracy, we must have full participation," said Andrew Young, a civil rights leader who went on to serve as a U.S. Congressman and mayor of Atlanta, Georgia. "A nation committed to full

Civil rights groups challenged several of these state voter-ID laws in court, arguing that they created a barrier to minority voting rights in violation of the VRA. "The VRA did not do enough," argued one analyst. "It guaranteed blacks the right to vote without intimidation, not that everyone would or could vote, or that every vote would count. The VRA gave us access to the ballot. It did not guarantee that we would get fair or adequate representation. The VRA gave us access. It did not guarantee us justice or accountability."[6]

The Fight Over Preclearance

As the 2007 expiration date of the VRA approached, many political leaders and analysts debated the law's value and impact. Some pointed to such controversial measures as voter-ID laws, partisan districting, purges of voter lists, and invalidation of ballots as evidence that African Americans and mem-

116

voter participation would experiment with weekend voting, mail-in voting, proportional representation, and full enforcement of the Voting Rights Act until our participation levels were closer to ninety percent rather than below sixty percent."[9]

The federal and state governments have enacted a number of laws and programs designed to increase voter registration and participation rates. For instance, the National Voter Registration Act of 1993 (commonly known as the Motor-Voter Bill) made registration procedures more uniform and convenient for minorities and low-income voters. The law enabled prospective voters to register by mail, when they applied for or renewed a driver's license, and through a variety of other state agencies.

The disputed presidential election of 2000—which was so close that the outcome was eventually decided by the U.S. Supreme Court—convinced many states to update their election rules and take steps to increase voter turnout. Several states passed laws enabling voters to cast their ballots early in order to avoid the rush on election day. Others tried to make voting easier by establishing vote centers in convenient locations, such as shopping malls or college campuses. These efforts helped increase turnout for the 2004 presidential election to 56.7 percent of eligible voters—the highest level since 1968.

bers of other minority groups remained vulnerable as targets for disenfranchisement. They argued that the continued use of such measures proved that the VRA was still necessary to protect minority voting rights.

Opponents of renewing the VRA focused mainly on the preclearance provision, which required covered jurisdictions to obtain federal approval before making any changes to their election practices. Critics claimed that this provision placed an unfair burden on certain states that had long since addressed discrimination that had occurred a generation earlier. They pointed out, for example, that states in the South still had to get federal preclearance in order to move a polling place from one church to another. "Congress is declaring from on high that states with voting problems 40 years ago can simply never be forgiven, that Georgians must eternally wear the scarlet letter because of the actions of their grandparents and great-grandparents,"

The Congressional Black Caucus, seen here in 2007, has emerged as an important voting bloc within the U.S. Congress.

declared Congressman Lynn Westmoreland, a Republican from Georgia. "We have repented and we have reformed."[7]

As evidence that his state had changed its ways, Westmoreland pointed out that a larger percentage of black residents than white residents had voted in recent elections. He also noted that Georgia voters had elected four African Americans to the U.S. Congress, 50 to the state legislature, and 600 to local offices in 2006.

Several national political commentators also mentioned the large number of black elected officials in the South as evidence that the preclearance provision of the VRA was no longer needed. "Today there are 43 African-American members of the House and Senate and more than 9,000 elected state and local officials. The state with the largest number? Mississippi," wrote George F. Will.

"So why the continuing pretense that the right to vote is, for African Americans, precarious and, unless the full VRA is preserved forever, perishable?"[8]

Voting Discrimination Continues

The National Commission on the Voting Rights Act was established to help determine whether minority voters had continued to experience widespread discrimination since the VRA was last renewed in 1982. Chaired by Bill Lann Lee, a former assistant attorney general for civil rights under President Bill Clinton, the commission held hearings in cities across the country in 2005. The members also examined federal court records and Department of Justice reports and interviewed civil rights leaders and election experts.

Lee presented the commission's findings to Congress during the debate over renewal of the VRA. He noted that the preclearance provision had resulted in 626 challenges to state election-law changes and redistricting plans since 1982. During this period, the federal government had refused to preclear 91 different changes submitted by the state of Georgia alone.

An incident in the covered jurisdiction of Kilmichael, Mississippi, served as an example of the type of discrimination that was prevented by the preclearance provision of the VRA. In 2001, the town council suddenly cancelled a local election three weeks before it was scheduled to take place. Many residents believed that white members of the council took this action because they feared that a black candidate would be elected mayor for first time in the town's history. Upon reviewing the cancellation under the preclearance provision, the Department of Justice decided that it was racially motivated and ordered the election to go on as planned.

Supporters of renewal also presented evidence of Native-American voting-rights abuses in South Dakota to show what could happen if the VRA was not enforced. South Dakota is home to nine federally recognized Native-American tribes that collectively make up 8.3 percent of the state's population. The VRA of 1975 was extended to cover several South Dakota counties with significant Native-American populations, requiring these counties to provide language assistance to voters and preclear all election-law changes. But the state and local governments decided to ignore the VRA. Only 10 out of 600 election-law changes were submitted for preclearance between 1975 and 2002.

Some of the most egregious voting-rights abuses took place in Buffalo County, where Native Americans accounted for 83 percent of the total population of 2,000. In order to maintain control over the three-member county commission, white political leaders packed 1,500 Native Americans into one voting district. This districting scheme allowed the county's 17 percent white population to elect two members of the commission. The American Civil Liberties Union (ACLU) Voting Rights Project sued the county under the VRA in 2003 and forced it to adopt a more equitable districting plan.

These examples were cited by VRA supporters as clear evidence that it was still needed to protect minority voters from discriminatory state voting laws. "The evidence demonstrates unfortunately that the persistence, degree, geographic breadth, and methods of voting discrimination are substantial and ongoing," Lee declared. "The voting discrimination that Congress intended to eliminate by enacting and reauthorizing the Voting Rights Act has held steady. The temporary provisions of the Act, in fact, have prevented and remedied such discrimination. They continue to do so to this day."[10]

VRA Increases Minority Representation and Influence

Supporters of renewal of the VRA also pointed out that the law was clearly successful in giving minorities a greater voice in government. A 2007 study by a team of political scientists found "a substantial relationship between the VRA and the election of nonwhite officials at the national, state, and local levels."[11] Within 20 years of the law's passage, 255 cities across the country had elected African-American mayors. Some of these mayors presided over major cities in the South, including Marion Barry in Washington, D.C., Andrew Young in Atlanta, Ernest Morial in New Orleans, and Henry Arrington in Birmingham, Alabama.

By 2000, two states where some of the worst voting-rights abuses had occurred back in the 1960s had the largest numbers of black elected officials in the nation. Mississippi boasted 850 African-American leaders in state and local governments, while Alabama had 725. These numbers represented tremendous progress from the days of Freedom Summer and the Selma-Montgomery March. But critics argued that minorities were still underrepresented in these states. Since the population of Alabama is 25 percent black, for example, they pointed out that a proportionate share of the total of nearly 4,400 elected officials would be 1,100, rather than 725.

The 2007 study found that minorities were underrepresented in the U.S. Congress as well. In 2000, minorities made up 31 percent of the national population but held only 12 percent of seats in the U.S. Congress. As evidence of the VRA's continued effectiveness, however, the political scientists noted that the vast majority of black and Hispanic members of Congress were elected to represent districts that were covered under the landmark law.

According to some observers, the ultimate test of racial equality in the American political system is whether black candidates can attract enough support from white voters to succeed at the national level. The first black presidential candidate to attract notable support from white voters was the Reverend Jesse Jackson in 1984. The prominent civil rights leader ran a spirited campaign that emphasized racial harmony. Although Jackson did not win the Democratic presidential nomination, he inspired millions of people to join his "rainbow coalition" of supporters from all races.

In 2008 Illinois Senator Barack Obama became the first African-American presidential candidate for a major U.S. political party.

Since that time, evidence suggests that a candidate's race has become a less significant factor in American voters' decision-making processes. In 2008, U.S. Senator Barack Obama of Illinois became the first African-American presidential nominee from a major party. Obama formally accepted the Democratic nomination on August 28, the 45th anniversary of the historic March on Washington. Some observers noted that Obama's success in breaking through the barriers of race in national politics helped fulfill the dream Martin Luther King, Jr., spoke about on that occasion.

Congress Extends the VRA for 25 Years

Despite the fight over preclearance, the renewal of the Voting Rights Act received broad bipartisan support in Congress. Most supporters agreed that the VRA had made important progress toward eliminating the barriers to

President George W. Bush signed landmark Voting Rights Act renewal legislation on July 27, 2006.

minority voter registration and participation, resulting in a significant increase in minority officeholders at all levels of government. But they were also convinced that discriminatory election practices remained a problem in some parts of the country, making minority voters vulnerable to disenfranchisement (see "Senator Barack Obama Supports Renewal of the VRA," p. 212).

Congress ultimately voted to extend all provisions of the Voting Rights Act for 25 more years. The new law—officially called the Fannie Lou Hamer, Rosa Parks, and Coretta Scott King Voting Rights Act Reauthorizataion and Amendments Act of 2006—passed in the Senate by a unanimous vote of 98-0 and in the House by an impressive margin of 390-33. The introduction to the legislation noted that "the purpose of this Act is to ensure that the right of all citizens to vote, including the right to register to vote and cast meaningful votes, is preserved and protected as guaranteed by the Constitution."

President George W. Bush signed the bill into law on July 27, 2006. "In the four decades since the VRA was first passed, we've made progress toward equality, yet the work for a more perfect union is never ending," he remarked. "We'll continue to build on the legal equality won by the civil rights movement to help ensure that every person enjoys the opportunity that this great land of liberty offers."[12] The signing ceremony was attended by members of the Hamer, Parks, and King families, as well as by such prominent black leaders as Jesse Jackson and NAACP Chairman Julian Bond.

Many people took advantage of the occasion to reflect back on the heroic struggle that led to the passage of the VRA, and to celebrate the landmark law's contributions toward ensuring that all Americans enjoy full and equal participation in the democratic process. "In this country, we are engaged in an intergenerational quest to perfect a flawed democracy, one whose founding principles held that the right to equality was so basic a truth as to be 'self-evident,' but restricted the vote to a small portion of its population," noted the NAACP's Legal Defense Fund. "The Voting Rights Act of 1965, which outlaws and guards against many barriers to minority voter participation, is a critical link in the lineage of struggle to enfranchise the politically marginalized, a struggle to ensure that the words 'American Democracy' are not a contradiction in terms."[13]

Notes:

[1] NAACP Legal Defense Fund, "Impact of the VRA in America Today." Available online at http://www.naacpldf.org/vra.aspx?day=19.

[2] Bolick, Clint. "Bad Fences: To Preserve American Democracy, We Must Return to the Original Aims of the Voting Rights Act," *National Review,* April 3, 1995, p. 51.

[3] Barone, Michael, quoted in Will, George F. "VRA, All of It, Forever?" *Newsweek,* October 25, 2005, p. 70.

[4] Quoted in Palast, Greg. "Vanishing Votes." *The Nation,* May 17, 2004, p. 20.

[5] Quoted in Palast.

[6] Editors of *Black Issues in Higher Education, The Unfinished Agenda of the Selma-Montgomery Voting Rights March.* Hoboken, NJ: John Wiley and Sons, 2005, p. 3.

[7] Quoted in Kellman, Laurie. "House Renews Voting Rights Act Unchanged." CBS News Online, July 14, 2006. Available online at http://www.cbsnews.com/stories/2006/07/14/ap/politics/mainD8IRN HO85.shtml.

[8] Will, "VRA, All of It, Forever?"

[9] Young, Andrew. *An Easy Burden: A Memoir of the Civil Rights Movement.* New York: Harper-Collins, 1996.

[10] Lee, Bill Lan. "Testimony before the Subcommittee on the Constitution, U.S. House of Representatives," March 8, 2006. Available online at http://judiciary.house.gov/media/pdfs/lee030806.pdf.

[11] Pei-te Lien, et al. Study reported in *PS: Political Science and Politics,* July 2007. Quoted in "New Study Explores Impact of Voting Rights Act on Election of Nonwhite Officials in the U.S.," *U.S. Newswire,* July 23, 2007.

[12] Bush, George W. "Remarks upon Signing the Fannie Lou Hamer, Rosa Parks, and Coretta Scott King Voting Rights Reauthorization and Amendments Act of 2006," July 27, 2006. Available online at http://www.whitehouse.gov/news/releases/2006/07/print/20060727.html.

[13] NAACP Legal Defense Fund, "The Struggle for the Right to Vote." Available online at http://www.naacpldf.org/vra.aspx?day=1.

BIOGRAPHIES

Ella Baker (1903-1986)
Civil Rights Activist and Co-founder of the
Student Nonviolent Coordinating Committee
(SNCC)

Ella Josephine Baker was born in Norfolk, Virginia, on December 13, 1903, but she spent most of her childhood in the small town of Littleton, North Carolina. She was the second of three children raised by Blake and Georgianna Baker, who supported their children by farming.

Baker grew up in a home environment that placed great importance on religious faith, family loyalty, and service to the wider community. Her mother, various aunts, and other women in the neighborhood all became important role models to Baker. She was deeply influenced by their quiet strength and pride, which shone forth even though they lived under the dark shadow of the South's Jim Crow laws.

Baker spent her early years attending local schools, but in 1918 her parents decided that the education she was receiving was not acceptable. They sent her to Shaw University, an all-black school in Raleigh, North Carolina, that offered both high school and college instruction. Baker spent the next nine years attending school at Shaw before graduating—first in her class—in 1927.

An Activist in Harlem

After earning her college degree, Baker immediately moved to Harlem, a mostly black neighborhood in the heart of New York City that had become famous around the world as a center of African-American literature, art, music, and culture. This phenomenon, known as the Harlem Renaissance, was in full swing by the time Baker arrived in 1927.

Baker loved Harlem's energy and spirit, and she applauded the declarations of racial pride made by Harlem Renaissance leaders like W.E.B. DuBois and Langston Hughes. Determined to make her own contributions to the city's success, she wrote articles for Harlem newspapers and took a leadership position with the Young Negroes Cooperative League (YNCL).

In 1929 the United States was rocked by the Great Depression, a decade-long economic downturn characterized by farm failures, factory closures, and mass unemployment. Like virtually every other part of America, Harlem was hit hard by these terrible conditions. In 1935 Baker was hired by the Works Progress Administration (WPA), a federal relief agency, to educate Harlem residents about making sound financial decisions in hard economic times.

Joins the Staff of the NAACP

In 1938 Baker left the WPA to join the New York office of the National Association for the Advancement of Colored People (NAACP), the largest African-American civil rights organization in the country. She initially joined the NAACP as an assistant field secretary, but by 1942 she had been promoted to director of branches. In this capacity Baker helped NAACP offices all across the nation organize fundraising and membership drives.

During these years Baker became the NAACP's leading voice for expanding the fight for civil rights so that the African-American "grassroots"—local communities and working-class blacks—could have a greater role in the struggle. She praised the efforts of the national leadership, but she asserted that the movement would be more effective if it made more of an effort to expand beyond its middle-class membership. Baker and other field staff thus turned their attention to recruiting factory workers, maids, and waitresses. This campaign succeeded in swelling NAACP membership in many parts of the country.

Baker resigned from her position with the national NAACP in 1946, but she remained active in the organization. She even served a four-year term as president of the New York City branch from 1954 until 1958. During this same period, Baker joined with fellow activists Stanley Levison and Bayard Rustin to establish In-Friendship, a group to aid victims of racial terrorism in the South.

Baker also served on New York City's Commission on School Integration. This committee had been formed by the city in the wake of the 1954 *Brown v. Board* Supreme Court decision outlawing segregated schools. She played an important role in shaping the city's open-enrollment plan for public schools, one of the first in the country. Under this plan, students could enroll in public schools outside their own neighborhoods without having to change their residency or pay extra tuition or transportation expenses.

Key Ally to Martin Luther King

In the late 1950s Baker assumed greater prominence on the national civil rights stage. In January 1957 she helped civil rights leader Martin Luther King, Jr., establish the Southern Christian Leadership Conference (SCLC). Under King's direction, this organization became one of the most important voices in the fast-growing civil rights movement. In January 1958 Baker accepted King's offer to move to Atlanta and serve as director of SCLC's Crusade for Citizenship, an education and action campaign for the enforcement of voting rights for black citizens.

Baker's experiences in Atlanta with the SCLC included moments of triumph mixed with times of great frustration. She took great satisfaction in her work in African-American communities, which ranged from voter registration drives to organizing campaigns of nonviolent protest against Jim Crow. But she also encountered sexism from some of her SCLC colleagues, and she felt that King and other members of the organization did not always do enough to empower local communities. Baker wanted to develop a great coalition of leaders at the local level and keep authority from being concentrated in hands of a few. As she repeatedly declared, "strong people don't need strong leaders."

In early 1960 Baker's outspoken support for grassroots activism took her in a new direction. Deeply impressed by the February 1960 sit-in protests that black college students had carried out in Greensboro, North Carolina, Baker convinced King to organize a conference of African-American student activists at Shaw University in April. During the conference, Baker urged the 300 attendees to form a new civil rights group instead of joining existing organizations. She warned that if they were absorbed into traditional civil rights groups, their energy and spirit would fade. The students took her words to heart and, with Baker's help, created the Student Nonviolent Coordinating Committee (SNCC).

Advisor and Mentor to SNCC

In August 1960 Baker left SCLC so that she could give all of her energy and support to SNCC. She became one of the organization's most trusted advisors, even though she was forty years older than many SNCC members. She reminded SNCC leaders like John Lewis that the voices of all members deserved to be heard, and helped steer the organization clear of choices that might erode its independence or distract it from its civil rights mission.

"[Baker's] leadership and presence helped fashion the practice and philosophy of the group and ... the public image it projected," wrote one biographer. "Men were persuaded to accept an organization whose intellectual, spiritual, and political guide was—rather than a towering male patriarch or a messiah of some kind—an unassuming middle-aged woman."[1]

Over the next few years, Baker played an important role in developing some of SNCC's most important activities, including the 1961 Freedom Rides, which were organized to protest segregated transportation facilities in the South. She also helped with the Freedom Vote in Mississippi. This mock election destroyed the argument often employed by Southern whites that African Americans were simply uninterested in exercising their voting rights. When the Freedom Vote election was completed, more than 80,000 black Mississippi residents had cast ballots—even though the state only had 20,000 registered African-American voters. These results gave further momentum to the growing demand for passage of a federal Voting Rights Act.

Baker also helped organize the Mississippi Freedom Democratic Party (MFDP) in 1964. The MFDP was formed as an alternative to the established Mississippi Democratic Party, which was all-white. That summer, a delegation from the MFDP traveled to the Democratic National Convention and claimed that its interracial membership was better suited to represent the state than the all-white delegation. The MFDP was turned back by national party leaders, but its protest against racism and discrimination within the party received national attention. Alarmed by the negative attention, the Democratic Party subsequently passed a rule mandating that all state delegations would have to be racially mixed.

In 1964 Baker decided to return to New York City. A few months later, she celebrated with millions of other Americans when the 1965 Voting Rights Act was signed into law. But she maintained her outspoken ways and political activism for the next two decades. In addition to her continued work on civil rights issues, she joined protests against the Vietnam War and participated in various women's rights campaigns.

Baker died in New York on December 13, 1986, which was her eighty-third birthday. As news of her death traveled across the country, civil rights leaders and activists who had worked with her over the years reminded the nation of the important role Baker played in extending voting rights to all Americans.

Sources:

Grant, Joanne. *Ella Baker: Freedom Bound.* New York: John Wiley and Sons, 1998.

Mueller, Carol. "Ella Baker and the Origins of Participatory Democracy." In *Women in the Civil Rights Movement: Trailblazers and Torchbearers, 1941-1965.* Bloomington: University of Indiana Press, 1993.

Ransby, Barbara. *Ella Baker and the Black Freedom Movement: A Radical Democratic Vision.* Chapel Hill: University of North Carolina Press, 2002.

Williams, Juan, and Julian Bond. *Eyes on the Prize: America's Civil Rights Years, 1954-1965.* New York: Viking Penguin, 1988.

Notes

[1] Ransby, Barbara. *Ella Baker and the Black Freedom Movement: A Radical Democratic Vision.* Chapel Hill: University of North Carolina Press, 2002, p. 365.

James Farmer (1920-1999)
Director of the Congress of Racial Equality (CORE) during the Civil Rights Movement

James Leonard Farmer, Jr., was born on January 12, 1920, in Marshall, Texas. His mother was Pearl Marion Houston Farmer, a former teacher. His father was James Leonard Farmer, Sr., an ordained Methodist minister who served as a campus chaplain and professor of philosophy and religion at several small black Methodist colleges in the South.

Education was a big priority in the Farmer household, and young James thrived in this setting. At the age of fourteen he enrolled in Wiley College, a small black liberal arts school in Marshall that also offered high school level courses. Farmer originally intended to become a doctor, but his discomfort with the sight of blood led him to set his sights elsewhere. He ultimately decided to follow his father's example and pursue a career in the ministry, in part because he thought that such a career would give him opportunities to campaign against racial discrimination, poverty, and other social problems. "It did not occur to me that in the civil rights struggle I would see more blood than I ever would have seen in a doctor's office or a hospital operating room," he later admitted in his autobiography, *Lay Bare the Heart*. But he acknowledged that this realization might not have stopped him, for he felt pulled to "wage war on racism."[1]

A Believer in Peaceful Protest

After graduating from Wiley in 1938, Farmer moved on to Howard University, a prestigious African-American school in Washington, D.C. As he pursued his religious studies he became fascinated by Mohandas Gandhi, who was carrying out a long, unrelenting campaign of nonviolent resistance to free India from British rule. He gradually became convinced that Gandhi's philosophy of forcing social change through peaceful protest could work in the United States as well. During this same period Farmer became a staff member for the Fellowship of Reconciliation (FOR), a national peace group.

Farmer graduated from Howard with a master's degree in theology in 1941. He then moved to Chicago, where he and several friends launched a series of small but trailblazing anti-discrimination protests. In 1942, for example, Farmer led a civil rights sit-in at a Chicago restaurant that refused to serve African Americans in the main eating area. This protest, which was perhaps the first civil rights sit-in in U.S. history, ended in victory when the frustrated restaurant owner agreed to end his discriminatory policies.

Farmer and his allies decided to call their group the Committee of Racial Equality (CORE). They proclaimed that CORE intended to fight racial segregation and discrimination in America by using the same sorts of bold but peaceful protest campaigns that Gandhi used. Two years later the group changed its name to the Congress of Racial Equality.

Farmer was elected national chairman of CORE, but much of the group's early leadership consisted of white, middle-class men from the North. Farmer and other CORE leaders often disagreed on the priorities and tactics the organization should take, and in late 1944 he left CORE to focus on FOR and labor union organizing. In 1949 he married Lula Patterson, with whom he eventually had two children.

Leading a Revitalized CORE

After the loss of its leading founder, CORE gradually faded from public prominence. But it never actually disbanded, and in the late 1950s the organization's philosophy of using peaceful protest and civil disobedience to advance civil rights was embraced by African-American college students, workers, and community leaders who had no affiliation with the group. The 1955 Montgomery bus boycott sparked a new wave of peaceful civil rights demonstrations across the South, and CORE received new life.

Farmer was delighted by the growth of the civil rights movement—and pleased that his philosophy of nonviolent protest was becoming such a central part of the movement. In 1959 the National Association for the Advancement of Colored People (NAACP) hired Farmer to develop a direct action program for the organization. Like other established civil rights groups, the NAACP had previously focused on making civil rights gains through the courts and Congress. And despite their discomfort with some direct protests, NAACP leaders recognized that they needed to develop their resources in that area. But Farmer never felt fully accepted within the NAACP, and in 1961 he left the organization to take the leadership reins at CORE.

Upon rejoining CORE, Farmer moved decisively to put the group's resources to work. He joined with the leadership of the Student Nonviolent Coordinating Committee (SNCC) to organize a series of Freedom Rides across the Jim Crow South. These rides, which featured a mix of white and African-American volunteers, were meant to defy the South's practice of segregating buses, waiting rooms, and other public transportation facilities by race.

Over the ensuing months, Farmer and other Freedom Riders were subjected to beatings, bombings, unfair arrest and jail, and a steady drumbeat of harassment and death threats from enraged white racists in many Southern cities. But the Freedom Rides succeeded in publicizing the outrageous discrimination that existed all across the South. It also gave the entire civil rights movement a sense that there was no turning back in the quest to claim equal voting rights and end segregation.

Farmer himself realized that the Freedom Rides acquired a great symbolic value within the movement. When U.S. Attorney General Robert F. Kennedy wanted CORE and SNCC to agree to a "cooling off" period in which the Freedom Rides would be suspended, Farmer flatly refused to consider the request. "My objective is not just to make a *point,* but to bring about a real change in the situation," he declared. "We will continue the Ride until people can sit wherever they wish on buses and use the facilities in any waiting room available to the public.... We have been cooling off for 350 years. If we cool off any more we will be in a deep freeze. The Freedom Ride will go on."[2]

Fighting for Voting Rights

Farmer himself was arrested numerous times in the early 1960s, and on one occasion he spent forty days in a Jackson, Mississippi, jail after he tried to enter a white restroom at a local bus station. He was in a Louisiana jail on August, 28, 1963, when the famous March on Washington took place. But even though he could not be there in person, Farmer sent a letter that was read to the assembled crowd. "We will not stop our demands for freedom," Farmer wrote, "until the heavy weight of centuries of oppression is removed from our backs and like proud men everywhere we can stand tall together again."

Under Farmer's leadership, CORE became an important force in organizing voter registration drives in the South in 1963 and 1964. The group's activities in this area helped create further momentum for the passage of the 1964 Civil Rights Act and the Voting Rights Act of 1965. But even as these triumphs occurred, Farmer's continued insistence on nonviolent protest came under fire from militant black activists. In addition, Farmer became increasingly convinced that personality conflicts and petty jealousies within the larger civil rights movement were robbing it of much of its potential vitality and power.

Restless and frustrated, Farmer left CORE in 1966. He was asked to head a new federal literacy program, but President Lyndon B. Johnson blocked funding for the program—possibly as a way to punish Farmer for his public opposition to the Vietnam War, which the president supported.

Farmer accepted a faculty position at Lincoln University, a black college in Oxford, Pennsylvania, and taught there from 1966 to 1968. He then decided to run for political office in New York City, but he was defeated in his effort to win a seat in the U.S. House of Representatives by Shirley Chisholm, a black woman. In 1969 Farmer took a job in the administration of President Richard M. Nixon. As assistant secretary for administration in the Department of Health, Education, and Welfare, Farmer helped establish new affirmative action hiring and promotion policies. But he left a year later out of frustration with many of the Nixon administration's policy positions.

Farmer never regained the prominence he had known as director of CORE in the early 1960s, but he continued to work on civil rights and labor issues for the rest of his life. He also became a professor of civil rights history at Mary Washington College in Fredericksburg, Virginia, in 1985. That same year he published his autobiography, *Lay Bare the Heart*, which was praised by critics as a fascinating and brutally honest account of the civil rights era.

In Farmer's later years he struggled mightily against the ravages of diabetes, which blinded him and forced him to undergo amputations of both legs. In 1998, though, he received the Presidential Medal of Freedom, the nation's highest civilian honor. U.S. Senator Charles Robb and Congressman John Lewis—who had worked with Farmer during the civil rights era—wrote a tribute to him for the occasion. "James Farmer has ... spent a lifetime teaching America the value of equality and opportunity," they stated. "He has taught America that its most volatile social problems could be solved nonviolently. He has reminded us of the countless acts of courage and conviction needed to bring about great change. He has shown us the idealism needed to act and the pragmatism needed to succeed. His respect for humanity and his belief in justice will forever inspire those of us privileged to call him mentor and friend."[3] Farmer died one year later, on July 9, 1999, in Fredericksburg.

Sources:

Farmer, James. *Lay Bare the Heart: An Autobiography of the Civil Rights Movement.* 1985. Fort Worth, TX: Texas Christian University Press, 1998.

Morris, Aldon D. *Origins of the Civil Rights Movements: Black Communities Organizing for Change.* New York: Free Press, 1984.

Notes

[1] Farmer, James. *Lay Bare the Heart: An Autobiography of the Civil Rights Movement.* 1985. Fort Worth, TX: Texas Christian University Press, 1998, p. 127.

[2] Farmer, p. 206.

[3] Lewis, John, and Charles Robb. "A Tribute to an American Freedom Fighter." Available online at www.medaloffreedom.com/JamesFarmer.htm.

Fannie Lou Hamer (1917-1977)
Civil Rights Activist and Leader of the
Mississippi Freedom Democratic Party (MFDP)

Fannie Lou Townsend was born on October 6, 1917, in Montgomery County, Mississippi. She later moved with her family to Sunflower County in the Mississippi Delta, where she would spend most of her life. Fannie Lou grew up in an impoverished family of sharecroppers. She began picking cotton at age six, following the example of her 19 older brothers and sisters. Influenced by her mother, who taught her to be proud of her heritage, and by the stories of redemption she learned in the Baptist church, Fannie Lou decided at a young age that the unjust conditions experienced by her family needed to change. "I always said if I lived to get grown, and had a chance, I was going to do something for the black man of the South," she later recalled, "if it would cost me my life."[1]

After marrying Perry "Pap" Hamer in 1944, Fannie Lou Hamer settled with her husband on a plantation near Ruleville, where the couple earned a meager living by sharecropping and performing other work for the landowners. Though she did not take part in civil rights activities for the first four decades of her life, Hamer continued to nurture hopes for a better way of life. In the summer of 1962, at age 44, she began her career as an activist after attending a voting rights gathering at a local church. "Until then, I'd never heard of no mass meeting and I didn't know that a Negro could register and vote,"[2] she recalled.

In fact, registering to vote in a county where 70 percent of blacks were disenfranchised was not a simple matter, but Hamer threw herself into the effort with great enthusiasm. After repeated attempts, she mastered the complicated registration exam and was authorized to participate in elections. For daring to do so, she lost her job and house, was shot at, and was forced to leave Ruleville for a time because of continued threats on her life. Hamer persevered, though, and by 1963 she had become a prominent member of the Mississippi chapter of the Student Nonviolent Coordinating Committee (SNCC), a leading civil rights group.

Hamer's association with SNCC brought more harassment. In June 1963 the intimidation turned to ugly violence when she and other activists were severely beaten by police after being arrested in Winona, Mississippi. Hamer suffered permanent kidney damage and blindness in one eye from the attack, but her determination to continue her civil rights mission remained strong. She continued to lead efforts to register black voters throughout the state.

Challenging Injustice with the MFDP

Seeking other means to focus attention on the electoral process, Hamer became a candidate for a seat in Congress in the spring of 1964. She garnered only a small number of votes, but her candidacy helped publicize voting rights and other issues and served as a powerful symbol of African-American empowerment. While she was on the campaign trail, Hamer helped spearhead a new effort to address party politics in South. Since the late 1800s, white Democrats had dominated all elective offices in the region, and the Democratic Party in Mississippi remained deeply opposed to voting-rights reforms or efforts to integrate the party. In response, Hamer and other activists formed the all-inclusive Mississippi Freedom Democratic Party (MFDP) in April 1964 as an alternative to the regular state party. The MFDP selected its own delegates later that summer, and in August they headed to Atlantic City, New Jersey, to attend the Democratic National Convention.

The MFDP delegates planned to challenge the legitimacy of the white delegates selected by the regular Mississippi Democratic Party on the grounds that blacks had been systematically excluded from the selection process. The MFDP delegates' greatest hope was that they would gain the support of other Democrats from across the nation and be seated at the convention. Failing that, they knew that their actions would at least focus public attention on voting rights abuses in Mississippi.

The presence of Hamer and the other MFDP delegates was not welcomed by President Lyndon Johnson and most other party leaders. They felt that the MFDP posed a threat to their plans to show American voters an orderly, unified convention. The president was especially sensitive about racial issues. Johnson had helped achieve passage of the Civil Rights Act of 1964 just months earlier, and he feared that the MFDP protest would detract from this accomplishment while further alienating white Democrats in the South.

The heavy media coverage at the convention gave the MFDP a prominent stage, and Hamer made the most of it. A powerful singer who often energized crowds with her songs, she performed moving spirituals that captured the attention of conventioneers and film crews. At an official hearing, she provided moving testimony about the discrimination she had experienced in Mississippi, including a detailed account of the beating she had suffered in Winona. At the conclusion of her remarks, she issued a stark challenge to the members of the party: "If the Freedom Democratic Party is not seated now, I question America. Is this America, the land of the free and the home of the brave, where ... our lives be threatened daily because we want to live as decent human beings?"[3]

Ultimately, Democratic leaders offered the MFDP a compromise: two of their delegates could be seated at the convention, but in a nonvoting capacity as observers. Many civil rights leaders urged the Mississippi activists to accept the offer, but Hamer opposed it. "We didn't come all this way for no two seats," she declared, and the MFDP delegation voted to refuse the compromise.

As Hamer and her colleagues returned home, they were deeply discouraged and did not yet realize the full significance of their actions. In years to come, however, historians would point to their stand at the convention as an important development in the civil rights struggle. It forced the Democratic Party to enact reforms that ultimately allowed for greater minority participation. This transformation was evident at the 1968 national convention, when Hamer and many of her black colleagues were seated as part of an integrated Mississippi delegation. In addition, the media attention focused on Hamer and others in 1964 inspired individuals all across the country to support future voting rights reforms. Among those who closely monitored the events in Atlantic City was Lyndon Johnson. Though he opposed the demands of the MFDP at the convention, many observers believe that the delegates' display of courage and determination was a factor in the president's decision to back voting rights legislation the following year.

Fighting On

When Congress convened in 1965, the MFDP challenged the seating of Mississippi's representatives in the House. The activists argued that the white lawmakers had won their offices in a fraudulent election that prohibited participation by all citizens. The challenge played out over several months but, once again, the MFDP's demands were ultimately denied. This setback deepened Hamer's doubts about the effectiveness of relying on government institutions and political parties to achieve social change. As a result, she began to focus more of her energies on forming locally oriented organizations in Mississippi to address specific needs. She played a prominent role in a Head Start preschool education program in Sunflower County, supported daycare programs, and helped establish farm and livestock cooperatives. Her most ambitious agricultural endeavor was the Freedom Farm, which she founded near Ruleville in 1969, though financial difficulties and mismanagement forced its closure in the mid-1970s.

Hamer did not totally abandon politics, however. She ran unsuccessfully for a seat in the Mississippi Senate in 1971 and that same year became a member of the policy council of the National Women's Political Caucus. Hamer also devoted significant time to speaking engagements throughout the country in the late 1960s and early 1970s, which helped raise funds for her projects and allowed her to support progressive causes. She maintained her busy schedule through the early 1970s despite suffering from chronic pain and other problems that had persisted after her beating. By the mid-1970s, heart disease, diabetes, and cancer also took a toll, and she was largely confined to her hometown. She died there on March 14, 1977, at the age of 59.

Sources:
Lee, Chana Kai. *For Freedom's Sake: The Life of Fannie Lou Hamer.* Urbana: University of Illinois Press, 1999.

Mills, Kay. *This Little Light of Mine: The Life of Fannie Lou Hamer.* New York: Dutton, 1993.

Notes
[1] Quoted in Mills, Kay. *This Little Light of Mine: The Life of Fannie Lou Hamer.* New York: Dutton, 1993, p. 13.

[2] Quoted in Lee, Chana Kai. *For Freedom's Sake: The Life of Fannie Lou Hamer.* Urbana: University of Illinois Press, 1999, p. 25.

[3] Quoted in Lee, p. 132.

Lyndon B. Johnson (1908-1973)
President of the United States Who Signed the Voting Rights Act into Law

Lyndon Baines Johnson was born near the small central Texas town of Stonewall on August 27, 1908. Johnson was the eldest of five children born to Sam Ealy Johnson, Jr., a state legislator, farmer, and newspaper owner, and Rebekah (Baines) Johnson, a homemaker who also worked for a time as a newspaper editor.

In 1927 Johnson enrolled in Southwest Texas State Teacher's College (SWTSTC) in San Marcos, Texas. After his junior year he took a one-year break from his studies to earn money for tuition. He accepted a job as a teacher in Cotulla in southern Texas. Johnson's experiences at Cotulla made an enormous and lasting impression on him. Surrounded by crushing poverty and whites who treated Hispanic residents with casual cruelty, Johnson received a grim education in the ways that social injustice continued to trouble America.

After earning his bachelor's degree in 1930 and working briefly as a teacher in Houston, Johnson took up politics. In 1931 he moved to Washington, D.C., to become an assistant to a Texas congressional representative. During this period, he became an ardent supporter of President Franklin D. Roosevelt and his "New Deal" policies of economic and social reform. Johnson's growing political connections led to a job with the National Youth Administration. In 1937 Johnson's reputation as a promising young Democrat—as well as the financial resources provided by the family of his wife, Claudia Alta "Lady Bird" Johnson—helped him to win a seat in the U.S. House of Representatives.

Four years later, Johnson made a bid for the U.S. Senate. When he lost an election swirling with rumors of questionable vote counting, Johnson returned to his seat in the House of Representatives. He remained there for the next seven years, but in 1944 he squeaked out an 87-vote victory to become a U.S. Senator. After settling into his new position, Johnson proved himself a master of political maneuvering in Washington, D.C. He steadily rose through the ranks and in 1956 claimed the coveted post of senate majority leader. Wielding his power deftly, he helped engineer the passage of a wide range of important legislation in the late 1950s. During this time, Johnson cemented his reputation as a "wheeler-dealer" politician who could hammer out compromises and achieve results. Critics, though, asserted that he was an opportunist who lacked strong moral convictions.

Johnson and Civil Rights

As a white Democrat from a southern state, Lyndon Johnson was an unlikely figure to advance the rights of minorities. As it turned out, it took him many years to evolve into a champion of civil rights. Initially, he was unwilling to challenge most of the political and social discrimination that dominated his home state and other parts of the South. He opposed most civil rights measures that came before Congress during his first two decades in Washington. But his memories of working with impoverished Hispanic children during his teaching days gave him a deep empathy for those who had failed to benefit from the country's prosperity. In addition, his formative political years as a New Deal Democrat had shown him how progressive government policies could help those in need.

Other factors also led Johnson to adjust his stance on civil rights in the late 1950s. Johnson wanted to run for the presidency some day. He knew that it would be difficult to make a bid for the White House if he was known as a typical southern politician who stonewalled any attempt at social and political reform. Moreover, he had the foresight to see that the South's segregationist policies were obstructing its development. These different influences first became evident when Johnson formally supported the Civil Rights Act of 1957—although many liberal activists criticized him for weakening the legislation to ensure its passage.

Johnson's presidential aspirations in 1960 were thwarted by John F. Kennedy, a young senator from Massachusetts who won the Democratic nomination. Kennedy recognized Johnson's value in attracting southern votes, however, and made the Texan his vice presidential running mate. The Kennedy-Johnson ticket narrowly defeated Republican presidential nominee Richard M. Nixon and vice-presidential candidate Henry Cabot Lodge, Jr., in the November election.

Johnson was a loyal member of the Kennedy administration until November 1963, when the president was tragically assassinated in Dallas, Texas. Johnson was quickly sworn in as the 36th president of the United States. As he entered the White House, a civil rights bill that Kennedy had introduced in the spring of 1963 was languishing in Congress. Many observers expected Johnson to water down or abandon the legislation. Instead, the president made it one of his highest priorities. Employing his expertise in congressional diplomacy, Johnson helped the bill survive a long battle in the House and Senate that extended into the following year. On July 2, he signed the Civil Rights Act of 1964 into law.

The Civil Rights Act was a decisive moment in the struggle for equal rights in the United States, but the work was far from finished. The following month, African-American civil rights activists from Mississippi reminded the president of that fact when they challenged his party over the issue of voting rights at the 1964 Democratic National Convention.

In the 1964 president election, Johnson defeated Republican candidate Barry Goldwater by a landslide, and the Democrats gained a sizable majority in Congress. Riding a wave of support, the president introduced a series of so-called Great Society initiatives. These proposals called for the establishment of the Medicare and Medicaid public health care programs as well as a range of antipoverty and education initiatives. Martin Luther King, Jr., and other civil rights activists were encouraged by Johnson's bold action, but they wanted something else. Even as the Great Society bills were being readied for Congress, they continued to urge the president to propose new legislation to directly address the issue of voting rights.

Seizing the Moment

Johnson's views on a voting rights bill were mixed. In December 1964 he told King that he would not push the issue of voting rights in 1965 because he did not want to alienate southern legislators before they approved his Great Society measures. At the same time, though, he instructed his attorney general to begin drafting just such legislation. The president's directive was likely a case of shrewd advance planning, so that a voting rights bill could be quickly presented to Congress if and when the time seemed right.

The events that would create that opportunity began to unfold in the early months of 1965, as civil rights groups launched a series of voting rights protests in Selma, Alabama. Johnson disapproved of this campaign, in part because it put him in a difficult political spot. He was opposed to committing federal forces to protect the civil rights activists because he believed that the presence of U.S. marshals or army troops would create a poisonous climate across the South. But he knew that if he refused to provide federal protection to the demonstrators, any violence that befell them would reflect badly on him and his administration.

Such criticism landed squarely at the door of the White House after Alabama state troopers attacked peaceful marchers at Selma's Edmund Pettus Bridge on March 7. Afterwards, civil rights leader John Lewis declared that "I don't know how President Johnson can send troops to Vietnam, and he can't send troops to Selma, Alabama."[1] Similar statements were heard all across the country, and a new wave of demonstrations on behalf of voting rights erupted.

On Monday, March 15, 1965, just a week after the initial violence in Selma, Johnson responded decisively. Addressing a joint session of Congress, he delivered a speech that is considered one of the finest of his career. He framed racial discrimination as a challenge to the country's ideals of democracy and opportunity, and he challenged the nation to "overcome the crippling legacy of bigotry and injustice." Johnson also urged Congress to ensure genuine voting rights for all Americans. Spurred on by Johnson's speech and widespread public support, Congress passed the Voting Rights Act of 1965 several months later. Johnson signed the bill into law on August 6.

The Quagmire of Vietnam

Enactment of the Voting Rights Act and passage of the Great Society program marked the peak of Johnson's influence, but his presidency was soon overwhelmed by another issue—the Vietnam War. The president had deepened U.S. involvement in Vietnam beginning in the summer of 1964 and rapidly increased the number of troops in the years that followed. By early 1968, there were 700,000 U.S. soldiers fighting in southeast Asia, and casualties were steadily mounting. Despite the large commitment of forces, the conflict turned into a military stalemate, and Americans became bitterly divided over its continuation. The optimistic war predictions Johnson delivered to the nation proved false, and trust in his leadership began to evaporate.

Though Johnson had the opportunity to run for reelection in 1968, the president's approval ratings were dismal and the strain of the war took a visible toll on his health. On March 31, 1968, he made a televised address in which he announced a new effort to reach a negotiated settlement in Vietnam. He then stunned the nation by declaring that "I shall not seek, nor will I accept, the nomination of my party for another term as your President." In his remaining months in office, Johnson pursued a peace agreement to end the Vietnam War, but these efforts failed. After leaving the White House in January 1969, he returned to his Texas ranch. He died there four years later, on January 22, 1973, after suffering a heart attack.

Sources:

Bernstein, Irving. *Guns or Butter: The Presidency of Lyndon Johnson.* New York: Oxford University Press, 1996.

Dalleck, Robert. *Flawed Giant: Lyndon Johnson and His Times, 1961-1973.* New York: Oxford University Press, 1998.

Kotz, Nick. *Judgment Days: Lyndon Baines Johnson, Martin Luther King, Jr., and the Laws That Changed America.* Boston: Houghton Mifflin, 2005.

Unger, Irwin, and Debi Unger. *LBJ: A Life.* New York: John Wiley, 1999.

Notes

[1] Quoted in Kotz, Nick. *Judgment Days: Lyndon Baines Johnson, Martin Luther King, Jr., and the Laws that Changed America.* Boston: Houghton Mifflin, 2005, p. 285.

Martin Luther King, Jr. (1929-1968)
Civil Rights Leader and President of the
Southern Christian Leadership Conference
(SCLC)

Michael Luther King was born in Atlanta, Georgia, on January 15, 1929 (he was renamed Martin when he was about six years old). He was born into a family with a proud history of religious and community leadership. His grandfather, A.D. Williams, had been the longtime pastor of Atlanta's Ebenezer Baptist Church and a founder of the city's chapter of the National Association for the Advancement of Colored People (NAACP). His father, Martin Luther King, Sr., also served the Baptist Church as a minister. He was promoted from associate pastor to lead pastor of the Ebenezer congregation after Williams's death in 1931. Martin was one of three children born to King Sr. and his wife, Alberta (Williams) King, a former schoolteacher.

Young Martin was raised in a financially secure middle-class home, unlike most other black youth of the 1930s and 1940s. Bright and curious, he recognized early on that he was far more fortunate than other young African Americans. This knowledge undoubtedly contributed to his eventual decision to wage social protest against discrimination and injustice in American society.

King thrived in grammar school and high school, and in 1944 he enrolled at Atlanta's all-black Morehouse College at age 15. After earning his bachelor's degree from Morehouse in 1948, he decided to study at Crozer Theological Seminary in Chester, Pennsylvania. King was an outstanding student at Crozer. In addition to serving as student body president and being named valedictorian of his 1951 graduating class, he also received a J. Lewis Crozer Fellowship, the school's most prestigious scholarship.

King then enrolled at Boston University to continue his education. He concluded his doctorate schoolwork in 1953 and received his Ph.D. in systematic theology two years later, after completing his dissertation. He also started a family during this same period. In 1953 he married Coretta Scott, and in 1955 they had the first of their four children.

A Voice for Justice in Montgomery

King launched his career as a Baptist minister in September 1954, when he accepted the pastor position at Dexter Avenue Baptist Church in Montgomery, Alabama. He had been at this post only a little over a year when events elsewhere in Montgomery caught his attention. On December 1, 1955, a mild-mannered African-American woman named Rosa Parks was arrested after she refused to give up her seat on a city bus to a white passenger. Parks's defiance of the city's segregation laws sparked a remarkable response from the city's African-American community. Sick and tired of living under the misery of Jim Crow laws, Montgomery's black population decided to join Parks in making a stand against segregation and discrimination.

Led by King and other black ministers across Montgomery, African-American residents launched a massive boycott of the city's segregated bus system. The boycott took a tremendous toll on the city's white-owned businesses and instilled a new sense of pride within the black community. It also vaulted King, the leading spokesman for the city's blacks during the boycott, to a position of national prominence. The bus boycott lasted until December 1956, when the U.S. Supreme Court ruled that Alabama's segregation laws were unconstitutional. After this ruling, the city reluctantly desegregated its bus system.

Following this victory, King led a group of other black ministers across the South in founding the Southern Christian Leadership Conference (SCLC). This organization was dedicated to tearing down the barriers of racial discrimination and distrust that had haunted America for so many generations. But King and his followers in SCLC were determined to make these changes by following the example of Mohandas Gandhi, who had led a successful campaign of nonviolent resistance to free India from British rule earlier in the twentieth century. Writing in his 1958 book *Stride Toward Freedom*, King explained his embrace of peaceful protests: "If the American Negro and other victims of oppression succumb to the temptation of using violence in the struggle for freedom, future generations will be the recipients of a desolate night of bitterness, and our chief legacy to them will be an endless reign of meaningless chaos."[1]

A Growing Movement

In 1959 King traveled to India in an effort to gain further insights into Gandhi's philosophy of nonviolent social protest. After returning to the United States he made his hometown of Atlanta the base of his growing civil rights work. He resigned from his church in Montgomery so that he could become co-pastor of Atlanta's Ebenezer Baptist Church with his father.

From 1960 to 1962, the civil rights movement continued to grow in size and strength. Acts of civil disobedience sprouted all across the South, triggering fear and fury in the hearts of white racists. These peaceful demonstrations included sit-ins at segregated lunch counters, Freedom Rides to challenge segregated bus systems, and protest marches that featured both black and white participants. Important new civil rights groups like the Student Nonviolent Coordinating Committee (SNCC) were founded during this period as well. But throughout this swirl of activity, King remained the leading voice of the movement. Idealistic, eloquent, and dedicated to his cause, King traveled all around the country to spread his message of racial equality and reconciliation. "We have learned to fly the air like birds and swim the sea like fish," he declared in 1963. "But we have not learned the simple art of living together as brothers."[2]

In the spring of 1963 King went to Birmingham, Alabama, to lead SCLC demonstrations against the city's racist leadership and its continued embrace of Jim Crow laws. Over the next few weeks, people all across the country saw televised images of Birmingham police attacking unarmed African-American demonstrators with snarling dogs and high-pressure fire hoses. These broadcasts produced a dramatic shift in public opinion in favor of the civil rights protestors. King, meanwhile, turned his arrest for disturbing the peace into an advantage. Sitting in a city jail cell, he wrote "Letter from Birmingham Jail," one of the most famous documents of the civil rights era. In this letter, King vowed that the African-American civil rights movement would wait no longer for equal rights in American society. "For years now I have heard the word 'Wait!'" he wrote. "It rings in the ear of every Negro with piercing familiarity. This 'Wait' has almost always meant 'Never.'"[3]

The events in Birmingham marked a turning point in the quest for civil rights. President John F. Kennedy responded to the violence by submitting major new civil rights legislation to the U.S. Congress. One year later, this legislation became law with the signing of the Civil Rights Act of 1964. As this legislation made its way through Congress, King and other civil rights leaders organized a massive March on Washington for Jobs and Freedom on August 28, 1963. This march brought more than 250,000 black and white participants together in Washington, D.C. This milestone in the civil rights era was highlighted by King's famous "I Have a Dream" speech, which he issued from the steps of the Lincoln Memorial.

Praise and Criticism

By the time President Lyndon B. Johnson signed the Civil Rights Act on July 2, 1964, King was universally recognized as the most important figure in the African-American civil rights movement. *Time* named him its Man of the Year for 1963, and in 1964 King received the prestigious Nobel Peace Prize. But he also had powerful enemies. FBI Director Herbert Hoover, for example, approved numerous illegal spying activities against the civil rights leader.

King also had critics within the black community. King and SCLC sometimes experienced tensions with the leadership of SNCC and other civil rights organizations that wanted to maintain their independence. Other African-American leaders, like Roy Wilkins of the NAACP, disapproved of some of the social protest strategies that King and others employed. And in the mid-1960s, a new generation of radical voices led by Malcolm X and Stokely Carmichael attracted growing support in the ghettos of Northern cities. These men spoke about violent resistance to racial injustice in positive terms. They also urged blacks to abandon the idea of an integrated society in favor of one that was completely self-sufficient. At times, these militant voices openly dismissed King's message of peaceful protest and racial reconciliation.

King heard these criticisms, but he remained firmly loyal to his principles. In early 1965 he helped organize a voter-registration campaign in Selma, Alabama. This campaign was marred by a savage attack by state troopers on peaceful marchers on March 7. But just like in Birmingham two years earlier, photographs and film footage documenting this "Bloody Sunday" attack increased public sympathy for the civil rights cause. One week later, Johnson gave a nationally televised speech in which he insisted that full voting rights could no longer be withheld from African Americans. On August 6, 1965, the Voting Rights Act was signed into law.

This triumph delighted King, but he did not rest. Instead, he turned his attention to the problems of urban poverty and slum housing in America. He launched programs in Chicago and other cities to publicize these issues. In addition, he emerged as a powerful critic of the Vietnam War. His opposition to the war put a severe strain on his relationship with President Johnson and his administration.

To the Mountaintop

In the spring of 1968 King traveled to Memphis, Tennessee, where the city's sanitation workers had called a strike to protest poor wages and gain union recognition. King wanted to show his support for the workers, who he felt suffered from many of the problems that afflicted poor people all around the country. On April 3, he delivered a civil rights speech in which he declared that "Like anybody, I would like to live a long life; longevity has its place. But I'm not concerned about that now. I just want to do God's will. And He's allowed me to go up to the mountain. And I've looked over. And I've seen the promised land. I may not get there with you. But I want you to know tonight that we as a people will get to the promised land."[4]

That address—known as King's "I've Been to the Mountaintop" speech— was the last one that the civil rights leader ever delivered. The next day he was assassinated while standing on the balcony of a downtown hotel. The news of his death sparked riots in major cities across the country, and was viewed as a national tragedy in countless black and white homes across America.

Today, King is remembered as one of the most influential Americans in the nation's history. Each year his birthday, January 15, is celebrated as a national holiday. In addition, the Lorraine Hotel in Memphis—where King was shot and killed—has been transformed into a testament to his civil rights legacy. It is now the home of the National Civil Rights Museum.

Sources:

Branch, Taylor. *Parting the Waters: America in the King Years 1954-1963.* New York: Simon and Schuster, 1988.

Dyson, Michael Eric. *I May Not Get There with You: The True Martin Luther King Jr.* New York: Free Press, 2000.

King, Martin Luther, Jr. *The Autobiography of Martin Luther King Jr.* Edited by Clayborne Carson. New York: IPM/Warner, 2001.

King, Martin Luther, Jr. *A Call to Conscience: The Landmark Speeches of Martin Luther King Jr.* Edited by Clayborne Carson. New York: IPM/Warner, 2001.

King, Martin Luther, Jr. *The Trumpet of Conscience.* New York: Harper, 1968.

Oates, Stephen B. *Let the Trumpet Sound: A Life of Martin Luther King Jr.* New York: Harper, 1982.

Notes

[1] King, Martin Luther, Jr. *Stride Toward Freedom.* New York: Harper, 1958.

[2] King, Martin Luther, Jr. *Strength to Love.* New York: Harper, 1963.

[3] King, Martin Luther, Jr. *Why We Can't Wait.* New York: Harper, 1964.

[4] King, Martin Luther, Jr. "I've Been to the Mountaintop." Speech delivered April 3, 1968, Memphis, Tennessee. In *A Testament of Hope: The Essential Writings and Speeches of Martin Luther King, Jr.* New York: HarperCollins, 1986, p. 279. Text available online at http://www.americanrhetoric.com /speeches/mlkivebeentothemountaintop.htm.

John Lewis (1940-)
Chairman of the Student Nonviolent
Coordinating Committee (SNCC) and
U.S. Congressman

John Robert Lewis was born on February 21, 1940, in Troy, Alabama. He was the third of ten children born to Eddie and Willie Mae Lewis, who supported their family by raising cotton and peanuts as tenant farmers. They did not own the land they farmed, but leased it in exchange for a portion of their crops. Lewis recognized at an early age that the tenant farming system kept families like his locked in poverty, and he grew determined to forge a different path with his life.

At first, Lewis thought he would become a minister. He had a strong religious faith, and by the time he was a teenager he had overcome his shy nature to make guest preaching appearances at Baptist churches throughout the area. Lewis was also inspired to pursue the ministry by the example of Martin Luther King, Jr., a young Southern clergyman whose sermons were broadcast every week on a black radio station.

Lewis graduated from high school in 1957. He then enrolled at the American Baptist Theological Seminary in Nashville, Tennessee, to study for the ministry. As he began his studies there, though, he felt a great restlessness inside him. Lewis hated the many ways in which African Americans were terrorized and discriminated against in the South. As early events in the civil rights movement began to unfold, like the Montgomery bus boycott of 1955, he became convinced that he needed to be a part of that effort. "I was stirred … to put myself in the path of history," he recalled. "I wanted to be involved. I didn't want to stand on the sidelines anymore."[1]

Founding SNCC

The first step that Lewis took into civil rights activism was to challenge the policy that prohibited black students from enrolling at Alabama's Troy

State College. He was helped in this effort by King and Ralph David Abernathy, leaders of a newly formed civil rights organization called the Southern Christian Leadership Conference (SCLC). King and Abernathy admired the bravery and idealism of Lewis, and they assisted him in determining the best way to legally challenge Troy State. But Lewis reluctantly abandoned his lawsuit several weeks later at the urging of his mother, who was terrified that their whole family might be targeted for violence because of his stand.

This setback deeply depressed Lewis, but he refused to give up his dreams of civil rights activism. Instead, he returned to Nashville and enrolled at Fisk University, one of the South's finest black colleges. At Fisk he divided his time between philosophy studies and explorations of nonviolent forms of social protest. During this time, a clergyman and teacher named James Lawson became an important mentor to Lewis. Lawson convinced him that the black community could effectively protest Southern segregation through a campaign of peaceful protests and civil disobedience of Jim Crow laws.

In early 1960 Lewis organized several student sit-ins at segregated Nashville lunch counters. These sit-ins, which included both black and white volunteers, sparked a furious response from white residents. They lashed out at the protestors with racial taunts and physical attacks, and the demonstrators were arrested multiple times for disturbing the peace. But Lewis and his friends returned to the lunch counters again and again, to the growing dismay of their tormentors.

In April 1960 Lewis was invited to attend a conference of African-American student activists at Shaw University in Raleigh, North Carolina. During this meeting, veteran civil rights activist Ella Baker urged the student activists to establish a new civil rights group that could take full advantage of their youthful spirit and thirst for action. Lewis heartily endorsed this view, and by the end of the conference he had helped found the Student Nonviolent Coordinating Committee (SNCC). SNCC quickly became one of the most important groups of the entire civil rights era.

Leading with Heart and Conviction

Lewis was a leader of SNCC from the group's first days of existence. He was quiet and soft spoken, but he became widely known for his personal integrity, his fearlessness, and his dedication to the philosophy of peaceful protest. Throughout the early 1960s, he could be found organizing and participating in sit-ins, Freedom Rides, and protest marches. He never backed down, despite vicious physical attacks from white mobs and many nights spent in jail cells across the South.

In 1963 Lewis was unanimously elected chairman of SNCC. Later that year he was the youngest keynote speaker at the famous March on Washington. In his speech, Lewis boldly criticized President John F. Kennedy for not being more supportive of civil rights.

In 1964 Lewis was an important force in the Mississippi Freedom Summer, a campaign to obtain greater voting rights for African Americans living in the state. He helped organize SNCC voter registration drives and community action programs all across Mississippi. "Southern states were riddled with legal obstacles to keep black men and women from voting—poll taxes, literacy tests," recalled Lewis in his memoir *Walking with the Wind.* "But those states were perfectly willing to resort to terrorism as well.... We would learn almost immediately that voter registration was as threatening to the entrenched white establishment in the South as sit-ins or Freedom Rides, and that it would prompt the same violent response."[2]

In early 1965 the drive for equal voting rights took Lewis to Selma, Alabama. On March 7 he and fellow activist Hosea Williams organized a group of peaceful marchers for a march to Montgomery, the state capital. But as Lewis and the other marchers crossed the Edmund Pettus Bridge on the outskirts of town, they were confronted by a large group of Alabama state troopers. When Lewis and Williams refused the troopers' orders to disperse the marchers, the troopers launched a brutal assault on the protestors. Men, women, and children were all targeted on that day, which quickly became known in civil rights lore as "Bloody Sunday." Pictures from the attack—including one of Lewis on the ground trying to ward off a blow from a baton-wielding trooper—stunned people all across America and produced a surge in sympathy for the voting rights cause.

Lewis later said that the marches "represented America at her best.... We had a mission to do what we could to make things better for all humankind. People *believed* that. It was not a show. It was not caught up in the political whim of the day. There was a deep and abiding sense that we *had to put our bodies on the line* for what was right. It was like a holy crusade. People were not trying to score political points. They were just trying to make things better, make things right for all America."[3]

Witness to the Passage of the Voting Rights Act

One week after the shocking events of Bloody Sunday, President Lyndon B. Johnson delivered a nationally televised address to Congress. He declared that the nation could no longer withhold voting rights and other civil rights from African Americans. He framed the issue as a basic question of morality and justice. After this speech, Lewis and King organized a march of 25,000 black and white supporters from Selma to Montgomery. Their intention was to show that while they appreciated the speech, they intended to keep marching and demonstrating until meaningful voting rights legislation was actually signed into law.

Their wish came true on August 6. Congress passed the landmark Voting Rights Act that day, and Lewis was invited to the White House signing ceremony along with King and several other prominent activists. "After signing the bill, Johnson gave pens to Dr. King, Rosa Parks and several other civil rights 'leaders,' including me," Lewis wrote in his memoir. "I still have mine today, framed on the wall of my living room in Atlanta, along with a copy of the bill itself. That day was a culmination, a climax, the end of a very long road. In a sense it represented a high point in modern America, probably the nation's finest hour in terms of civil rights."[4]

The following year, Lewis's leadership of SNCC came to an unhappy end. Stokely Carmichael and other black militants within the group became increasingly influential. They wanted to kick whites out of the organization and renounce nonviolent protest. When Lewis objected to these calls, he was ousted from his position after a tense power struggle with Carmichael, James Forman, and their supporters.

Disappointed but unbowed, Lewis returned to Fisk University and earned his bachelor's degree in 1967. He then went to work for the Field Foundation as a community organizer. In 1970 he was promoted to director of the organization's Voter Education Project (VEP), which worked to organize and educate southern black voters. In 1977 Lewis left the foundation to take a job with the administration of President Jimmy Carter. He was given the director's reins for ACTION, a federal agency that provided assistance to economically troubled communities.

A Distinguished Congressman

In 1982 Lewis entered the world of politics as a legislator. He won election to the Atlanta City Council, where he became known as a reliable champion of the poor and elderly. In 1986 he won a special run-off election for the Democratic nomination for a seat in the U.S. Congress. He defeated Julian Bond, a fellow civil rights veteran from SNCC, in a close and bitter election.

Since first reaching Congress in 1986, Lewis has represented his Georgia district for seven consecutive terms. He is both influential and widely respected in Washington, D.C., and his continued leadership on civil rights issues is well-known. In 1998 he published a memoir called *Walking with the Wind*, which has been praised as one of the finest books about the civil rights movement. Lewis has received numerous awards and honors as well, including the Eleanor Roosevelt Award for Human Rights in 1998 and the John F. Kennedy "Profile in Courage" Award for lifetime achievement. In 2004 a monument honoring Lewis's civil rights work was unveiled at the foot of Edmund Pettus Bridge in Selma, the site of the 1965 Bloody Sunday march.

Sources:

Bausum, Anne. *Freedom Riders: John Lewis and Jim Zwerg on the Front Lines of the Civil Rights Movement.* Washington, DC: National Geographic Society, 2006.

Lewis, John, with Michael D'Orso. *Walking with the Wind: A Memoir of the Movement.* New York: Simon and Schuster, 1998.

Williams, Juan, and Julian Bond. *Eyes on the Prize: America's Civil Rights Years, 1954-1965.* New York: Viking Penguin, 1988.

Notes

[1] Lewis, John, with Michael D'Orso. *Walking with the Wind: A Memoir of the Movement.* New York: Simon and Schuster, 1998, p. 75.

[2] Lewis, p. 182.

[3] "Keeping the Faith: Civil Rights and the Baby Boom." John Lewis Interview with Seth Goddard. Available online at www.life.com/Life/boomers.lewis.html.

[4] Lewis, p. 347.

George Wallace (1919-1998)
Governor of Alabama and Segregationist Leader

George Corley Wallace was born on August 25, 1919, in Clio, Alabama. He grew up in a rural county where his father, George Wallace, Sr., farmed cotton and his grandfather was a probate judge. His mother was Mozell (Smith) Wallace, who devoted her time to caring for her four children.

Wallace's first passion was boxing, and his skill in the ring earned him a state Golden Gloves championship. He showed a similar zeal for politics at a young age. Wallace became a page for the Alabama Senate at age 15 and was elected class president at the University of Alabama, where he earned a law degree in 1942. After serving as a crew member on B-29 bombing missions during World War II, he returned to Alabama and began his political career in earnest, winning a seat in the state legislature in 1947. Wallace was elected to a judge's seat on the circuit court five years later.

Initially, Wallace took a somewhat moderate stance on race. While he did not oppose the state's systematic segregation, he earned a reputation for treating African Americans fairly in his courtroom. In addition, his early political campaigns tended to focus on progressive social issues rather than racial divisions. "I started off talking about schools and highways and prisons and taxes,"[1] he later explained.

In the mid-1950s, though, such issues were of secondary importance to most white voters in the South. They were far more concerned about the controversy over civil rights reform. When Wallace made his first run for governor in 1958, he lost to an opponent who was an outspoken supporter of white supremacy. Deciding that his moderation had cost him the election, Wallace created a new political image in preparation for the next governor's race in 1962. He cast himself as a hard-line opponent of civil rights reform and won publicity by temporarily defying federal efforts to investigate voting records in his home county. His reactionary stance helped him win the election, and in his January 1963 inaugural speech, he declared his position in no uncertain terms: "Segregation now! Segregation tomorrow! Segregation forever!"

Defying Change

Throughout his campaign, Wallace had vowed to resist the integration of Alabama schools with all the powers of his office. In June 1963 he fulfilled his promise at the University of Alabama when two black students attempted to enroll at the school. The incident sparked a showdown with the Kennedy administration, which deployed National Guard troops to make sure that the students would be admitted. Wallace eventually stood aside, but his defiant statements and actions established him as the nation's most prominent defender of segregation.

Wallace clashed with federal authorities again in the fall of 1963. The governor used state police and National Guard troops to prevent African-American students from sitting in integrated public school classrooms. He did not relent until federal authorities intervened.

Wallace's actions, and the support he received from his constituents, were based on white racism. But the governor was careful to justify his resistance to integration on the basis of other principles. Like generations of Southern leaders before him, he proclaimed the sanctity of states' rights and argued that the federal government and the Supreme Court were improperly intruding in local affairs in their reform efforts. Playing on the fears of the Cold War era, he frequently justified his opposition to civil rights protestors by claiming that they were communist subversives. As to his personal views, he asserted that "I am no racist.... If I hate a creature that God made because of his color, that is evil. But I am a segregationist because I believe that segregation of the races is best for both people."[2] Some historians suggest that Wallace's true opinions didn't match this rhetoric, and they note passages in the governor's official correspondence that espouse a belief in black inferiority—a common view among white Southern political leaders of the era.

Whatever his personal convictions, Wallace's deeds and defiant words helped create an atmosphere in which violent opposition to the civil rights cause and disregard for federal law became more acceptable. On September 15, 1963, a bomb exploded at the Sixteenth Street Baptist Church in Birmingham, killing four black children who were preparing for services. In the wake of this ugly and cowardly attack, commentators across the country—including President John F. Kennedy—insisted that Wallace deserved some of the blame for the violence.

Showdown in Selma

When Dr. Martin Luther King, Jr., and his colleagues in the Southern Christian Leadership Conference (SCLC) launched their voting-rights campaign in Selma, Alabama, in early 1965, Wallace initially allowed local authorities to handle the situation. That position changed in early March, when the activists began planning a 50-mile march from Selma to the state capitol. Wallace decided that the march should be stopped. He would later claim that he made this decision in order to protect the marchers from violent clashes with local citizens along the route, but he gave other reasons in a news conference the day before the event. He charged that the protesters would be disrupting traffic and commerce and warned that law enforcement would use "whatever measures necessary" to prevent the marchers from walking to Montgomery. In addition to his other motivations, Wallace clearly despised the idea of giving ground to the protestors. "I'm not going to have a bunch of niggers walking along a highway in this state as long as I'm the governor,"[3] he told his advisors in private.

The showdown came at the Edmund Pettus Bridge in Selma on March 7, where police thrashed the marchers with clubs, tear gas, and bullwhips. When news film of the incident was broadcast across the country later that evening, it provoked widespread support for the protestors and focused intense hostility on Wallace. In the aftermath, some insiders claimed that the police on the scene had disobeyed the governor's instructions to avoid violence. But Albert Lingo, head of the Alabama state troopers who carried out the attack, maintained that the command to use clubs on the marchers had come directly from the governor.

When the Reverend James Reeb, a white civil rights activist, was killed in Selma two days after the march, the governor found himself under even greater pressure. Attempting to defuse some of the criticism, Wallace requested a meeting with President Lyndon Johnson, who severely chastised the governor in private and then used their joint press conference to announce that he would soon send voting rights legislation to Congress. Johnson's actions were a clear sign that the events in Selma were provoking the very reforms that Wallace opposed. A week later, federal district judge Frank M. Johnson ruled that protestors could stage a second Selma to Montgomery march. The judge also required Wallace to protect the marchers' safety—by requesting federal assistance if necessary. The governor chose the latter option, and federal military forces were on hand as the march began four days later. When it concluded in Montgomery on March 25, Wallace looked out of a window of his office in the capitol building to see a crowd of 25,000 protesters on the front steps.

The Survivor

Wallace's image may have been diminished by the events of early 1965, but his political career was far from over. In fact, he remained immensely popular among his core supporters in Alabama. Though state law prevented him from running for a second consecutive term as governor, he arranged for his wife, Lurleen, to run in the 1966 election. She won handily, which in effect allowed her husband to continue operating as governor. Following Lurleen's death in 1968, Wallace himself was elected governor in 1970 and reelected in 1974.

During these years, Wallace also made three attempts to capture the presidency of the United States. In 1968 he ran as the American Independent Party candidate. He won five southern states and 13 percent of the national vote on the strength of a culturally conservative message that made thinly veiled appeals to racism. In 1972 he decided to make another run for the presidency. He was a formidable candidate for the Democratic nomination until May 15, when he was shot five times by a mentally unstable man at a Maryland campaign rally. Wallace survived, but the attack paralyzed him below the waist. He spent the rest of his life in a wheelchair and suffered chronic pain.

Even this turn of events did not force Wallace to leave the political stage. He made a final unsuccessful run for the White House in 1976 and then, after four years out of office, was elected as Alabama's governor for the fourth time in 1982. By this point in his career, he had renounced his segregationist views. In fact, he repeatedly apologized to the African-American community for his past actions. Skeptics charged that this was merely an opportunistic attempt to retain power after blacks had gained the vote, but others judged it a sign that the nation's extreme political divisions over the issue of race were easing. Wallace's ailments grew worse in the final decade of his life, and he spent much of that period confined to his bed. He passed away on September 13, 1998, at the age of 79.

Sources:

Carter, Dan T. *The Politics of Rage: George Wallace, the Origins of the New Conservatism, and the Transformation of American Politics*. New York: Simon & Schuster, 1995.

Lesher, Stephen. *George Wallace: American Populist*. Reading, MA: Addison-Wesley, 1994.

Notes

[1] Quoted in Carter, Dan T. *The Politics of Rage: George Wallace, the Origins of the New Conservatism, and the Transformation of American Politics*. New York: Simon and Schuster, 1995, p. 109.

[2] Quoted in Lesher, Stephen. *George Wallace: American Populist*. Reading, MA: Addison-Wesley, 1994, p. 280.

[3] Quoted in Carter, p. 247.

PRIMARY SOURCES

Alabama Literacy Test Samples

Prior to 1965, many states in the South used elaborate voter-registration procedures as part of a systematic effort to prevent African Americans from voting. Prospective voters in Alabama, for instance, were required to fill out a four-page application form and then submit to an extensive literacy test.

In Part A of the test, the applicant had to read a section of the U.S. Constitution aloud, and then write out a section of the Constitution as it was read aloud by the registrar. In Part B, the prospective voter had to answer four questions based on these sections from the Constitution. In Part C, the applicant had to answer four more questions designed to test general knowledge about state and national government.

Although the content of state literacy tests changed frequently, the samples below provide an idea of the types of questions that appeared on Alabama voter exams. They were taken from a workbook used by volunteer teachers to help prepare black citizens to register, and the answers are included.

Part B, Sample 1

1. What body can try impeachments of the president of the United States?
   <u>Senate</u>

2. Check the applicable definition for responsibility:

   <u>X</u> a duty

   _____ a speech

   _____ failure

3. Name the attorney general of the United States. <u>Nicholas Katzenbach</u>

4. Women may now serve on juries in Alabama State courts. <u>True</u>

Part B, Sample 2

1. Can the president of the United States be impeached? <u>Yes</u>

2. Check the applicable definition for "representative":

   _____ agreement between states

   <u>X</u> person chosen to act for others

   _____ good character

3. FBI stands for the <u>Federal Bureau of Investigation.</u>

4. Each county in Alabama may decide by vote whether or not it will have legalized sale of alcoholic beverages. <u>True</u>

Part B, Sample 3

1. Can the president of the United States be removed from office for conviction of bribery? <u>Yes</u>

2. Check the applicable definition for "treaty":

<u>X</u> agreement between nations

_____ a tax

_____ a written oration

3. Name the man who is nationally known for heading the Federal Bureau of Investigation for many years. <u>Herbert Hoover</u>

4. What officer is designated by the Constitution to be president of the Senate of the United States? <u>Vice President</u>

Part B, Sample 4

1. Can you be imprisoned, under Alabama law, for a debt? <u>No</u>

2. In addition to becoming a U.S. citizen by birth, a person may become a citizen by:

_____ immigration

<u>X</u> naturalization

_____ voting

3. Name one person by name or title who is part of the judicial branch of government in Alabama. <u>Chief Justice Livingston</u>

4. The first sentence of the United States Constitution is called the Preamble. <u>True</u>

Part C, Sample 1

1. If a person charged with treason denies his guilt, how many persons must testify against him before he can be convicted? <u>Two</u>

2. At what time of day on January 20 each four years does the term of the president of the United States end? <u>12 noon</u>

3. If the president does not wish to sign a bill, how many days is he allowed in which to return it to Congress for reconsideration? <u>Ten</u>

4. If a bill is passed by Congress and the President refuses to sign it and does not send it back to Congress in session within the specified period of time, is the bill defeated or does it become law? <u>It becomes law unless Congress adjourns before the expiration of 10 days.</u>

Part C, Sample 2

1. If a person seeks to search your home, what kind of paper must he have before you are compelled to allow him to do it? <u>Search warrant</u>

2. If the United States wishes to purchase land for an arsenal and have exclusive legislative authority over it, consent is required from <u>Legislature.</u>

3. Prior to the adoption of the United States Constitution, the organization of states was known as the <u>Confederation.</u>

4. Tribunals are <u>courts.</u>

Part C, Sample 3

1. Can the state coin money with the consent of Congress? <u>No</u>

2. Name one area of authority over state militia reserved exclusively to the states. <u>The appointment of officers</u>

3. The power of granting patents, that is, of securing to inventors the exclusive right to their discoveries, is given to the Congress for the purpose of <u>promoting progress.</u>

4. The only legal tender which may be authorized by states for payment of debts is <u>U.S. Currency.</u>

Part C, Sample 4

1. In what year did the Congress gain the right to prohibit the migration of persons to the states? <u>1808</u>

2. Who is the commander-in-chief of the army and navy of the United States? <u>The President</u>

3. Which of the Parts above, of the United States Constitution, deals with the federal government's authority to call the state militia into federal service? <u>Part 1</u>

4. The president is forbidden to exercise his authority of pardon in cases of <u>impeachment.</u>

Source: Veterans of the Civil Rights Movement, www.crmvet.org/info/litques.htm.

Learning the Bitter Truth about Jim Crow

During the Jim Crow era, which lasted from the late 1800s through the 1960s, African Americans in the South were expected to follow strict rules of behavior that demonstrated respect and submission toward whites. During the summer of 1955, an African-American teenager from Chicago named Emmett Till broke these unwritten rules of acceptable black behavior during a visit to Mississippi and was murdered by white segregationists. Despite strong evidence, an all-white jury refused to convict the killers.

The brutal murder of Emmett Till had a profound effect on 14-year-old Essie Mae Moody (whose name was changed to Annie Mae Moody due to a problem with her birth certificate). In this excerpt from her memoir Coming of Age in Mississippi, *she recalls the tense racial atmosphere in the Jim Crow South and her sudden realization that she could be killed "just because I was black."*

Not only did I enter high school with a new name, but also with a completely new insight into the life of Negroes in Mississippi. I was now working for one of the meanest white women in town, and a week before school started Emmett Till was killed.

Up until his death, I had heard of Negroes found floating in a river or dead somewhere with their bodies riddled with bullets. But I didn't know the mystery behind these killings then. I remember once when I was only seven I heard Mama and one of my aunts talking about some Negro who had been beaten to death. "Just like them lowdown skunks killed him they will do the same to us," Mama had said. When I asked her who killed the man and why, she said, "An Evil Spirit killed him. You gotta be a good girl or it will kill you too." So since I was seven, I had lived in fear of that "Evil Spirit." It took me eight years to learn what that spirit was.

I was coming from school the evening I heard about Emmett Till's death. There was a whole group of us, girls and boys, walking down the road headed home. A group of about six high school boys were walking a few paces ahead of me and several other girls. We were laughing and talking about something that had happened in school that day. However, the six boys in front of us weren't talking very loud. Usually they kept up so much noise. But today they were just walking and talking among themselves....

[Moody and the other girls eavesdrop and hear them discuss an African-American boy who was recently murdered for allegedly whistling at a white woman.]

Questions about who was killed, where, and why started running through my mind. I walked up to one of the boys.

"Eddie, what boy was killed?"

"Moody, where've you been?" he asked me. "Everybody talking about that fourteen-year-old boy who was killed in Greenwood by some white men. You don't know nothing that's going on besides what's in them books of yours, huh?"

Standing there before the rest of the girls, I felt so stupid. It was then that I realized I really didn't know what was going on all around me. It wasn't that I was dumb. It was just that ever since I was nine, I'd had to work after school and do my lessons on lunch hour. I never had time to learn anything, to hang around with people my own age. And you were never told anything by adults.

That evening when I stopped off at the house on my way to Mrs. Burke's, Mama was singing. Any other day she would have been yelling at Adline and Junior them to take off their school clothes. I wondered if she knew about Emmett Till. The way she was singing she had something on her mind and it wasn't pleasant either.

> I got a shoe, you got a shoe,
> All of God's chillum got shoes;
> When I get to hebben, I'm gonna put on my shoes,
> And gonna tromp all over God's hebben.
> When I get to hebben I'm gonna put on my shoes,
> And gonna walk all over God's hebben.

Mama was dishing up beans like she didn't know anyone was home. Adline, Junior, and James had just thrown their books down and sat themselves at the table. I didn't usually eat before I went to work. But I wanted to ask Mama about Emmett Till. So I ate and thought of some way of asking her.

"These beans are some good, Mama," I said, trying to sense her mood.

"Why is you eating anyway? You gonna be late for work. You know how Miss Burke is," she said to me.

"I don't have much to do this evening. I kin get it done before I leave work," I said.

The conversation stopped after that. Then Mama started humming that song again.

> When I get to hebben, I'm gonna put on my shoes,
> And gonna tromp all over God's hebben.

She put a plate on the floor for Jennie Ann and Jerry.

"Jennie Ann? You and Jerry sit down here and eat and don't put beans all over this floor."

Ralph, the baby, started crying, and she went in the bedroom to give him his bottle. I got up and followed her.

"Mama, did you hear about that fourteen-year-old Negro boy who was killed a little over a week ago by some white men?" I asked her.

"Where did your hear that?" she said angrily.

"Boy, everybody really thinks I am dumb or deaf or something. I heard Eddie them talking about it this evening coming from school."

"Eddie them better watch how they go around here talking. These white folks git a hold of it they gonna be in trouble," she said.

"What are they gonna be in trouble about, Mama? People got a right to talk, ain't they?"

"You go on to work before you is late. And don't you let on like you know nothing about that boy being killed before Miss Burke them. Just do your work like you don't know nothing," she said. "That boy's a lot better off in heaven than he is here," she continued and then started singing again.

On my way to Mrs. Burke's that evening, Mama's words kept running through my mind. "Just do your work like you don't know nothing." "Why is Mama acting so scared?" I thought. "And what is Mrs. Burke knew we knew? Why must I pretend I don't know? Why are these people killing Negroes? What did Emmett Till do besides whistle at that woman?"

By the time I got to work, I had worked my nerves up some. I was shaking as I walked up on the porch. "Do your work like you don't know nothing." But once I got inside, I couldn't have acted normal if Mrs. Burke were paying me to be myself.

I was so nervous, I spent most of the evening avoiding them going about the house dusting and sweeping. Everything went along fairly well until dinner was served.

"Don, Wayne, and Mama, y'all come on to dinner. Essie, you can wash up the pots and dishes in the sink now. Then after dinner you won't have as many," Mrs. Burke called to me.

If I had the power to mysteriously disappear at that moment, I would have. They used the breakfast table in the kitchen for most of their meals. The dining room was only used for Sunday dinner or when they had company. I wished they had company tonight so they could eat in the dining room while I was at the kitchen sink.

"I forgot the bread," Mrs. Burke said when they were all seated. "Essie, will you cut it and put it on the table for me?"

I took the cornbread, cut it in squares, and put it on a small round dish. Just as I was about to set it on the table, Wayne yelled at the cat. I dropped the plate and the bread went all over the floor.

"Never mind, Essie," Mrs. Burke said angrily as she got up and got some white bread from the breadbox.

I didn't say anything. I picked up the cornbread from around the table and went back to the dishes. As soon as I got to the sink, I dropped a saucer on the floor and broke it. Didn't anyone say a word until I had picked up the pieces.

"Essie, I bought some new cleanser today. It's setting on the bathroom shelf. See if it will remove the stains in the tub," Mrs. Burke said.

I went to the bathroom to clean the tub. By the time I got through with it, it was snow white. I spent a whole hour scrubbing it. I had removed the stains in no time but I kept scrubbing until they finished dinner.

When they had finished and gone into the living room as usual to watch TV, Mrs. Burke called me to eat. I took a clean plate out of the cabinet and sat down. Just as I was putting the first forkful of food in my mouth, Mrs. Burke entered the kitchen.

"Essie, did you hear about that fourteen-year-old boy who was killed in Greenwood?" she asked me, sitting down in one of the chairs opposite me.

"No, I didn't hear that," I answered, almost choking on the food.

"Do you know why he was killed?" she asked and I didn't answer.

"He was killed because he got out of his place with a white woman. A boy from Mississippi would have known better than that. This boy was from Chicago. Negroes up North have no respect for people. They think they can get away with anything. He just came to Mississippi and put a whole lot of notions in the boys' heads here and stirred up a lot of trouble," she said passionately.

"How old are you, Essie?" she asked me after a pause.

"Fourteen. I will soon be fifteen though," I said.

"See, that boy was just fourteen too. It's a shame he had to die so soon." She was so red in the face, she looked as if she was on fire.

When she left the kitchen I sat there with my mouth open and my food untouched. I couldn't have eaten now if I were starving. "Just do you work like you don't know nothing" ran through my mind again and I began washing the dishes.

I went home shaking life a leaf on a tree. For the first time out of all her trying, Mrs. Burke had made me feel like rotten garbage. Many times she had tried to instill fear within me and subdue me and had given up. But when she talked about Emmett Till there was something in her voice that sent chills and fear all over me.

Before Emmett Till's murder, I had known the fear of hunger, hell, and the Devil. But now there was a new fear known to me—the fear of being killed just because I was black. This was the worst of my fears. I knew once I got food, the fear of starving to death would leave. I also was told that if I were a good girl, I wouldn't have to fear the Devil or hell. But I didn't know what one had to do or not do as a Negro not to be killed. Probably just being a Negro period was enough, I thought.

Source: Moody, Anne. *Coming of Age in Mississippi.* 1968. New York: Bantam, 1976, pp. 121-26.

White Support for the Montgomery Bus Boycott

Not all whites in the South supported segregation. When civil rights leaders launched the Montgomery Bus Boycott in 1955 to protest segregation of the city's public transportation system, many white residents hoped it would succeed. One white woman who held this opinion was Virginia Foster Durr. Born in 1903, she was raised in Birmingham, Alabama. After marrying attorney Clifford Durr, she moved with him to Washington, D.C., for many years. The Montgomery Bus Boycott started a short time after she returned to her home state. In the following excerpt from an interview, Durr recalls the difficulties she and other whites faced when they were openly sympathetic to the protest.

I was born into a segregated system, and I took it for granted. Nobody told me any different. It really wasn't until I got to Washington that I began to realize how much at variance the South was from the rest of the country and how very wrong the system was. So when I came back to Montgomery, in 1951, after almost twenty years, I no longer took the system for granted.

The first thing that happened to whites like us who were sympathetic to the boycott was that we lost our businesses. People didn't come to us. We got a reputation. My husband got mighty little law business after he took a very decided stand [supporting the boycott]. People like my husband and Aubrey Williams [publisher of the *Southern Farmer*] realized that they were cutting their own throats. Aubrey lost all of his advertising, every bit of it.

The fact that our family stood by us even though they did not agree with us was our salvation. If they had disowned us, had not stood by us, we could not have stayed. We were lucky because Clifford was kin to so many people in Montgomery County. It was difficult for them to ostracize us on account of that strong feeling of kinship.

It all gets down to economics. White men were terrified that if they took any position at all they would lose their business, as my husband had. They couldn't sell real estate to blacks or they would get in bad with the bank. You had to have a great deal of security to be willing to take that kind of ostracism and disapproval.

"We're Not Moving to the Back, Mr. Blake," from *Eyes on the Prize: America's Civil Rights Years* by Juan Williams, Introduction by Julian Bond, copyright © 1987 by Blackside, Inc. Used by permission of Viking Penguin, a division of Penguin Group (USA) Inc.

There was another kind of terror. Some whites were scared that they wouldn't be invited to the ball, to the parties. It's a terror of being a social failure, of not making your way in the world. Now that's not nearly as bad as being lynched or killed or beaten up. But it is a terrible fear; that's the fear that possesses most men today.

I think the women played a tremendous part in the movement, the white and the black women. For years, we had an integrated prayer group here. We'd pray together every morning. That was broken up by one of those white Nazi groups. The husbands and uncles and brothers of these women took out advertisements in the papers, and many of them repudiated their own wives.

When I heard that the boycott had been successful, I felt pure, unadulterated joy. It was like a fountain of joy. Of course the blacks felt that way, but the white friends I had felt the way I did. We felt joy and release. It was as if a great burden had fallen off us.

Source: Williams, Juan. *Eyes on the Prize: America's Civil Rights Years, 1954-1965*. New York: Viking, 1987, pp. 82-83.

Ella Baker Describes the Founding of SNCC

In 1960 a group of African-American college students decided to challenge the segregation of private businesses in the South by sitting peacefully at a whites-only lunch counter in Greensboro, North Carolina. The sit-in movement expanded quickly throughout the region. Impressed by the energy and enthusiasm of the student activists, Ella Baker invited them to attend a conference at Shaw University in Raleigh, North Carolina. This meeting led to the founding of the Student Nonviolent Coordinating Committee (SNCC), a grassroots organization which played a major role in the civil rights movement. Baker reported on the successful conference in the following article, which appeared in The Southern Patriot.*

T he Student Leadership Conference made it crystal clear that current sit-ins and other demonstrations are concerned with something much bigger than a hamburger or even a giant-sized Coke.

Whatever may be the difference in approach to their goal, the Negro and white students, North and South, are seeking to rid America of the scourge of racial segregation and discrimination—not only at lunch counters, but in every aspect of life.

In reports, casual conversations, discussion groups, and speeches, the sense and the spirit of the following statement that appeared in the initial newsletter of the students at Barber-Scotia College, Concord, N.C., were re-echoed time and again:

"We want the world to know that we no longer accept the inferior position of second-class citizenship. We are willing to go to jail, be ridiculed, spat upon and even suffer physical violence to obtain First Class Citizenship."

By and large, this feeling that they have a destined date with freedom, was not limited to a drive for personal freedom, or even freedom for the Negro in the South. Repeatedly it was emphasized that the movement was concerned with the moral implications of racial discrimination for the "whole world" and the "Human Race."

This universality of approach was linked with a perceptive recognition that "it is important to keep the movement democratic and to avoid struggles for personal leadership."

It was further evident that desire for supportive cooperation from adult leaders and the adult community was also tempered by apprehension that adults might try to "capture" the student movement. The students showed willingness to be met on the basis of equality, but were intolerant of anything that smacked of manipulation or domination.

This inclination toward group-centered leadership, rather than toward a leader-centered group pattern of organization, was refreshing indeed to those of the older group who bear the scars of the battle, the frustrations and the disillusionment that come when the prophetic leader turns out to have heavy feet of clay.

However hopeful might be the signs in the direction of group-centered-ness, the fact that many schools and communities, especially in the South, have not provided adequate experience for young Negroes to assume initiative and think and act independently accentuated the need for guarding the student movement against well-meaning, but nevertheless unhealthy, over-protectiveness.

Here is an opportunity for adult and youth to work together and provide genuine leadership—the development of the individual to his highest potential for the benefit of the group.

Many adults and youth characterized the Raleigh meeting as the greatest or most significant conference of our period.

Whether it lives up to this high evaluation or not will, in a large measure, be determined by the extent to which there is more effective training in and understanding of non-violent principles and practices, in group dynamics, and in the re-direction into creative channels of the normal frustrations and hostilities that result from second-class citizenship.

Source: Baker, Ella. "Bigger Than a Hamburger." *The Southern Patriot,* May 1960.

James Farmer Remembers the Freedom Rides

The Congress of Racial Equality (CORE) was founded in 1942 with the goal of using the techniques of nonviolent resistance to fight racial discrimination in the United States. James Farmer became the organization's national director in 1961, the year that CORE played a leading role in organizing Freedom Rides in the South. These integrated bus trips through segregated areas often met with violent white resistance. In this excerpt from his memoir Lay Bare the Heart, *Farmer recalls his decision to participate in a Freedom Ride in Mississippi.*

Jeeps patrolled the streets. The atmosphere was warlike. As thirty or forty nonviolent black youths readied themselves for their ride into bigotry's main den, to beard the beast lurking there, individual apprehensions were eclipsed by collective determination.

The eclipse was only partial, though; fear shone through. If any man says that he had no fear in the action of the sixties, he is a liar. Or without imagination.

If there are those who think that the leaders were exceptions to that and were strangers to fear, let me quickly disabuse them of such a notion. Frankly, I was scared spitless and desperately wanted to avoid taking that ride to Jackson. Alabama had chewed up the original thirteen interracial CORE Freedom Riders; they had been brutalized, hospitalized, and in one case disabled—by flame, club, and pummeling fists. Across the Alabama line from Georgia, blacks had been brutally pistol-whipped and clubbed with blackjacks and fists and then thrown, bloodied, into the back of the bus. Whites had been clobbered even worse for trying to intervene—one suffered a stroke as a result and was paralyzed forever.

A bus had been burned to the ground in Anniston, Alabama, and the Freedom Riders, escaping with their lives, were hospitalized for smoke inhalation. In the Birmingham bus depot, Jim Peck, a white man, had been left for dead in a pool of his own blood. His head required fifty-three stitches. How many stitches could repair the heart that bled for the nation?

And, fortuitously, I had missed that carnage on the ride from Atlanta to Montgomery due to the death of my father. But how would I escape Mississippi? If Alabama had been purgatory, Mississippi would be hell.

Black students from Nashville, members of SNCC, their numbers augmented by youthful black CORE members from New Orleans, had dashed in to catch in midair the baton dropped by the initial thirteen. They had not asked if I would ride with them; they assumed that I would.

I had different thoughts, though. I had decided not to ride. Definitely, at any cost, not to go. Catalogued in my mind were all the necessary excuses. When the inevitable question came, I was ready with answers.

But that decision had not come without inner pain. After all, when I took over the helm of CORE, four months earlier, I had said that I would be no armchair general, tied to the tent. I would not *send* troops, but would go with them. But that was bravado born of remoteness from reality. Who would expect me to risk being cut down so early in the promise of a leadership career? Everyone would understand when they thought about it. There would be many other battles, much time to show courage. And how could I let myself be wiped out now, before anyone outside the inner circle of the movement even knew I was there? Not now, maybe later. And my father had just died. I should not follow him so soon. Two deaths in two weeks would be too much for my mother. The family needed me now.

Yet, a grain of ambivalence stuck in my craw. Maybe a "still, small voice" would speak. A part of me hoped so. But if it spoke, I was certain that I would close my ears. Though, just in case, I had packed my suitcase and tossed it into the trunk of a staff car. And along with it my inner turmoil.

When the kids boarded the buses, I watched as a father seeing his children leave the home, as they must, and race into an uncertain future. Typically, the father was sad because he could not go with them; they had to go alone.

On the first bus, the Trailways, they were not alone. With them was a young black Methodist minister, the Reverend James Lawson. A man of much imagination, Jim Lawson must have had the same apprehensions that I had. But he had decided to go anyway. Courage, after all, is not being unafraid, but doing what needs to be done in spite of fear. He fairly leaped onto the bus, with a grim gladness. The students on board smiled and gave me a "thumbs up" gesture and shouted, "See you later, Jim." I returned the gesture and the smile, hoping that they would see me later, *much* later.

The second bus, the Greyhound, was boarded by some SNCC people, but mostly by CORE people. The CORE contingent had come at my urging, transmitted by my staff in New York, to keep the "revolution" going. They fully expected the protection my presence would provide. They filed in and took seats. I stood outside and waved farewell. The windows were open and I extended my hand through to shake hands with a pretty, seventeen-year-old CORE girl from New Orleans. She shook the hand with some puzzlement. "My prayers are with you, Doris," I said. "Have a safe trip, and when it's over, we'll get together and decide what we have to do next to finish the job."

Doris Castle's eyes, strafed with fear, became huge balls of terror. "You're coming with us, aren't you, Jim?" she whispered. I went through my pre-arranged litany of excuses: I'd been away from the office for four weeks; my desk was piled high with papers. People would be angry with CORE if they got no timely response to their letters, would not contribute money. Someone had to raise money to fuel these buses, to keep the revolution going. As national director, I had a solemn responsibility to mind the store. All of us want to be where the action is, but no such luck. Some of us are stuck with the dull jobs, the supportive ones. I could not be there in person, but she knew I'd be there in spirit.

Eyes wide, she shook her head slowly, brushing away all my words. Brain did not believe what ears were hearing. She spoke softly, in a stage whisper. But the words hit like a trip-hammer, driving me, it seemed, partway into the pavement. "Jim. *Please.*"

"Get my luggage," I shouted to a CORE staffer standing nearby. "Put it on the damn bus. I'm going."

Doris didn't smile, she just looked. And she suddenly looked tired. Kids grow up fast under fire, and sometimes grow old. Like in war.

Source: Farmer, James. *Lay Bare the Heart: An Autobiography of the Civil Rights Movement.* Fort Worth: Texas Christian University Press, 1998. First published by Arbor House, 1985.

Registering Voters during Freedom Summer

In June 1964, more than 1,000 college students from across the country arrived in Mississippi to help register African-American voters as part of a project known as Freedom Summer. Within days, three civil rights workers disappeared and were presumed to have become the victims of racist violence. This incident increased the tension and fear felt by both the student activists and the rural black Mississippi residents they were trying to register. In the following excerpt from an interview, Peter Orris, a 19-year-old white volunteer, recalls his experiences during Freedom Summer.

Following the disappearance of Goodman, Chaney, and Schwerner, there was a decision made by the SNCC leadership that those of us that were going to go to the southwest area of Mississippi shouldn't go right away, because the situation was too tense and the possibility of mass violence and many more deaths was present. So they decided that we should go in the interim to Holmes County in the Delta and do the voter registration there. So we went to a town called Mileston, which was outside of Tchula, in Holmes County. And we spent two to three weeks there, working on voter registration. What that meant was going to people's houses who we knew were not registered to vote and we would begin to talk to people about the Freedom Democratic party, about registering to vote, about the programs that were being put forward, about being ready to drive people to the courthouse, and going with them while they registered.

When we'd go to a new farmer's house, the first problem was that we were white northerners on a mission, so to speak—all of those things were fraught with danger for the people that we were talking to. You'd get there, and the people would be sitting down and you'd shake their hands. Now, that was an unusual thing for a white person to do to a black person in Mississippi at that time. The next thing was that you would avoid a situation in which you were standing over and talking down to people—a body message about the power relationship. So we would always sit down, we'd sit on the steps, walking up to the porch. We'd either be on an equal eye level or on a lower level. We were much younger than many of the people we were speaking to, and it was necessary to establish a relationship or an understanding of the respect that we paid to them for their age and their situation. Frequently, people would respond by not looking us in the eye. At the end of every phrase there would be a "ma'am" or a "sir," depending on who was there. And they would say yes to everything we said. We'd say, "Would you like to be involved in the voter registration project? Will you go down to vote?" "Yes, sir." And we knew we were not getting across, we knew they were just waiting for us to go away because we were a danger to them, and in many ways we were. We had much less to risk than they did. This was their lives, their land, their family, and they were going to be here when we were gone.

Source: Hampton, Henry, and Steve Fayer with Sarah Flynn. *Voices of Freedom: An Oral History of the Civil Rights Movements from the 1950s through the 1980s.* New York: Bantam, 1991, pp. 191-92.

Powerful Testimony from Fannie Lou Hamer

The 1964 Freedom Summer voting-rights campaign culminated in the formation of the Mississippi Freedom Democratic Party (MFDP). The MFDP was intended to provide an integrated alternative to the regular state Democratic Party, which was controlled by white segregationists. The MFDP sent delegates to the Democratic National Convention in Atlantic City, New Jersey, and petitioned the Credentials Committee to be seated in place of the regular party delegates. The most powerful testimony at the hearing came from Fannie Lou Hamer, who described the harassment and brutality she and other black Mississippi residents endured for trying to exercise their voting rights.

Mr. Chairman, and to the Credentials Committee, my name is Mrs. Fannie Lou Hamer, and I live at 626 East Lafayette Street, Ruleville, Mississippi, Sunflower County, the home of Senator James O. Eastland, and Senator [John C.] Stennis.

It was the 31st of August in 1962 that eighteen of us traveled twenty-six miles to the county courthouse in Indianola to try to register to become first-class citizens. We was met in Indianola by policemen, Highway Patrolmen, and they only allowed two of us in to take the literacy test at the time. After we had taken this test and started back to Ruleville, we was held up by the City Police and the State Highway Patrolmen and carried back to Indianola where the bus driver was charged that day with driving a bus the wrong color.

After we paid the fine among us, we continued on to Ruleville, and Reverend Jeff Sunny carried me four miles in the rural area where I had worked as a timekeeper and sharecropper for eighteen years. I was met there by my children, who told me the plantation owner was angry because I had gone down—tried to register.

After they told me, my husband came, and said the plantation owner was raising Cain because I had tried to register. And before he quit talking the plantation owner came and said, "Fannie Lou, do you know—did Pap tell you what I said?"

And I said, "Yes, sir."

He said, "Well I mean that."

Said, "If you don't go down and withdraw your registration, you will have to leave." Said, "Then if you go down and withdraw," said, "you still might have to go because we're not ready for that in Mississippi."

And I addressed him and told him and said, "I didn't try to register for you. I tried to register for myself."

I had to leave that same night.

On the 10th of September 1962, sixteen bullets was fired into the home of Mr. and Mrs. Robert Tucker for me. That same night two girls were shot in Ruleville, Mississippi. Also, Mr. Joe McDonald's house was shot in.

And June the 9th, 1963, I had attended a voter registration workshop; was returning back to Mississippi. Ten of us was traveling by the Continental Trailway bus. When we got to Winona, Mississippi, which is Montgomery County, four of the people got off to use the washroom, and two of the people to use the restaurant....

The four people that had gone in to use the restaurant was ordered out. During this time I was on the bus. But when I looked through the window and saw they had rushed out I got off of the bus to see what had happened. And one of the ladies said, "It was a State Highway Patrolman and a Chief of Police ordered us out."

I got back on the bus and one of the persons had used the washroom got back on the bus, too.

As soon as I was seated on the bus, I saw when they began to get the five people in a highway patrolman's car. I stepped off of the bus to see what was happening and somebody screamed from the car that the five workers was in and said, "Get that one there." And when I went to get in the car, when the man told me I was under arrest, he kicked me.

I was carried to the county jail and put in the booking room. They left some of the people in the booking room and began to place us in cells. I was placed in a cell with a young woman called Miss Ivesta Simpson. After I was placed in the cell I began to hear sounds of licks and screams. I could hear the sounds of licks and horrible screams. And I could hear somebody say, "Can you say, 'yes, sir,' nigger? Can you say 'yes, sir'?"

And they would say other horrible names.

She would say, "Yes, I can say 'yes, sir.'"

"So, well, say it."

She said, "I don't know you well enough."

They beat her, I don't know how long. And after a while she began to pray, and asked God to have mercy on those people.

And it wasn't too long before three white men came to my cell. One of these men was a State Highway Patrolman and he asked me where I was from. And I told him Ruleville.

He said, "We are going to check this." And they left my cell and it wasn't too long before they came back. He said, "You are from Ruleville all right," and he used a curse word. And he said, "We're going to make you wish you was dead."

I was carried out of that cell into another cell where they had two Negro prisoners. The State Highway Patrolmen ordered the first Negro to take the blackjack. The first Negro prisoner ordered me, by orders from the State Highway Patrolman, for me to lay down on a bunk bed on my face. And I laid on my face, the first Negro began to beat me.

And I was beat by the first Negro until he was exhausted. I was holding my hands behind me at that time on my left side, because I suffered from polio when I was six years old.

After the first Negro had beat until he was exhausted, the State Highway Patrolman ordered the second Negro to take the blackjack.

The second Negro began to beat and I began to work my feet, and the State Highway Patrolman ordered the first Negro who had beat to sit on my feet—to keep me from working my feet. I began to scream and one white man got up and began to beat me in my head and tell me to hush.

One white man—my dress had worked up high—he walked over and pulled my dress. I pulled my dress down and he pulled my dress back up.

I was in jail when Medgar Evers was murdered.

All of this is on account of we want to register, to become first-class citizens. And if the Freedom Democratic Party is not seated now, I question America. Is this America, the land of the free and the home of the brave, where we have to sleep with our telephones off of the hooks because our lives be threatened daily, because we want to live as decent human beings, in America?

Thank you.

Source: Hamer, Fannie Lou. "Testimony before the Credentials Committee, Democratic National Convention," 1964. Available online at http://www.americanrhetoric.com /speeches/fannielouhamercredentialscommittee.htm.

Martin Luther King's Letter from a Selma, Alabama, Jail

On February 1, 1965—just a few weeks after he was honored with the Nobel Peace Prize—the Reverend Martin Luther King, Jr., was arrested for participating in a voting-rights protest in Selma, Alabama. During his incarceration, he wrote a letter describing the systematic denial of African-American voting rights that continued to take place in the South, despite the passage of the Civil Rights Act of 1964. In this excerpt from the letter, which was published in the New York Times *on February 5, King calls on the American people to support the campaign for full and equal black voting rights.*

Dear Friends: When the King of Norway participated in awarding the Nobel Peace Prize to me he surely did not think that in less than sixty days I would be in jail. He, and almost all world opinion will be shocked because they are little aware of the unfinished business in the South.

By jailing hundreds of Negroes, the city of Selma, Alabama, has revealed the persisting ugliness of segregation to the nation and the world. When the Civil Rights Act of 1964 was passed many decent Americans were lulled into complacency because they thought the day of difficult struggle was over.

Why are we in jail? Have you ever been required to answer 100 questions on government, some abstruse even to a political scientist specialist, merely to vote? Have you ever stood in line with over a hundred others and after waiting an entire day seen less than ten given the qualifying test?

THIS IS SELMA, ALABAMA. THERE ARE MORE NEGROES IN JAIL WITH ME THAN THERE ARE ON THE VOTING ROLLS.

But apart from voting rights, merely to be a person in Selma is not easy. When reports asked Sheriff Clark if a woman defendant was married, he replied, "She's a nigger woman and she hasn't got a Miss or a Mrs. in front of her name."

This is the U.S.A. in 1965. We are in jail simply because we cannot tolerate these conditions for ourselves or our nation.

We need the help of all decent Americans. Our organization, SCLC, is not only working in Selma, Ala., but in dozens of other Southern communities. Our self-help projects operate in South Carolina, Georgia, Louisiana, Mississippi and other states. Our people are eager to work, to sacrifice, to be jailed—but their income, normally meager, is cut off in these crises. Your help can make the difference. Your help can be a message of unity which the thickest jail walls cannot muffle. With warmest good wishes from all of us.

Sincerely,

MARTIN LUTHER KING, JR.

Source: King, Martin Luther, Jr. "A Letter from a Selma, Alabama, Jail," originally published as an advertisement, *New York Times*, February 5, 1965.

John Lewis Remembers "Bloody Sunday"

Civil rights leader John Lewis was an important figure in the long and dangerous campaign for equal voting rights for African Americans. Raised in the heart of the Jim Crow South, Lewis became dedicated to the civil rights cause in the late 1950s. Over the next several years he organized sit-ins at segregated lunch counters and restaurants, participated in Freedom Rides, and led voter registration drives during the Mississippi Freedom Summer. By 1963, when he was elected chairman of the Student Nonviolent Coordinating Committee (SNCC), Lewis had been arrested two dozen times.

In early 1965 Lewis's activism took him to Selma, Alabama, where he helped organize a peaceful protest march to the state capitol in Montgomery to publicize the ongoing quest for equal voting rights in the South. But this March 7 demonstration was crushed by Alabama state troopers who savagely beat the marchers—including women and children—as they crossed the Edmund Pettus Bridge. Photographs and footage from this incident, which came to be known as "Bloody Sunday," stunned America. In the following excerpt from his memoir Walking with the Wind, *Lewis recalls the violence that greeted the Selma marchers on that infamous day.*

It was mid-afternoon now, and time to assemble. A team of doctors and nurses from a group called the Medical Committee for Human Rights had arrived the day before on a flight from New York and set up a makeshift clinic in the small parsonage beside the church. We expected a confrontation. We knew Sheriff Clark had issued yet another call the evening before for even more deputies. Mass arrests would probably be made. There might be injuries. Most likely, we would be stopped at the edge of the city limits, arrested and maybe roughed up a bit. We did not expect anything worse than that.

And we did *not* expect to march all the way to Montgomery. No one knew for sure, until the last minute, if the march would even take place. There had been a measure of planning, but nowhere near the preparations and logistics necessary to move that many people in an orderly manner down fifty-four miles of highway, a distance that would take about five days for a group that size to cover.

Many of the men and women gathered on that ballfield had come straight from church. They were still wearing their Sunday outfits. Some of

---

Abridged from *Walking with the Wind: A Memoir of the Movement* by John Lewis with Michael D'Orso. Copyright © by John Lewis. Used with permission of Simon & Schuster Adult Publishing Group.

the women had on high heels. I had on a suit and tie, a light tan raincoat, dress shoes and my backpack. I was no more ready to hike half a hundred miles than anyone else. Like everyone around me, I was basically playing it by ear. None of us had thought much further ahead than that afternoon. Anything that happened beyond that—if we were allowed to go on, if this march did indeed go all the way to Montgomery—we figured we would take care of as we went along. The main thing was that we *do* it, that we march.

It was close to 4 P.M. when Andy [Andrew Young], Hosea [Williams], [James] Bevel and I gathered the marchers around us. A dozen or so reporters were there as well. I read a short statement aloud for the benefit of the press, explaining why we were marching today. Then we all knelt to one knee and bowed our heads as Andy delivered a prayer.

And then we set out, nearly six hundred of us, including a white SCLC staffer named Al Lingo—the same name as the commander of Alabama's state troopers.

We walked two abreast, in a pair of lines that stretched for several blocks. Hosea and I led the way. Albert Turner, an SCLC leader in Perry County, and Bob Mants were right behind us—Bob insisted on marching because I was marching; he told me he wanted to be there to "protect" me in case something happened.

Marie Foster and Amelia Boynton were next in line, and behind them, stretching as far as I could see, walked an army of teenagers, teachers, undertakers, beauticians—many of the same Selma people who had stood for weeks, months, *years,* in front of that courthouse.

At the far end, bringing up the rear, rolled four slow-moving ambulances.

I can't count the number of marches I have participated in in my lifetime, but there was something peculiar about this one. It was more than disciplined. It was somber and subdued, almost like a funeral procession. No one was jostling or pushing to get to the front, as often happened with these things. I don't know if there was a feeling that something was going to happen, or if the people simply sensed that this was a special procession, a "leaderless" march. There were no big names up front, no celebrities. This was just plain folks moving through the streets of Selma.

There was a little bit of a crowd looking on as we set out down the red sand of Sylvan Street, through the black section of town. There was some cheering and singing from those onlookers and from a few of the marchers, but then, as we turned right along Water Street, out of the black neighborhood now, the mood changed. There was no singing, no shouting—just the sound of scuffling feet. There was something holy about it, as if we were walking down a sacred path. It reminded me of Gandhi's march to the sea. Dr. King used to say there is nothing more powerful than the rhythm of marching feet, and that was what this was, the marching feet of a determined people. That was the only sound you could hear.

Down Water Street we went, turning right and walking along the river until we reached the base of the bridge, the Edmund Pettus Bridge.

There was a small posse of armed white men there, gathered in front of the *Selma Times-Journal* building. They had hard hats on their heads and clubs in their hands. Some of them were smirking. Not one said a word. I didn't think too much of them as we walked past. I'd seen men like that so many times.

As we turned onto the bridge, we were careful to stay on the narrow sidewalk. The road had been closed to traffic, but we still stayed on the walkway, which was barely wide enough for two people.

I noticed how steep it was as we climbed toward the steel canopy at the top of the arched bridge. It was too steep to see the other side. I looked down at the river and saw how still it was, still and brown. The surface of the water was stirred just a bit by the late-afternoon breeze. I noticed my trench coat was riffling a little from that same small wind.

When we reached the crest of the bridge, I stopped dead still.

So did Hosea.

There, facing us at the bottom of the other side, stood a sea of blue-helmeted, blue-uniformed Alabama state troopers, line after line of them, dozens of battle-ready lawmen stretched from one side of U.S. Highway 80 to the other.

Behind them were several dozen more armed men—Sheriff Clark's posse—some on horseback, all wearing khaki clothing, many carrying clubs the size of baseball bats.

On one side of the road I could see a crowd of about a hundred whites, laughing and hollering, waving Confederate flags. Beyond them, at a safe distance, stood a small, silent group of black people.

I could see a crowd of newsmen and reporters gathered in the parking lot of a Pontiac dealership. And I could see a line of parked police and state trooper vehicles. I didn't know it at the time, but Clark and Lingo were in one of those cars.

It was a drop of one hundred feet from the top of that bridge to the river below. Hosea glanced down at the muddy water and said, "Can you swim?"

"No," I answered.

"Well," he said, with a tiny half smile, "neither can I.

"But," he added, lifting his head and looking straight ahead, "we might have to."

Then we moved forward. The only sounds were our footsteps on the bridge and the snorting of a horse ahead of us.

I noticed several troopers slipping gas masks over their faces as we approached.

At the bottom of the bridge, while we were still about fifty feet from the troopers, the officer in charge, a Major John Cloud, stepped forward, holding a small bullhorn up to his mouth.

Hosea and I stopped, which brought the others to a standstill.

"This is an unlawful assembly," Cloud pronounced. *"Your march is not conducive to the public safety. You are ordered to disperse and go back to your church or to your homes."*

"May we have a word with the major?" asked Hosea.

"There is no word to be had," answered Cloud.

Hosea asked the same question again, and got the same response. Then Cloud issued a warning: *"You have two minutes to turn around and go back to your church."*

I wasn't about to turn around. We were there. We were not going to run. We couldn't turn and go back even if we wanted to. There were too many people.

We could have gone forward, marching right into the teeth of those troopers. But that would have been too aggressive, I thought, too provocative. God knew what might have happened if we had done that. These people were ready to be arrested, but I didn't want anyone to get hurt.

We couldn't go forward. We couldn't go back. There was only one option left that I could see.

"We should kneel and pray," I said to Hosea.

He nodded.

We turned and passed the word back to begin bowing down in a prayer-ful manner.

But that word didn't get far. It didn't have time. One minute after he had issued his warning—I know this because I was careful to check my watch—Major Cloud issued an order to his troopers.

"Troopers," he barked. *"Advance!"*

And then all hell broke loose.

The trooper and possemen swept forward as one, like a human wave, a blur of blue shirts and billy clubs and bullwhips. We had no chance to turn and retreat. There were six hundred people behind us, bridge railings to either side and the river below.

I remember how vivid the sounds were as the troopers rushed toward us—the clunk of the troopers' heavy boots, the whoops of rebel yells from the white onlookers, the clip-clop of horses' hooves hitting the hard asphalt of the highway, the voice of a woman shouting, "Get 'em! *Get* the niggers!"

And then they were upon us. The first of the troopers came over me, a large, husky man. Without a word, he swung his club against the left side of my head. I didn't feel any pain, just the thud of the blow, and my legs giving way. I raised an arm—a reflex motion—as I curled up in the "prayer for protection" position. And then the same trooper hit me again. And everything started to spin.

I heard something that sounded like gunshots. And then a cloud of smoke rose all around us.

Tear gas.

I'd never experienced tear gas before. This, I would learn later, was a particularly toxic form called C-4, made to induce nausea.

I began choking, coughing. I couldn't get air into my lungs. I felt as if I was taking my last breath. If there was ever a time in my life for me to panic, it should have been then. But I didn't. I remember how strangely calm I felt as I thought, This is it. People are going to die here. *I'm* going to die here….

I was bleeding badly. My head was no exploding with pain. That brief, sweet sense of just wanting to lie there was gone. I needed to get up. I'd faded out for I don't know how long, but now I was tuned back in.

There was mayhem all around me. I could see a young kid—a teenaged boy—sitting on the ground with a gaping cut in his head, the blood just gushing out. Several women, including Mrs. Boynton, were lying on the pavement and the grass median. People were weeping. Some were vomiting from the tear gas. Men on horses were moving in all directions, purposely riding over the top of fallen people, bringing their animals' hooves down on shoulders, stomachs and legs....

I was up now and moving, back across the bridge, with troopers and possemen and other retreating marchers all around me. At the other end of the bridge, we had to push through the possemen we'd passed outside the *Selma Times-Journal* building.

"Please, *no*," I could hear one woman scream.

"God, we're being *killed!*" cried another.

With nightsticks and whips—one posseman had a rubber hose wrapped with barbed wire—Sheriff Clark's "deputies" chased us all the way back into the Carver project and up to the front of Brown's Chapel, where we tried getting as many people as we could inside the church to safety. I don't even recall how I made it that far, how I got from the bridge to the church, but I did....

By nightfall, things had calmed down a bit. Hosea and I and the others had decided to call a mass meeting there in the church, and more than six hundred people, many bandaged from the wounds of that day, arrived. Clark's possemen had been ordered away, but the state troopers were still outside, keeping a vigil.

Hosea Williams spoke to the crowd first, trying to say something to calm them. Then I got up to say a few words. My head was throbbing. My hair was matted with blood clotting from an open gash. My trench coat was stained with dirt and blood.

I looked out on the room, crammed wall to wall and floor to ceiling with people. There was not a spot for one more body. I had no speech prepared. I had not had the time or opportunity to give much thought to what I would say. The words just came.

"I don't know how President Johnson can send troops to Vietnam," I said. "I don't see how he can send troops to the Congo. I don't see how he can send troops to *Africa,* and he can't send troops to Selma, Alabama."

There was clapping, and some shouts of "Yes!" and "Amen!"

"Next time we march," I continued, "we may have to keep going when we get to Montgomery. We may have to go on to *Washington*."

When those words were printed in *The New York Times* the next morning, the Justice Department announced it was sending FBI agents to Selma to investigate whether "unnecessary force was used by law officers and others." For two months we'd been facing "unnecessary force," but that apparently had not been enough. This, finally, was enough....

It was not until the next day that I learned what else had happened that evening, that just past 9:30 P.M., ABC Television cut into its Sunday night movie—a premier broadcast of Stanley Kramer's *Judgment at Nuremberg,* a film about Nazi racism—with a special bulletin. News anchor Frank Reynolds came onscreen to tell viewers of a brutal clash that afternoon between state troopers and black protest marchers in Selma, Alabama. They then showed fifteen minutes of film footage of the attack.

The images were stunning—scene after scene of policemen on foot and on horseback beating defenseless American citizens. Many viewers thought this was somehow part of the movie. It seemed too strange, too ugly to be real. It *couldn't* be real.

But it was. At one point in the film clip, Jim Clark's voice could be heard clearly in the background: "Get those goddamned niggers!" he yelled. "And get those goddamned *white* niggers."

The American public had already seen so much of this sort of thing, countless images of beatings and dogs and cursing and hoses. But something about that day in Selma touched a nerve deeper than anything that had come before. Maybe it was the concentrated focus of the scene, the mass movement of those troopers on foot and riders on horseback rolling into and over two long lines of stoic, silent, unarmed people. This wasn't like Birmingham, where chanting and cheering and singing preceded a wild stampede and scattering. This was a face-off in the most vivid terms between a dignified, composed, completely nonviolent multitude of silent protestors and the truly malevolent force of a heavily armed, hateful battalion of troopers. The sight of them rolling over us like human tanks was something that had never been seen before.

People just couldn't believe this was happening, not in America. Women and children being attacked by armed men on horseback—it was impossible to believe.

But it had happened. And the response from across the nation to what would go down in history as Bloody Sunday was immediate. By midnight that evening, even as I lay asleep in my room over at Good Samaritan [Hospital, where Lewis had been admitted late Sunday night], people from as far away as New York and Minnesota were flying into Alabama and driving to Selma, forming a vigil of their own outside Brown's Chapel. President Johnson, who had been contacted by the Justice Department almost immediately after the attack, watched the ABC footage that evening. He knew he would have to respond. Dr. King, too, was informed of what had happened as soon as the President—Andy Young called King in Atlanta, and the two agreed that now there *would* be a march. They made plans to file a request the first thing in the morning, asking for a federal injunction barring state interference in a massive Selma-to-Montgomery march.

That request arrived the next morning, Monday, in Montgomery, on the desk of Federal District Judge Frank Johnson—the same judge who had issued the injunction four years earlier providing us with safe passage out of Montgomery during the Freedom Ride.

Banner headlines, with four-column photographs—many showing the trooper clubbing me as I lay on the ground with my arm upraised—appeared that Monday morning in newspapers around the world. By midday I was receiving telegraphs and cards and flowers from total strangers. A wreath arrived from an elderly woman in Southern California. "A FORMER ALABAMIAN," the card read. "WE ARE WITH YOU."

Dr. King and Ralph Abernathy came to see me. They told me what was going on outside, that people all across the country were with us, that they were going to have this march. "It's going to happen, John," Dr. King told me. "Rest assured it is going to happen."

Source: Lewis, John. *Walking with the Wind: A Memoir of the Movement.* New York: Simon and Schuster, 1998.

Terror on the Edmund Pettus Bridge

No one who participated in the initial Selma-Montgomery Voting Rights March on March 7, 1965, was safe from the violent "Bloody Sunday" attack by state and local law enforcement officers. Sheyann Webb—who was six years old on the day she and other peaceful protesters tried to cross the Edmund Pettus Bridge—describes the terrifying scene in this excerpt from her memoir Selma, Lord, Selma.

Now the Edmund Pettus Bridge sits above the downtown; you have to walk up it like it's a hill. We couldn't see the other side, we couldn't see the troopers. So we started up and the first part of the line was over. I couldn't see all that much because I was so little; the people in front blocked my view.

But when we got up there on that high part and looked down we saw them. I remember the woman [next to me] saying something like, "Oh, My Lord" or something. And I stepped out to the side for a second and I saw them. They were in a line—they looked like a blue picket fence—stretched across the highway. There were others gathered behind that first line and to the sides, along the little service road in front of the stores and drive-ins, there was a group of white people. And further back were some of Sheriff Jim Clark's possemen on their horses. Traffic had been blocked.

At that point I began to get a little uneasy about things. I think everyone did. People quit talking; it was so quiet then that all you could hear was the wind blowing and our footsteps on the concrete sidewalk.

Well, we kept moving down the bridge. I remember glancing at the water in the Alabama River, and it was yellow and looked cold. I was told later that Hosea Williams said to John Lewis, "See that water down there? I hope you can swim, 'cause we're fixin' to end up in it."

The troopers could be seen more clearly now. I guess I was fifty to seventy-five yards from them. They were wearing blue helmets, blue jackets, and they carried clubs in their hands; they had those gas-mask pouches slung across their shoulders. The first part of the march line reached them and we all came to a stop. For a few seconds we just kept standing, and then I heard this voice speaking over the bullhorn saying that this was an unlawful assembly and for us to disperse and go back to the church.

I remember I held the woman's hand who was next to me and had it gripped hard. I wasn't really scared at that point. Then I stepped out a way and looked again and saw the troopers putting on their masks. That scared me. I had never faced the troopers before, and nobody had ever put on gas masks during the downtown marches. But this one was different; we were out of the city limits and on a highway. Williams said something to the troopers asking if we could pray—I didn't hear it but was told later that we could—and then I heard the voice again come over the bullhorn and tell us we had two minutes to disperse.

Some of the people around me began to talk then, saying something about, "Get ready, we're going to jail," words to that effect.

But I didn't know about that; the masks scared me. So the next thing I know—it didn't seem like two minutes had gone by—the voice was saying, "Troopers advance and see that they are dispersed." Just all of a sudden it was beginning to happen. I couldn't see for sure how it began, but just before it did I took another look and saw this line of troopers moving toward us; the wind was whipping at their pant legs....

All I knew is I heard all this screaming and the people were turning and I saw this first part of the line running and stumbling back toward us. At that point, I was just off the bridge and on the side of the highway. And they came running and some of them were crying out and somebody yelled, "Oh, God, they're killing us!" I think I just froze then. There were people everywhere, jamming against me, pushing against me. Then, all of a sudden, it stopped and everyone got down on their knees, and I did too, and somebody was saying for us to pray. But there was so much excitement it never got started, because everybody was talking and they were scared and we didn't know what was happening or was going to happen. I remember looking toward the troopers and they were backing up, but some of them were standing over some of our people who had been knocked down or had fallen. It seemed like just a few seconds went by and I heard a shout. "Gas! Gas!" And everybody started screaming again. And I looked and I saw the troopers charging us again and some of them were swinging their arms and throwing canisters of tear gas. And beyond them I saw the horsemen starting their charge toward us. I was terrified. What happened then is something I'll never forget as long as I live. Never. In fact, I still dream about it sometimes.

I saw those horsemen coming toward me and they had those awful masks on; they rode right through the cloud of gas. Some of them had clubs, others had ropes or whips, which they swung about them like they were driving cattle. I'll tell you, I forgot about praying, and I just turned and ran. And just as I was turning the tear gas got me; it burned my nose first and then got my eyes. I was blinded by tears. So I began running and not seeing where I was going. I remember being scared that I might fall over the railing and into the water. I don't know if I was screaming or not, but everyone else was…. It was like a nightmare seeing it through the tears. I just knew then that I was going to die, that those horses were going to trample me. So I kind of knelt down and held my hands and arms up over my head….

All of a sudden somebody was grabbing me under the arms and lifting me up and running. The horses went by and I kept waiting to get trampled on or hit, but they went on by and I guess they were hitting at somebody else. And I looked up and saw it was Hosea Williams who had me and he was running but we didn't seem to be moving, and I kept kicking my legs in the air, trying to speed up, and I shouted at him, "Put me down! You can't run fast enough with me!"

But he held on until we were off the bridge and down on Broad Street and he let me go. I didn't stop running until I got home. All along the way there were people running in small groups; I saw people jumping over cars and being chased by the horsemen who kept hitting them….

When I got into the house my momma and daddy were there and they had this shocked look on their faces and I ran in and tried to tell them what had happened. I was maybe a little hysterical because I kept repeating over and over, "I can't stop shaking, Momma, I can't stop shaking," and finally she grabbed me and sat down with me on her lap. But my daddy was like I'd never seen him before. He had a shotgun and yelled. "By God, if they want it this way, I'll give it to them!" And he started out the door. Momma jumped up and got in front of him shouting at him. And he said, "I'm ready to die; I mean it! I'm ready to die!" I was crying on the couch, I was so scared. But finally he put the gun aside and sat down. I remember just laying there on the couch, crying and feeling so disgusted. They had beaten us like we were slaves.

Source: Webb, Sheyann. *Selma, Lord, Selma.* Tuscaloosa: University of Alabama Press, 1980, pp. 92-99.

President Lyndon Johnson Delivers "The American Promise"

On March 15, 1965—one week after the infamous Bloody Sunday attack in Selma, Alabama—President Lyndon B. Johnson delivered a speech before the U.S. Congress entitled "The American Promise." In this address, which appears below in its entirety, Johnson informed Congress and the American people that he planned to introduce strong new legislation to secure African-American voting rights in the South. "No law that we now have on the books—and I have helped to put three of them there—can ensure the right to vote when local officials are determined to deny it," he explained. The president went on to ask all Americans to support the proposed legislation and the civil rights cause.

I speak tonight for the dignity of man and the destiny of democracy.

I urge every member of both parties, Americans of all religions and of all colors, from every section of this country, to join me in that cause.

At times history and fate meet at a single time in a single place to shape a turning point in man's unending search for freedom. So it was at Lexington and Concord. So it was a century ago at Appomattox. So it was last week in Selma, Alabama.

There, long-suffering men and women peacefully protested the denial of their rights as Americans. Many were brutally assaulted. One good man, a man of God, was killed.

There is no cause for pride in what has happened in Selma. There is no cause for self-satisfaction in the long denial of equal rights of millions of Americans. But there is cause for hope and for faith in our democracy in what is happening here tonight.

For the cries of pain and the hymns and protests of oppressed people have summoned into convocation all the majesty of this great Government—the Government of the greatest Nation on earth.

Our mission is at once the oldest and the most basic of this country: to right wrong, to do justice, to serve man.

In our time we have come to live with moments of great crisis. Our lives have been marked with debate about great issues; issues of war and peace, issues of prosperity and depression. But rarely in any time does an issue lay bare the secret heart of America itself. Rarely are we met with a challenge, not to our growth or abundance, our welfare or our security, but rather to the values and the purposes and the meaning of our beloved Nation.

The issue of equal rights for American Negroes is such an issue. And should we defeat every enemy, should we double our wealth and conquer the stars, and still be unequal to this issue, then we will have failed as a people and as a nation.

For with a country as with a person, "What is a man profited, if he shall gain the whole world, and lose his own soul?"

There is no Negro problem. There is no Southern problem. There is no Northern problem. There is only an American problem. And we are met here tonight as Americans—not as Democrats or Republicans—we are met here as Americans to solve that problem.

This was the first nation in the history of the world to be founded with a purpose. The great phrases of that purpose still sound in every American heart, North and South: "All men are created equal"—"government by consent of the governed"—"give me liberty or give me death." Well, those are not just clever words, or those are not just empty theories. In their name Americans have fought and died for two centuries, and tonight around the world they stand there as guardians of our liberty, risking their lives.

Those words are a promise to every citizen that he shall share in the dignity of man. This dignity cannot be found in a man's possessions; it cannot be found in his power, or in his position. It really rests on his right to be treated as a man equal in opportunity to all others. It says that he shall share in freedom, he shall choose his leaders, educate his children, and provide for his family according to his ability and his merits as a human being.

To apply any other test—to deny a man his hopes because of his color or race, his religion or the place of his birth—is not only to do injustice, it is to deny America and to dishonor the dead who gave their lives for American freedom.

THE RIGHT TO VOTE. Our fathers believed that if this noble view of the rights of man was to flourish, it must be rooted in democracy. The most basic right of all was the right to choose your own leaders. The history of this country, in large measure, is the history of the expansion of that right to all of our people.

Many of the issues of civil rights are very complex and most difficult. But about this there can and should be no argument. Every American citizen must have an equal right to vote. There is no reason which can excuse the denial of that right. There is no duty which weighs more heavily on us than the duty we have to ensure that right.

Yet the harsh fact is that in many places in this country men and women are kept from voting simply because they are Negroes.

Every device of which human ingenuity is capable has been used to deny this right. The Negro citizen may go to register only to be told that the day is wrong, or the hour is late, or the official in charge is absent. And if he persists, and if he manages to present himself to the registrar, he may be disqualified because he did not spell out his middle name or because he abbreviated a word on the application.

And if he manages to fill out an application he is given a test. The registrar is the sole judge of whether he passes this test. He may be asked to recite the entire Constitution, or explain the most complex provisions of State law. And even a college degree cannot be used to prove that he can read and write.

For the fact is that the only way to pass these barriers is to show a white skin.

Experience has clearly shown that the existing process of law cannot overcome systematic and ingenious discrimination. No law that we now have on the books—and I have helped to put three of them there—can ensure the right to vote when local officials are determined to deny it.

In such a case our duty must be clear to all of us. The Constitution says that no person shall be kept from voting because of his race or his color. We have all sworn an oath before God to support and to defend that Constitution. We must now act in obedience to that oath.

GUARANTEEING THE RIGHT TO VOTE. Wednesday I will send to Congress a law designed to eliminate illegal barriers to the right to vote.

The broad principles of that bill will be in the hands of the Democratic and Republican leaders tomorrow. After they have reviewed it, it will come here formally as a bill. I am grateful for this opportunity to come here tonight at the invitation of the leadership to reason with my friends, to give them my views, and to visit with my former colleagues.

I have had prepared a more comprehensive analysis of the legislation which I had intended to transmit to the clerk tomorrow but which I will submit to the clerks tonight. But I want to really discuss with you now briefly the main proposals of this legislation,

This bill will strike down restrictions to voting in all elections—Federal, State, and local—which have been used to deny Negroes the right to vote.

This bill will establish a simple, uniform standard which cannot be used, however ingenious the effort, to flout our Constitution.

It will provide for citizens to be registered by officials of the United States Government if the State officials refuse to register them.

It will eliminate tedious, unnecessary lawsuits which delay the right to vote.

Finally, this legislation will ensure that properly registered individuals are not prohibited from voting.

I will welcome the suggestions from all of the Members of Congress—I have no doubt that I will get some—on ways and means to strengthen this law and to make it effective. But experience has plainly shown that this is the only path to carry out the command of the Constitution.

To those who seek to avoid action by their National Government in their own communities; who want to and who seek to maintain purely local control over elections, the answer is simple:

Open your polling places to all your people.

Allow men and women to register and vote whatever the color of their skin.

Extend the rights of citizenship to every citizen of this land.

THE NEED FOR ACTION. There is no constitutional issue here. The command of the Constitution is plain.

There is no moral issue. It is wrong—deadly wrong—to deny any of your fellow Americans the right to vote in this country.

There is no issue of States fights or national rights. There is only the struggle for human rights.

I have not the slightest doubt what will be your answer.

The last time a President sent a civil rights bill to the Congress it contained a provision to protect voting rights in Federal elections. That civil rights bill was passed after 8 long months of debate. And when that bill came to my desk from the Congress for my signature, the heart of the voting provision had been eliminated.

This time, on this issue, there must be no delay, no hesitation and no compromise with our purpose.

We cannot, we must not, refuse to protect the right of every American to vote in every election that he may desire to participate in. And we ought not and we cannot and we must not wait another 8 months before we get a bill. We have already waited a hundred years and more, and the time for waiting is gone.

So I ask you to join me in working long hours—nights and weekends, if necessary—to pass this bill. And I don't make that request lightly. For from the window where I sit with the problems of our country I recognize that outside this chamber is the outraged conscience of a nation, the grave concern of many nations, and the harsh judgment of history on our acts.

WE SHALL OVERCOME. But even if we pass this bill, the battle will not be over. What happened in Selma is part of a far larger movement which reaches into every section and State of America. It is the effort of American Negroes to secure for themselves the full blessings of American life.

Their cause must be our cause too. Because it is not just Negroes, but really it is all of us, who must overcome the crippling legacy of bigotry and injustice. And we shall overcome.

As a man whose roots go deeply into Southern soil I know how agonizing racial feelings are. I know how difficult it is to reshape the attitudes and the structure of our society.

But a century has passed, more than a hundred years, since the Negro was freed. And he is not fully free tonight.

It was more than a hundred years ago that Abraham Lincoln, a great President of another party, signed the Emancipation Proclamation, but emancipation is a proclamation and not a fact.

A century has passed, more than a hundred years, since equality was promised. And yet the Negro is not equal.

A century has passed since the day of promise. And the promise is unkept.

The time of justice has now come. I tell you that I believe sincerely that no force can hold it back. It is right in the eyes of man and God that it should come. And when it does, I think that day will brighten the lives of every American.

For Negroes are not the only victims. How many white children have gone uneducated, how many white families have lived in stark poverty, how many white lives have been scarred by fear, because we have wasted our energy and our substance to maintain the barriers of hatred and terror?

So I say to all of you here, and to all in the Nation tonight, that those who appeal to you to hold on to the past do so at the cost of denying you your future.

This great, rich, restless country can offer opportunity and education and hope to all: black and white, North and South, sharecropper and city dweller. These are the enemies: poverty, ignorance, disease. They are the enemies and not our fellow man, not our neighbor. And these enemies too, poverty, disease and ignorance, we shall over, come.

AN AMERICAN PROBLEM. Now let none of us in any sections look with prideful righteousness on the troubles in another section, or on the problems of our neighbors. There is really no part of America where the promise of equality has been fully kept. In Buffalo as well as in Birmingham, in Philadelphia as well as in Selma, Americans are struggling for the fruits of freedom.

This is one Nation. What happens in Selma or in Cincinnati is a matter of legitimate concern to every American. But let each of us look within our own hearts and our own communities, and let each of us put our shoulder to the wheel to root out injustice wherever it exists.

As we meet here in this peaceful, historic chamber tonight, men from the South, some of whom were at Iwo Jima, men from the North who have carried Old Glory to far corners of the world and brought it back without a stain on it, men from the East and from the West, are all fighting together without regard to religion, or color, or region, in Viet-Nam. Men from every region fought for us across the world 20 years ago.

And in these common dangers and these common sacrifices the South made its contribution of honor and gallantry no less than any other region of the great Republic—and in some instances, a great many of them, more.

And I have not the slightest doubt that good men from everywhere in this country, from the Great Lakes to the Gulf of Mexico, from the Golden

Gate to the harbors along the Atlantic, will rally together now in this cause to vindicate the freedom of all Americans. For all of us owe this duty; and I believe that all of us will respond to it.

Your President makes that request of every American.

PROGRESS THROUGH THE DEMOCRATIC PROCESS. The real hero of this struggle is the American Negro. His actions and protests, his courage to risk safety and even to risk his life, have awakened the conscience of this Nation. His demonstrations have been designed to call attention to injustice, designed to provoke change, designed to stir reform.

He has called upon us to make good the promise of America. And who among us can say that we would have made the same progress were it not for his persistent bravery, and his faith in American democracy.

For at the real heart of battle for equality is a deep-seated belief in the democratic process. Equality depends not on the force of arms or tear gas but upon the force of moral right; not on recourse to violence but on respect for law and order.

There have been many pressures upon your President and there will be others as the days come and go. But I pledge you tonight that we intend to fight this battle where it should be fought: in the courts, and in the Congress, and in the hearts of men.

We must preserve the right of free speech and the right of free assembly. But the right of free speech does not carry with it, as has been said, the right to holler fire in a crowded theater. We must preserve the right to free assembly, but free assembly does not carry with it the right to block public thoroughfares to traffic.

We do have a right to protest, and a right to march under conditions that do not infringe the constitutional rights of our neighbors. And I intend to protect all those rights as long as I am permitted to serve in this office.

We will guard against violence, knowing it strikes from our hands the very weapons which we seek—progress, obedience to law, and belief in American values.

In Selma as elsewhere we seek and pray for peace. We seek order. We seek unity. But we will not accept the peace of stifled rights, or the order imposed by fear, or the unity that stifles protest. For peace cannot be purchased at the cost of liberty.

In Selma tonight, as in every—and we had a good day there—as in every city, we are working for just and peaceful settlement. We must all remember that after this speech I am making tonight, after the police and the FBI and the Marshals have all gone, and after you have promptly passed this bill, the people of Selma and the other cities of the Nation must still live and work together. And when the attention of the Nation has gone elsewhere they must try to heal the wounds and to build a new community.

This cannot be easily done on a battleground of violence, as the history of the South itself shows. It is in recognition of this that men of both races have shown such an outstandingly impressive responsibility in recent days—last Tuesday, again today,

RIGHTS MUST BE OPPORTUNITIES. The bill that I am presenting to you will be known as a civil rights bill. But, in a larger sense, most of the program I am recommending is a civil rights program. Its object is to open the city of hope to all people of all races.

Because all Americans just must have the right to vote. And we are going to give them that right.

All Americans must have the privileges of citizenship regardless of race. And they are going to have those privileges of citizenship regardless of race.

But I would like to caution you and remind you that to exercise these privileges takes much more than just legal right. It requires a trained mind and a healthy body. It requires a decent home, and the chance to find a job, and the opportunity to escape from the clutches of poverty.

Of course, people cannot contribute to the Nation if they are never taught to read or write, if their bodies are stunted from hunger, if their sickness goes untended, if their life is spent in hopeless poverty just drawing a welfare check.

So we want to open the gates to opportunity. But we are also going to give all our people, black and white, the help that they need to walk through those gates.

THE PURPOSE OF THIS GOVERNMENT. My first job after college was as a teacher in Cotulla, Texas, in a small Mexican-American school. Few of them could speak English, and I couldn't speak much Spanish. My students were poor and they often came to class without breakfast, hungry. They knew even in their youth the pain of prejudice. They never seemed to know why people disliked them. But they knew it was so, because I saw it in their eyes. I often walked home late in the afternoon, after the classes were finished, wishing there was more that I could do. But all I knew was to teach them the little that I knew, hoping that it might help them against the hardships that lay ahead.

Somehow you never forget what poverty and hatred can do when you see its scars on the hopeful face of a young child.

I never thought then, in 1928, that I would be standing here in 1965. It never even occurred to me in my fondest dreams that I might have the chance to help the sons and daughters of those students and to help people like them all over this country.

But now I do have that chance—and I'll let you in on a secret—I mean to use it. And I hope that you will use it with me.

This is the richest and most powerful country which ever occupied the globe. The might of past empires is little compared to ours. But I do not want to be the President who built empires, or sought grandeur, or extended dominion.

I want to be the President who educated young children to the wonders of their world. I want to be the President who helped to feed the hungry and to prepare them to be taxpayers instead of taxeaters.

I want to be the President who helped the poor to find their own way and who protected the right of every citizen to vote in every election.

I want to be the President who helped to end hatred among his fellow men and who promoted love among the people of all races and all regions and all parties.

I want to be the President who helped to end war among the brothers of this earth.

And so at the request of your beloved Speaker and the Senator from Montana; the majority leader, the Senator from Illinois; the minority leader, Mr. McCulloch, and other Members of both parties, I came here tonight—not as President Roosevelt came down one time in person to veto a bonus bill, not as President Truman came down one time to urge the passage of a railroad bill— but I came down here to ask you to share this task with me and to share it with the people that we both work for. I want this to be the Congress, Republicans and Democrats alike, which did all these things for all these people.

Beyond this great chamber, out yonder in 50 States, are the people that we serve. Who can tell what deep and unspoken hopes are in their hearts tonight as they sit there and listen. We all can guess, from our own lives, how difficult they often find their own pursuit of happiness, how many problems each little family has. They look most of all to themselves for their futures. But I think that they also look to each of us.

Above the pyramid on the great seal of the United States it says—in Latin—"God has favored our undertaking."

God will not favor everything that we do. It is rather our duty to divine His will. But I cannot help believing that He truly understands and that He really favors the undertaking that we begin here tonight.

Source: Woolley, John T., and Gerhard Peters. *The American Presidency Project* [online]. Santa Barbara, CA: University of California. Available online at http://www.presidency.ucsb.edu/ws/?pid=26805.

Johnson Signs the Voting Rights Act of 1965

President Lyndon B. Johnson signed the Voting Rights Act into law on August 6, 1965. He made the following remarks on that historic occasion. More than four decades later, the Voting Rights Act of 1965 is still considered to be one of the most important and influential laws in U.S. history. It put an end to the discriminatory practices that had been used to prevent African Americans from voting in the South, spurred a dramatic increase in the number of black registered voters and elected officials, and helped the nation live up to its founding principle that "all men are created equal."

Mr. Vice President, Mr. Speaker, Members of Congress, members of the Cabinet, distinguished guests, my fellow Americans:

Today is a triumph for freedom as huge as any victory that has ever been won on any battlefield. Yet to seize the meaning of this day, we must recall darker times.

Three and a half centuries ago the first Negroes arrived at Jamestown. They did not arrive in brave ships in search of a home for freedom. They did not mingle fear and joy, in expectation that in this New World anything would be possible to a man strong enough to reach for it.

They came in darkness and they came in chains.

And today we strike away the last major shackle of those fierce and ancient bonds. Today the Negro story and the American story fuse and blend.

And let us remember that it was not always so. The stories of our Nation and of the American Negro are like two great rivers. Welling up from that tiny Jamestown spring they flow through the centuries along divided channels.

When pioneers subdued a continent to the need of man, they did not tame it for the Negro. When the Liberty Bell rang out in Philadelphia, it did not toll for the Negro. When Andrew Jackson threw open the doors of democracy, they did not open for the Negro.

It was only at Appomattox, a century ago, that an American victory was also a Negro victory. And the two rivers—one shining with promise, the other dark-stained with oppression—began to move toward one another.

THE PROMISE KEPT. Yet, for almost a century the promise of that day was not fulfilled. Today is a towering and certain mark that, in this generation, that promise will be kept. In our time the two currents will finally mingle and rush as one great stream across the uncertain and the marvelous years of the America that is yet to come.

This act flows from a clear and simple wrong. Its only purpose is to right that wrong. Millions of Americans are denied the right to vote because of their color. This law will ensure them the right to vote. The wrong is one which no American, in his heart, can justify. The right is one which no American, true to our principles, can deny.

In 1957, as the leader of the majority in the United States Senate, speaking in support of legislation to guarantee the right of all men to vote, I said, "This right to vote is the basic right without which all others are meaningless. It gives people, people as individuals, control over their own destinies."

Last year I said, "Until every qualified person regardless of … the color of his skin has the right, unquestioned and unrestrained, to go in and cast his ballot in every precinct in this great land of ours, I am not going to be satisfied."

Immediately after the election I directed the Attorney General to explore, as rapidly as possible, the ways to ensure the right to vote.

And then last March, with the outrage of Selma still fresh, I came down to this Capitol one evening and asked the Congress and the people for swift and for sweeping action to guarantee to every man and woman the right to vote. In less than 48 hours I sent the Voting Rights Act of 1965 to the Congress. In little more than 4 months the Congress, with overwhelming majorities, enacted one of the most monumental laws in the entire history of American freedom.

THE WAITING IS GONE. The Members of the Congress, and the many private citizens, who worked to shape and pass this bill will share a place of honor in our history for this one act alone.

There were those who said this is an old injustice, and there is no need to hurry. But 95 years have passed since the 15th amendment gave all Negroes the right to vote.

And the time for waiting is gone.

There were those who said smaller and more gradual measures should be tried. But they had been tried. For years and years they had been tried, and tried, and tried, and they had failed, and failed, and failed.

And the time for failure is gone.

There were those who said that this is a many-sided and very complex problem. But however viewed, the denial of the right to vote is still a deadly wrong.

And the time for injustice has gone.

This law covers many pages. But the heart of the act is plain. Wherever, by clear and objective standards, States and counties are using regulations, or laws, or tests to deny the right to vote, then they will be struck down. If it is dear that State officials still intend to discriminate, then Federal examiners will be sent in to register all eligible voters. When the prospect of discrimination is gone, the examiners will be immediately withdrawn.

And, under this act, if any county anywhere in this Nation does not want Federal intervention it need only open its polling places to all of its people.

THE GOVERNMENT ACTS. This good Congress, the 89th Congress, acted swiftly in passing this act. I intend to act with equal dispatch in enforcing this act.

And tomorrow at 1 p.m., the Attorney General has been directed to file a lawsuit challenging the constitutionality of the poll tax in the State of Mississippi. This will begin the legal process which, I confidently believe, will very soon prohibit any State from requiring the payment of money in order to exercise the fight to vote.

And also by tomorrow the Justice Department, through publication in the Federal Register, will have officially certified the States where discrimination exists.

I have, in addition, requested the Department of Justice to work all through this weekend so that on Monday morning next, they can designate many counties where past experience clearly shows that Federal action is necessary and required. And by Tuesday morning, trained Federal examiners will be at work registering eligible men and women in 10 to 15 counties.

And on that same day, next Tuesday, additional poll tax suits will be filed in the States of Texas, Alabama, and Virginia.

And I pledge you that we will not delay, or we will not hesitate, or we will not turn aside until Americans of every race and color and origin in this country have the same right as all others to share in the process of democracy.

So, through this act, and its enforcement, an important instrument of freedom passes into the hands of millions of our citizens. But that instrument must be used. Presidents and Congresses, laws and lawsuits can open the doors to the polling places and open the doors to the wondrous rewards which await the wise use of the ballot.

THE VOTE BECOMES JUSTICE. But only the individual Negro, and all others who have been denied the right to vote, can really walk through those doors, and can use that right, and can transform the vote into an instrument of justice and fulfillment.

So, let me now say to every Negro in this country: You must register. You must vote. You must learn, so your choice advances your interest and the interest of our beloved Nation. Your future, and your children's future, depend upon it, and I don't believe that you are going to let them down.

This act is not only a victory for Negro leadership. This act is a great challenge to that leadership. It is a challenge which cannot be met simply by protests and demonstrations. It means that dedicated leaders must work around the clock to teach people their rights and their responsibilities and to lead them to exercise those rights and to fulfill those responsibilities and those duties to their country.

If you do this, then you will find, as others have found before you, that the vote is the most powerful instrument ever devised by man for breaking down injustice and destroying the terrible walls which imprison men because they are different from other men.

THE LAST OF THE BARRIERS TUMBLE. Today what is perhaps the last of the legal barriers is tumbling. There will be many actions and many difficulties before the rights woven into law are also woven into the fabric of our Nation. But the struggle for equality must now move toward a different battlefield.

It is nothing less than granting every American Negro his freedom to enter the mainstream of American life: not the conformity that blurs enriching differences of culture and tradition, but rather the opportunity that gives each a chance to choose.

For centuries of oppression and hatred have already taken their painful toll. It can be seen throughout our land in men without skills, in children without fathers, in families that are imprisoned in slums and in poverty.

RIGHTS ARE NOT ENOUGH. For it is not enough just to give men rights. They must be able to use those rights in their personal pursuit of happiness. The wounds and the weaknesses, the outward walls and the inward scars which diminish achievement are the work of American society. We must all now help to end them—help to end them through expanding programs already devised and through new ones to search out and forever end the special handicaps of those who are black in a Nation that happens to be mostly white.

So, it is for this purpose—to fulfill the rights that we now secure—that I have already called a White House conference to meet here in the Nation's Capital this fall.

So, we will move step by step—often painfully but, I think, with clear vision—along the path toward American freedom.

It is difficult to fight for freedom. But I also know how difficult it can be to bend long years of habit and custom to grant it. There is no room for injustice anywhere in the American mansion. But there is always room for understanding toward those who see the old ways crumbling. And to them today I say simply this: It must come. It is right that it should come. And when it has, you will find that a burden has been lifted from your shoulders, too.

It is not just a question of guilt, although there is that. It is that men cannot live with a lie and not be stained by it.

DIGNITY IS NOT JUST A WORD. The central fact of American civilization—one so hard for others to understand—is that freedom and justice and the dignity of man are not just words to us. We believe in them. Under all the growth and the tumult and abundance, we believe. And so, as long as some among us are oppressed—and we are part of that oppression—it must blunt our faith and sap the strength of our high purpose.

Thus, this is a victory for the freedom of the American Negro. But it is also a victory for the freedom of the American Nation. And every family across this great, entire, searching land will live stronger in liberty, will live more splendid in expectation, and will be prouder to be American because of the act that you have passed that I will sign today.

Thank you.

Source: Woolley, John T., and Gerhard Peters. *The American Presidency Project* [online]. Santa Barbara, CA: University of California. Available online at http://www.presidency .ucsb.edu/ws/?pid=27140.

Senator Barack Obama Supports Renewal of the VRA

In 2008, Democratic Senator Barack Obama of Illinois made history as the first African American to be nominated by a major political party for president of the United States. Two years earlier, as a member of Congress, he made the following speech in support of renewing all provisions of the Voting Rights Act of 1965. Obama credits the VRA for making important progress toward eliminating the barriers to minority voter registration and participation. But he argues that the VRA is still needed to address discriminatory election practices that remain in force in some parts of the country.

M r. President, I rise today, both humbled and honored by the opportunity to express my support for renewal of the expiring provisions of the Voting Rights Act of 1965.

I want to thank the many people inside and outside of Congress who worked so hard over the past year to get us here. We owe a debt of gratitude to the leadership on both sides of the aisle, and we owe special thanks to Chairmen [F. James] Sensenbrenner and [Arlen] Specter, Ranking Members [John] Conyers and [Patrick] Leahy, and Rep. Mel Watt. Without their work and dedication—and the support of voting rights advocates around the country—I doubt this bill would have come before us so soon.

And I want to thank both chambers, and both sides of the aisle, for getting this done with the same broad support that drove the original Act 40 years ago. At a time when Americans are frustrated with the partisan bickering that too often stalls our work, the refreshing display of bipartisanship we are seeing today reflects our collective belief in the success of the Act and reminds us of how effective we can be when we work together.

Nobody can deny that we've come a long way since 1965.

Look at registration numbers. Only two years after passage of the original Act, registration numbers for minority voters in some states doubled. Soon after, not a single state covered by the Voting Rights Act had registered less than half of its minority voting-age population.

Look at the influence of African-American elected officials at all levels of government. There are African-American members of Congress. Since 2001, our nation's top diplomat has been an African American.

In fact, most of America's elected African-American officials come from the states covered by Section 5 of the Voting Rights Act—states like Mississippi and Alabama and Louisiana and Georgia.

But to me, the most striking evidence of our progress can be found right across this building, in my dear friend, Congressman John Lewis, who was on the front lines of the civil rights movement, risking life and limb for freedom. And on March 7, 1965, he led 600 peaceful protestors demanding the right to vote across the Edmund Pettus Bridge in Selma, Alabama.

I've often thought about the people on the Edmund Pettus Bridge that day. Not only John Lewis and Hosea Williams leading the march, but the hundreds of everyday Americans who left their homes and their churches to join it. Blacks and whites, teenagers and children, teachers and bankers and shopkeepers—a beloved community of God's children ready to stand for freedom.

And I wonder, where did they find that kind of courage? When you're facing row after row of state troopers on horseback armed with billy clubs and tear gas... When they're coming toward you spewing hatred and violence, how do you simply stop, kneel down, and pray to the Lord for salvation?

But the most amazing thing of all is that after that day—after John Lewis was beaten within an inch of his life, after people's heads were gashed open and their eyes were burned and they watched their children's innocence literally beaten out of them.... After all that, they went back to march again.

They marched again. They crossed the bridge. They awakened a nation's conscience, and not five months later, the Voting Rights Act of 1965 was signed into law. And it was reauthorized in 1970, 1975, and 1982.

Now, in 2006, John Lewis, the physical scars from those marches still visible, is an original cosponsor of the fourth reauthorization of the Voting Rights Act, and he was joined last week by 389 of his House colleagues in voting for its passage.

There are some who argue the Act is no longer needed, that the protections of Section 5's "pre-clearance" requirement—a requirement that ensures certain states are upholding the right to vote—are targeting the wrong states. But the evidence refutes that notion. Of the 1,100 objections issued by the Department of Justice since 1965, 56% occurred since the last reauthorization in 1982. So, despite the progress these states have made in upholding the right to vote, it's clear that problems still exist.

Others have argued against renewing Section 203's protection of language minorities. Unfortunately, these arguments have been tied to the debate over immigration and muddle a non-controversial issue—protecting the right to vote—with one of today's most contentious debates.

But let's remember: you can't request language assistance if you're not a voter, and you can't be a voter if you're not a citizen. And while voters, as citizens, must be proficient in English, many are simply more confident that they can cast ballots printed in their native languages without making errors.

A representative of the Southwestern Voter Registration Project is quoted as saying: "Citizens who prefer Spanish registration cards do so because they feel more connected to the process; they also feel they trust the process more when they understand it." These sentiments—connection to and trust in our democratic process—are exactly what we want from our voting rights legislation.

Our challenges don't end at reauthorizing the Voting Rights Act either. We have to prevent the problems we've seen in recent elections from happening again. We've seen political operatives purge voters from registration rolls for no legitimate reason, prevent eligible ex-felons from casting ballots, distribute polling equipment unevenly, and deceive voters about the time, location and rules of elections. Unfortunately, these efforts have been directed primarily at minorities, the disabled, low-income individuals, and other historically disenfranchised groups.

The Help America Vote Act was a big step in the right direction, but we need to do more. We need to fully fund HAVA. We need to enforce critical requirements like statewide registration databases. We need to make sure polling equipment is distributed equitably and that the equipment works. And we need to work on getting more people to the polls on election day.

We need to make sure that minority voters are not the subject of deplorable intimidation tactics when they do get to the polls. In 2004, Native American voters in South Dakota were confronted by men posing as law enforcement. These hired intimidators joked about jail time for ballot missteps, and followed voters to their cars to record their license plate numbers.

In Lake County, Ohio, some voters received a memo on bogus Board of Elections letterhead informing voters who registered through Democratic and NAACP drives that they could not vote.

In Wisconsin, a flier purporting to be from the "Milwaukee Black Voters League" was circulated in predominantly African-American neighborhoods with the following message: "If you've already voted in any election this year, you can't vote in the presidential election. If you violate any of these laws, you can get ten years in prison and your children will get taken away from you."

So, we have much more work to do. This occasion is cause for celebration, but it's also an opportunity to renew our commitment to voting rights. As Congressman Lewis said last week: "It's clear that we have come a great distance, but we still have a great distance to go."

The memory of Selma still lives on in the spirit of the Voting Rights Act. Since that day, the Voting Rights Act has been a critical tool in ensuring that all Americans not only have the right to vote, but the right to have their vote counted. Those of us concerned about protecting those rights can't afford to sit on our laurels upon reauthorization of this bill. We must take advantage of this rare united front and continue the fight to ensure unimpeded access to the polls for all Americans. In other words, we need to take the spirit that existed on that bridge, and we have to spread it across this country.

Two weeks after the first march was turned back, Dr. King told a gathering of organizers and activists and community members that they should not despair because the arc of the moral universe is long, but it bends towards justice. That's because of the work that each of us do to bend it towards justice. It's because of people like John Lewis and Fannie Lou Hamer and Coretta Scott King and Rosa Parks, all the giants upon whose shoulders we stand that we are the beneficiaries of that arc bending towards justice.

That's why I stand here today. I would not be in the United States Senate had it not been for the efforts and courage of so many parents and grandparents and ordinary people who were willing to reach up and bend that arc in the direction of justice. I hope we continue to see that spirit live on, not just during this debate, but throughout all our work here in the Senate. Thank you.

Source: Obama, Barack. "Remarks of Senator Barack Obama in Support of H.R. 9, the Voting Rights Act," July 20, 2006. Available online at http://obama.senate.gov/speech/060720-remarks_of_sena_8.

IMPORTANT PEOPLE, PLACES, AND TERMS

14th Amendment
Ratified in 1868, this constitutional amendment granted citizenship to all persons born or naturalized in the United States and guaranteed "equal protection of the laws" to all American citizens.

15th Amendment
Ratified in 1870, this constitutional amendment guaranteed the right of all male citizens to vote, without regard to race, color, or previous condition of servitude.

19th Amendment
This constitutional amendment, ratified in 1920, gave women the right to vote.

Affirmative action
A broad term used to describe policies that attempt to increase minority involvement in government, business, and education.

Baker, Ella (1903-1986)
Civil rights activist and co-founder of the Student Nonviolent Coordinating Committee (SNCC).

Black Codes
The name given to various laws passed in the South after the Civil War to limit the rights of African Americans to own property, work, travel, and vote.

Bloody Sunday
A term used in reference to March 7, 1965, when a voting rights march in Selma, Alabama, was shattered by state troopers who used tear gas, clubs, and whips on the peaceful demonstrators.

Boycott

The refusal to buy or use products or otherwise deal with businesses or other institutions as a way to register dissatisfaction or unhappiness with their practices.

Brown v. Board of Education

A 1954 Supreme Court ruling that declared the segregation of public schools unconstitutional and launched the civil rights movement.

Clark, Jim (1922-2007)

Segregationist sheriff of Dallas County, Alabama, who assaulted peaceful protesters during the Selma voting-rights campaign.

Congress of Racial Equality (CORE)

A civil rights organization that played a leading role in organizing Freedom Rides and other peaceful protests during the 1960s.

CORE

See Congress of Racial Equality.

Covered jurisdiction

States and counties with a history of discriminatory election practices that were covered under the special or emergency provisions of the Voting Rights Act. These provisions required the jurisdictions to allow federal officials to oversee voter registration and pre-clear all election-law changes with the federal government.

Descriptive representation

A situation in which an elected official shares social or cultural attributes—such as race or gender—with a particular voter.

Disenfranchise

To deny or take away a citizen's voting rights.

Evers, Medgar (1925-1963)

Field secretary for the NAACP in Mississippi who was murdered by white supremacists angered by his civil rights work.

Farmer, James (1920-1999)

Director of the Congress of Racial Equality (CORE) during the civil rights movement.

Franchise
The right to vote.

Freedom Rides
Peaceful civil rights protests in which black and white activists traveled together on interstate buses to challenge segregated transportation facilities in the South.

Freedom Summer
An African-American voter registration drive that was carried out by civil rights activists in Mississippi in 1964.

Gerrymandering
The practice of drawing the boundaries of election districts in order to favor a particular political party or group of voters.

Grandfather clause
Discriminatory measures passed by white legislators in several southern and western states that allowed illiterate men to vote only if they could prove that their grandfathers were allowed to vote. This law permitted illiterate white men to exercise their voting rights, but disqualified most African Americans since many of their grandfathers had been slaves.

Hamer, Fannie Lou (1917-1977)
Civil rights activist and leader of the Mississippi Freedom Democratic Party (MFDP).

Jim Crow
Post-Reconstruction laws that established segregation and discrimination against blacks in virtually all aspects of daily life across the South.

Johnson, Frank M. (1918-1999)
White federal judge who issued a number of important rulings during the 1950s and 1960s that benefited the civil rights cause.

Johnson, Lyndon B. (1908-1973)
President of the United States who signed the Voting Rights Act of 1965 into law.

King, Martin Luther, Jr. (1929-1968)
Civil rights leader and president of the Southern Christian Leadership Conference (SCLC).

Language minority
American citizens who speak a language other than English. The Voting Rights Act of 1975 was extended to provide bilingual ballots and voting assistance for these citizens.

Lewis, John (1940-)
Chairman of the Student Nonviolent Coordinating Committee (SNCC) and U.S. congressman from Georgia.

Literacy test
A test used to assess whether citizens' reading and writing skills made them "qualified" to vote. Such tests were used in the South to prevent African Americans from registering to vote, and were suspended under the Voting Rights Act of 1965.

Majority-minority district
An election district created with the goal of maximizing the number of minority voters in order to increase the chances of electing minority officials.

March on Washington
Historic 1963 demonstration for civil rights in the nation's capital, highlighted by Martin Luther King, Jr.'s famous "I Have a Dream" speech.

MFDP
See Mississippi Freedom Democratic Party.

Mississippi Freedom Democratic Party (MFDP)
Founded in 1964 to register discontent with the segregationist state Democratic Party in Mississippi, this activist group waged an unsuccessful effort to be seated at the Democratic National Convention that year.

Montgomery Bus Boycott
A year-long civil rights protest, launched in 1955, that succeeded in ending segregation of the city's public transportation system.

NAACP
See National Association for the Advancement of Colored People.

National Association for the Advancement of Colored People (NAACP)
A civil rights organization founded in 1909 by a multiracial group to lobby for political and social changes that would grant equal rights to African Americans.

Parks, Rosa (1913-2005)
African-American woman whose refusal to give up her seat to a white man on a segregated city bus launched the Montgomery Bus Boycott.

Poll tax
A fee citizens were required to pay in order to vote. Such fees had the effect of discriminating against low-income voters and were eventually outlawed.

Preclearance
A controversial provision of the Voting Rights Act that requires states and counties with a history of voting-rights abuses to seek permission from the federal government before making any election-law changes.

Race-based districting
The practice of using the race of voters as a primary factor in drawing election district boundaries.

Reconstruction
The post-Civil War era, from 1868 to 1877, when the South was under Northern military control and rights for African Americans were enforced and expanded.

SCLC
See Southern Christian Leadership Conference.

Segregation
The forced separation of people by race.

Selma-Montgomery Voting Rights March
A 1965 civil rights protest designed to call public attention to voting-rights abuses in Alabama that was shattered by police brutality.

Separate but equal
A doctrine stating that government-mandated segregation of the races is legal as long as the facilities provided for the different groups are equal.

Sit-ins

A movement in which African Americans and mixed groups of white and black demonstrators defied Southern segregation laws by sitting at white-only lunch counters and other public facilities.

SNCC

See Student Nonviolent Coordinating Committee (SNCC).

Southern Christian Leadership Conference (SCLC)

A civil rights organization founded in 1957 by the Reverend Martin Luther King, Jr., and other ministers in the South.

Student Nonviolent Coordinating Committee (SNCC)

A prominent civil rights organization founded by college activists in 1960.

Substantive representation

A situation in which an elected official shares policy goals or political positions with a particular voter.

Till, Emmett (1941-1955)

A Chicago teenager who broke unwritten rules of acceptable black behavior during a 1955 visit to Mississippi and was murdered by white segregationists. Despite strong evidence, an all-white jury refused to convict the murderers.

Voting Rights Act of 1965

Landmark legislation that put an end to discriminatory practices that had been used to prevent African Americans from voting in the South, and led to an immediate increase in the number of black registered voters and elected officials.

VRA

See Voting Rights Act of 1965.

Wallace, George (1919-1998)

Governor of Alabama and segregationist leader.

X, Malcolm (1925-1965)

Nation of Islam minister and civil rights figure who advocated black nationalism and the use of force in defending oneself from white violence.

CHRONOLOGY

1776

Voting rights in the newly created United States are granted only to white male property-owners; women, blacks, Catholics, Jews, Quakers, and white men without landholdings are excluded.

1792

New Hampshire becomes the first state to do away with the rule that only property owners and taxpayers can vote. Other states follow suit.

1848

The Treaty of Guadalupe-Hidalgo ends the Mexican-American War and gives Mexicans living in Arizona, California, New Mexcio, Texas, and Nevada the right to vote—provided they are proficient in English.

1856

All white male citizens of the United States receive the right to vote, although exceptions are made for those convicted of certain crimes.

1865

After the Civil War ends in victory for the North, slavery is outlawed in the United States with the passage of the Thirteenth Amendment to the U.S. Constitution. *See p. 8.*

1866

The Civil Rights Act of 1866 is passed, granting citizenship to all native-born Americans. Voting rights, however, are still subject to various restrictions.

Oklahoma passes a "grandfather clause" that exempts men from literacy test requirements if they can prove that their grandfathers could vote. This law permits illiterate white men to exercise their voting rights, but disqualifies most African Americans since most of their grandfathers had been slaves. Other Southern states pass similar laws in the ensuing years. *See p. 14.*

1868

The Fourteenth Amendment to the U.S. Constitution becomes law. It grants citizenship to all persons born or naturalized in the United States—regardless of skin color—and guarantees all U.S. citizens equal protection under the law. *See p. 8.*

1869

The Fifteenth Amendment to the U.S. Constitution is passed, formally giving African-American men the right to vote. It is ratified on February 3, 1870. *See p. 8.*

1870

During the post-Civil War period known as Reconstruction, Hiram Revels becomes the first African American elected to the U.S. Senate and Joseph Hayne Rainey becomes the first African-American legislator in the U.S. House of Representatives. *See p. 8.*

1877

Reconstruction comes to an end in the South, ushering in a new era of white discrimination against African Americans in the voting booth and in virtually every other area of economic, political, and social life. *See p. 9.*

1882

The Chinese Exclusion Act is passed, barring Chinese Americans from voting or holding U.S. citizenship.

1887

The Dawes General Allotment Act is passed, barring Native Americans who refuse to give up their tribal affiliations from holding U.S. citizenship.

1888

Florida becomes the first of the Southern states to pass laws designed to strip voting rights from African Americans. Other states across the South follow suit, and black voting registration plummets across the region. *See p. 13.*

1896

The U.S. Supreme Court issues its infamous *Plessy v. Ferguson* ruling, which declares that states can segregate public transportation, schools, and other facilities by race if those facilities provided to blacks and whites are "separate but equal." *See p. 11.*

1909

The National Association for the Advancement of Colored People (NAACP) is established. *See p. 17.*

1915

The U.S. Supreme Court rules in *Guinn v. United States* that Oklahoma's "grandfather clause" is unconstitutional.

1916-1919

An estimated half-million blacks relocate from the South to the North to escape discriminatory Jim Crow laws. This exodus continues throughout the 1920s. *See p. 16.*

1920

American women receive the right to vote with the passage and ratification of the Nineteenth Amendment to the U.S. Constitution. *See p. 18.*

1924

Native Americans receive full citizenship—including full voting rights—as a result of the passage of the Indian Citizenship Act of 1924. Many Native Americans, though, continue to endure discriminatory state laws designed to suppress their voting power. *See p. 19.*

1937

The U.S. Supreme Court upholds the constitutionality of Georgia poll taxes in *Breedlove v. Suttles.* The decision is a huge victory for segregationists who use prohibitively high poll taxes to keep African Americans from exercising their right to vote.

1940

Only 3 percent of eligible African Americans in the South are registered to vote. *See p. 21.*

1943

The Chinese Exclusion Act is repealed, giving Chinese immigrants the right to citizenship and the right to vote.

1946

Filipinos are granted the right to become U.S. citizens.

1952

The McCarran-Walter Act gives first-generation Japanese Americans the right to become citizens.

1954

In one of the landmark rulings in the history of the U.S. Supreme Court, the Court delivers a unanimous decision in *Brown v. Board of Education* that racial segregation in public schools is unconstitutional. *See p. 26.*

1955

Emmett Till, a fourteen-year-old African-American youth from Chicago, is murdered in Mississippi by white supremacists. *See p. 29.*

The Montgomery Bus Boycott is launched after Rosa Parks, a black woman, refuses to give up her bus seat to a white man. *See p. 30.*

1957

Congress passes the Civil Rights Act of 1957, which authorizes the U.S. Attorney General to file lawsuits on behalf of African Americans and other minority groups that face discrimination or harassment when they attempt to vote.

The Southern Christian Leadership Conference (SCLC), a civil rights group devoted to nonviolent forms of social protest, is founded. Martin Luther King, Jr., is elected its first president. *See p. 33.*

1959

The U.S. Supreme Court rules in *Lassiter v. Northampton County Board of Elections* that literacy tests for voting in North Carolina are constitutional, even though they are clearly designed to suppress African-American voting.

1960

February 1—Four African-American college students launch a sit-in to protest segregated lunch counters at a North Carolina Woolworth's store. The success of this sit-in triggers a wave of similar protests across the South. *See p. 34.*

April—The Student Nonviolent Coordinating Committee (SNCC) is founded. *See p. 36.*

May 9—Congress passes the Civil Rights Act of 1960.

November—Democratic candidate John F. Kennedy defeats Republican nominee Richard M. Nixon to become president of the United States. *See p. 37.*

December—The U.S. Supreme Court rules in *Boynton v. Virginia* that states cannot legally segregate bus and train terminals, restrooms, waiting areas, and other interstate transportation facilities. *See p. 37.*

1961

The Student Nonviolent Coordinating Committee (SNCC) launches its first voter registration project in Mississippi. *See p. 62.*

May 4—The first Freedom Ride leaves Washington, D.C. to challenge the South's continued segregation of buses, bus stations, and other public transportation facilities. *See p. 38.*

November 1—A new rule issued by the federal Interstate Commerce Commission takes effect, demanding that all public transportation facilities in the United States be desegregated. *See p. 40.*

1963

John Lewis is unanimously elected chairman of SNCC.

SNCC launches its Freedom Ballot initiative in Mississippi to call attention to ongoing state-sponsored suppression of the black vote. *See p. 62.*

April—Martin Luther King, Jr., issues his famous "Letter from Birmingham Jail." *See p. 45.*

June 11—The University of Alabama is integrated over the objections of Governor George Wallace, who stands aside only when confronted by federal marshals. *See p. 46.*

June 12—Civil rights activist Medgar Evers is murdered in Mississippi. *See p. 48.*

August 28—The famous March on Washington takes place in Washington, D.C. Highlights of the huge civil rights demonstration include Martin Luther King, Jr.'s famous "I Have a Dream" speech. *See p. 52.*

November 22—President Kennedy is assassinated in Dallas, Texas, and Lyndon B. Johnson takes the oath of office as the nation's 36th president. *See p. 55.*

1964

A coalition of civil rights organizations known as the Council of Federated Organizations (COFO) mounts its Freedom Summer voter registration effort in Mississippi. *See p. 64.*

February 4—The Twenty-fourth Amendment to the U.S. Constitution is ratified, outlawing poll taxes. *See p. 58.*

June 21—Three civil rights workers disappear in Mississippi; their murdered bodies are discovered 44 days later. *See p. 65.*

July 2—The Civil Rights Act of 1964 is signed into law, making it illegal to discriminate on the basis of race, national origin, religion, and gender in voting, public places, the workplace, and schools. *See p. 60.*

August—The Mississippi Freedom Democratic Party (MFDP) challenges the legitimacy of the all-white Mississippi Democratic Party delegation at the Democratic National Convention. *See p. 68.*

1965

January 18—Voting rights protests organized by activists from the SCLC and SNCC begin in Selma, Alabama. *See p. 82.*

February 1—Martin Luther King, Jr., and 250 other protestors are arrested in Selma. *See p. 82.*

March 7—Peaceful protesters taking part in the Selma-Montgomery Voting Rights March are viciously assaulted by club-wielding Alabama state troopers. Media coverage of the "Bloody Sunday" attack increases public calls for new voting rights legislation. *See p. 85.*

March 9—Martin Luther King, Jr., aborts a second Selma-to-Montgomery march over the objections of other civil rights activists. *See p. 88.*

March 9—A white Unitarian minister, James Reeb, is beaten to death in Selma by white supremacists. *See p. 89.*

March 15—Johnson appears before Congress and announces his support for new legislation designed to ensure full voting rights for African Americans. *See p. 89.*

March 21-25—The Selma-to-Montgomery Voting Rights March finally takes place and is completed without violence, thanks to heavy federal protection for the marchers. *See p. 90.*

August 6—President Johnson signs the Voting Rights Act into law. *See p. 94.*

1966

In *South Carolina v. Katzenbach*, the U.S. Supreme Court upholds the constitutionality of the Voting Rights Act. *See p. 98.*

1968

Shirley Chisholm of New York becomes the first African-American woman to be elected to Congress. *See p. 100.*

Black voter registration surges all across the South. In Mississippi alone, black voter registration increases from less than 7 percent to nearly 60 percent from 1964 to 1968. *See p. 100.*

April 4—Martin Luther King, Jr., is assassinated in Memphis, Tennessee. His murder sparks riots in many cities across the country. *See p. 104.*

1970

Congress renews the temporary provisions of the Voting Rights Act for five years. *See p. 108.*

1971

The Congressional Black Caucus is founded. *See p. 100.*

1972

Two African Americans—Barbara Jordan of Texas and Andrew Young in Georgia— become the first blacks elected to represent Southern states in the U.S. Congress since 1901. *See p. 100.*

1974

The Supreme Court rules in *Richardson v. Ramirez* that states have the right to deny voting rights to convicted criminals. *See p. 113.*

1975

President Gerald Ford signs legislation reauthorizing temporary provisions of the Voting Rights Act for another seven years. *See p. 108.*

1982

Congress reauthorizes special provisions of the Voting Rights Act for 25 years. *See p. 110.*

1992

Language minority provisions of the Voting Rights Act are strengthened and extended for another 15 years.

1993

The National Voter Registration Act, more commonly known as the "Motor Voter" Bill, makes it easier for minority and low income voters to register. *See p. 117.*

2000

Studies conducted after the disputed 2000 election find high rates of invalidated ballots in minority voting districts nationwide. *See p. 114.*

2002

Congress passes the Help America Vote Act, which requires states to computerize lists of registered voters in an effort to prevent voter fraud. *See p. 115.*

2006

On July 27, President George W. Bush signs a 25-year extension of the Voting Rights Act. *See p. 122.*

2008

On August 28, Senator Barack Obama of Illinois officially accepts the Democratic nomination to become the first black presidential candidate for a major political party in U.S. history. *See p. 121.*

SOURCES FOR FURTHER STUDY

Carson, Clayborne, et al, eds. *The Eyes on the Prize Civil Rights Reader: Documents, Speeches, and Firsthand Accounts from the Black Freedom Struggle, 1954-1990.* New York: Penguin, 1991. A fine collection of speeches, personal letters, interviews, and other sources that document America's struggles to move on from its history of racial injustice and build a more equal society.

Cox, Julian. *Road to Freedom: Photographs of the Civil Rights Movement, 1956-1968.* Atlanta: High Museum of Art, 2008. This collection of emotionally powerful images was organized by Julian Cox, curator of photography at Atlanta's High Museum of Art. It uses photographs from the civil rights era to document all of the major milestones, events, and individuals of the movement.

Davis, Townsend. *Weary Feet, Rested Souls: A Guided History of the Civil Rights Movement.* New York: Norton, 1998. This terrific resource for young adults uses maps, photographs, and other illustrations to describe events in Selma, Montgomery, Little Rock, and other American cities and towns that became flashpoints in the civil rights struggles of the 1950s and 1960s.

Editors of Black History in Education. *The Unfinished Agenda of the Selma-Montgomery Voting Rights March.* Hoboken, NJ: John Wiley and Sons, 2005. Published 40 years after the historic Selma voting rights campaign, this book analyzes the march's continuing impact on American society and culture. Full of letters, interviews, speeches, and other primary documents by prominent individuals associated with the civil rights struggle, the book also assesses the state of minority voting rights in the twenty-first century.

Garrow, David J. *Protest at Selma: Martin Luther King Jr. and the Voting Rights Act of 1965.* Yale University Press, 1980. A Pulitzer Prize-winning biographer of King, Garrow turns his focus in this book to Selma, Alabama, in 1965, when it became the focal point for the civil rights movement's battle to secure equal voting rights for African Americans. This work covers the efforts of leaders like King, John Lewis, and Hosea Williams in Selma, as well as the horrible "Bloody Sunday" attack on peaceful marchers by Alabama state troopers and its aftermath.

Lewis, John, with Michael D'Orso. *Walking with the Wind: A Memoir of the Movement.* New York: Simon and Schuster, 1998. John Lewis, a leading figure of the civil rights movement who went on to become a respected U.S. Congressman, offers a powerful and eloquent account of the trials and triumphs of the civil rights struggle. His memoir also provides a fascinating look at one African-American man's spiritual journey from childhood through adulthood.

NAACP Legal Defense Fund. "The VRA in 28 Days." Available online at http://www.naacp ldf.org/vra.aspx?day=0. This extensive Web site was prepared to coincide with both the 40th anniversary of the Voting Rights Act and Black History Month. In addition to 28 daily articles covering topics related to African-American voting rights, the site features audio files of interviews, information about legal cases, and sources for further reading.

United States Department of Justice, Civil Rights Division, Voting Section. "Introduction to Federal Voting Rights Laws." Available online at http://www.usdoj.gov/crt/voting/intro /intro_b.htm. This government Web site provides an overview of the background and provisions of major voting rights legislation, including the Voting Rights Act of 1965 and its various renewals and amendments.

Williams, Juan. *Eyes on the Prize: America's Civil Rights Years, 1954-1965*. New York: Viking, 1987. This is a companion book to the six-part *Eyes on the Prize* PBS television series about the civil rights movement and its impact on American society and culture. Richly illustrated with photographs from the era, it paints an absorbing portrait of the movement and its many brave and talented participants.

BIBLIOGRAPHY

Books

Bausum, Anne. *Freedom Riders: John Lewis and Jim Zwerg on the Front Lines of the Civil Rights Movement.* Washington, DC: National Geographic Society, 2006.

Branch, Taylor. *At Canaan's Edge: America in the King Years 1965-1968.* New York: Simon and Schuster, 2006.

Branch, Taylor. *Parting the Waters: America in the King Years 1954-1963.* New York: Simon and Schuster, 1988.

Carson, Clayborne, et al, eds. *The Eyes on the Prize Civil Rights Reader: Documents, Speeches, and Firsthand Accounts from the Black Freedom Struggle, 1954-1990.* New York: Penguin, 1991.

Carter, Dan T. *The Politics of Rage: George Wallace, the Origins of the New Conservatism, and the Transformation of American Politics.* New York: Simon & Schuster, 1995.

Cox, Julian. *Road to Freedom: Photographs of the Civil Rights Movement, 1956-1968.* Atlanta: High Museum of Art, 2008.

Crawford, Vicki L., ed. *Women in the Civil Rights Movement: Trailblazers and Torchbearers, 1941-1965.* Bloomington: University of Indiana Press, 1993.

Davis, Townsend. *Weary Feet, Rested Souls: A Guided History of the Civil Rights Movement.* New York: Norton, 1998.

Dyson, Michael Eric. *I May Not Get There with You: The True Martin Luther King Jr.* New York: Free Press, 2000.

Editors of Black History in Education. *The Unfinished Agenda of the Selma-Montgomery Voting Rights March.* Hoboken, NJ: John Wiley and Sons, 2005.

Farmer, James. *Lay Bare the Heart: An Autobiography of the Civil Rights Movement.* 1985. Fort Worth: Texas Christian University Press, 1998.

Garrow, David J. *Protest at Selma: Martin Luther King Jr. and the Voting Rights Act of 1965.* New Haven, CT: Yale University Press, 1980.

King, Martin Luther, Jr. *The Autobiography of Martin Luther King Jr.* Edited by Clayborne Carson. New York: IPM/Warner, 2001.

King, Martin Luther, Jr. *A Call to Conscience: The Landmark Speeches of Martin Luther King Jr.* Edited by Clayborne Carson. New York: IPM/Warner, 2001.

Kotz, Nick. *Judgment Days: Lyndon Baines Johnson, Martin Luther King, Jr., and the Laws That Changed America.* Boston: Houghton Mifflin, 2005.

Laney, Garrine P. *The Voting Rights Act of 1965: Historical Background and Current Issues.* New York: Novinka Books, 2003.

Lewis, John, with Michael D'Orso. *Walking with the Wind: A Memoir of the Movement.* New York: Simon and Schuster, 1998.

Morris, Aldon D. *Origins of the Civil Rights Movements: Black Communities Organizing for Change.* New York: Free Press, 1984.

Ransby, Barbara. *Ella Baker and the Black Freedom Movement: A Radical Democratic Vision.* Chapel Hill: University of North Carolina Press, 2002.

Oates, Stephen B. *Let the Trumpet Sound: A Life of Martin Luther King Jr.* New York: Harper, 1982.

U.S. Commission on Civil Rights. *A Citizen's Guide to Understanding the Voting Rights Act.* Washington, DC: U.S. Commission on Civil Rights, 1984.

Williams, Juan. *Eyes on the Prize: America's Civil Rights Years, 1954-1965.* New York: Viking, 1987.

Periodicals

Bolick, Clint. "Bad Fences: To Preserve American Democracy, We Must Return to the Original Aims of the Voting Rights Act." *National Review,* April 3, 1995, p. 51.

Burke, Lewis W. "Killing, Cheating, Legislating, and Lying." *South Carolina Law Review* 57, 2006, p. 859.

"Civil Rights Movement (Voting Rights)." *CQ Researcher,* Sep. 15, 2006, p. 758.

Cose, Ellis. "Back on the Bridge: It's Been 40 Years since the Unrest in Selma. A Lot Has Changed, but Not Enough." *Newsweek,* August 8, 2005, p. 30.

Henderson, Wade. "Voting Rights Act Reauthorization: What You Need to Know." *National Voter,* June 2006, p. 10.

Hull, Elizabeth. "Felons Deserve the Right to Vote." *USA Today (Magazine),* January 2004, p. 50.

Lewis, John. "Reflections on Judge Frank M. Johnson." *Yale Law Journal* 109, 2000, p. 1253.

Miller, John J. "Every Man's Burden: Will the Voting Rights Act Be Necessary Forever?" *National Review,* April 10, 2006, p. 22.

"New Study Explores Impact of Voting Rights Act on Election of Non-White Officials in the U.S." *U.S. Newswire,* July 23, 2007.

Palast, Greg. "Vanishing Votes." *The Nation,* May 17, 2004, p. 20.

Slater, Michael. "Voter Fraud?" *National Voter,* October 2007, p. 4.

Will, George. "VRA, All of It, Forever? The Voting Rights Act of 1965 Was the Noblest Law of the 20th Century. Some of Its Provisions, However, Are Now Weird—and Worse." *Newsweek,* Oct 10, 2005, p. 70.

Woodwell, William H., Jr. "Thinking Outside the Ballot Box." *National Voter,* June 2006, p. 4.

Online

American Civil Liberties Union, Voting Rights Project. "Voting Rights Act: Timeline." Available online at http://www.votingrights.org/timeline.

"The History of Jim Crow." Available online at http://www.jimcrowhistory.org/history/history
.html.

Leadership Conference on Civil Rights. "Protecting Minority Rights: The Voting Rights Act
at Work 1982-2005," February 1, 2006. Available online at http://www.civilrights.org
/press_room/press-releases.

NAACP Legal Defense Fund. "The VRA in 28 Days." Available online at http://www.naacpldf
.org/vra.aspx.

PBS. "Eyes on the Prize: America's Civil Rights Years, 1954-1965." Available online at
www.pbs.org/wgbh/amex/eyesontheprize/index.html.

Seattle Times. "Martin Luther King Jr. and the Civil Rights Movement." Available online at
www.seattletimes.nwsource.com/special/mlk.

"Voices of Civil Rights." Available online at http://www.voicesofcivilrights.org.

DVD

American Experience: Citizen King. PBS, 2004.

4 Little Girls. HBO, 1997.

Free at Last: Civil Rights Heroes. World Almanac Video, 2004.

Voices of Civil Rights. History Channel, 2006.

PHOTO AND ILLUSTRATION CREDITS

Cover photo: Photo by Peter Pettus, Prints & Photographs Division, Library of Congress, LC-DIG-pmsca-08102.

Chapter One: National Photo Company Collection, Prints and Photographs Division, Library of Congress, LC-DIG-npcc-12928 (p. 11), LC-DIG-npcc-16220 (p. 15); Department of Agriculture, Office of the Secretary, Office of Information, U.S National-al Archives and Records Administration (p. 13); Photograph by John Vachon, Photographs and Prints Division, Schomburg Center for Research in Black Culture, The New York Public Library, Astor, Lenox and Tilden Foundations (p. 16); Photo by Cornelius M. Battey, Prints and Photographs Division, Library of Congress, LC-USZ62-16767 (p. 18).

Chapter Two: AP Photo (p. 26); Photo by Thomas J. O'Halloran, U.S. News & World Report Magazine Photograph Collection, Prints and Photographs Division, Library of Congress, LC-DIG-ppmsca-03089 (p. 28); Gene Herrick/AP Photo (p. 31); Nashville Public Library, Special Collections (p. 34); Photo by Dick DeMarsico, New York World-Telegram and the Sun Photograph Collection, Prints and Photographs Division, Library of Congress, LC-USZ62-134715 (p. 36); str/AP Photo (p. 39).

Chapter Three: Photo by Warren K. Leffler, U.S. News & World Report Magazine Photograph Collection, Prints and Photographs Division, Library of Congress, LC-DIG-ppmsca-04294 (p. 47), LC-U9-10364-37 (p. 52); Photo by John Loengard/Life Magazine/Time & Life Pictures/Getty Images (p. 48); UPI/Newscom (p. 53); Photo by Abbie Rowe, National Park Service/John Fitzgerald Kennedy Presidential Library, Boston, AR-7969-E (p. 55).

Chapter Four: LBJ Library, Photo by Yoichi Okamoto (p. 59); JAB/AP Photo (p. 61); Herbert Randall Freedom Summer Photographs, McCain Library and Archives, The University of Southern Mississippi (p. 63); AP Photo (p. 67); Photo by Warren K. Leffler, U.S. News & World Report Magazine Photograph Collection, Prints and Photographs Division, Library of Congress, LC-DIG-ppmsca-04299 (p. 69); Yankee Poster Collection, Prints and Photographs Division, Library of Congress, LC-USZ62-134339 (p. 71).

Chapter Five: LBJ Library Photo by Yoichi Okamoto (p. 76); Horace Cort/AP Photo (p. 84); AP Photo (p. 86); stf/AP Photo (p. 88); Photo by Stanley Wolfson, New York World-Telegram and the Sun Photograph Collection, Prints and Photographs Division, Library of Congress, LC-USZ62-135695 (p. 91).

Chapter Six: LBJ Library, Photo by Yoichi Okamoto (p. 95); Moncrief Photograph Collection, D#399, Mississippi Department of Archives & History, [http://mdah.state,ms .us] (p. 99); Department of Defense, Dept. of the Air Force, U.S. National Archives & Records Administration (p. 101); Herald Examiner Collection/Los Angeles Public Library (p. 103).

Chapter Seven: Congressional Portrait Collection, Prints and Photographs Division, Library of Congress, LC-USZ62-98041 (p. 109); Photo by Michael Gross, U.S. Department of State (p. 114); Office of U.S. Speaker of the House Nancy Pelosi (p. 118); Office of U.S. Senator Barack Obama (p. 121); White House photo by Paul Morse (p. 122).

Biographies: National Association for the Advancement of Colored People, Prints and Photographs Division, Library of Congress, LC-USZ62-118852 (p. 127); Photo by Walter Albertin, New York World-Telegram and the Sun Photograph Collection, Prints and Photographs Division, Library of Congress, LC-USZ62-119481 (p. 132); Photo by Warren K. Leffler, U.S. News & World Report Magazine Photograph Collection, Prints and Photographs Division, Library of Congress, LC-DIG-ppmsc-01267 (p. 137); Prints and Photographs Division, Library of Congress, LC-USZ62-21755 (p. 141); MRP Photos/Newscom (p. 146); Office of U.S. Congressman John Lewis (p. 151); UPI/Newscom (p. 156).

INDEX